MARTHA
JEFFERSON

MARTHA JEFFERSON

AN INTIMATE LIFE WITH
Thomas Jefferson

WILLIAM G. HYLAND JR.

ROWMAN & LITTLEFIELD
Lanham • Boulder • New York • London

Published by Rowman & Littlefield
A wholly owned subsidiary of The Rowman & Littlefield Publishing Group, Inc.
4501 Forbes Boulevard, Suite 200, Lanham, Maryland 20706
www.rowman.com

Unit A, Whitacre Mews, 26-34 Stannary Street, London SE11 4AB

British Library Cataloguing in Publication Information Available

Library of Congress Cataloging-in-Publication Data

Hyland, William G., Jr., 1956–
    Martha Jefferson : an intimate life with Thomas Jefferson / William G. Hyland Jr.
        pages cm
    Includes bibliographical references and index.
    ISBN 978-1-4422-3983-8 (cloth : alk. paper) —
    ISBN 978-1-4422-3984-5 (electronic)
    1. Jefferson, Martha, 1748–1782. 2. Presidents' spouses—United States—Biography.
3. Governors' spouses—Virginia—Biography. 4. Jefferson, Thomas, 1743–1826. I. Title.
    E332.25.H95 2015
    973.4'6092—dc23
    [B]   2014021736

♾™ The paper used in this publication meets the minimum requirements of American National Standard for Information Sciences—Permanence of Paper for Printed Library Materials, ANSI/NISO Z39.48-1992.

Printed in the United States of America

If in the house of Hades men forget their dead,
Yet will I even there remember my dear companion.

—Homer, *The Iliad*, XXII, 389, inscribed (in Greek)
by Thomas Jefferson on the gravestone of Martha, his wife, 1782

Contents

Abbreviations
Used in Notes

Anas: *The Complete Anas of Thomas Jefferson*, ed. Frank B. Sawvel.

Bear: James A. Bear, Jr., *Jefferson at Monticello: Recollections of a Monticello Slave and of a Monticello Overseer* (Charlottesville: University Press of Virginia, 1999).

Brodie: Fawn Brodie, *Thomas Jefferson: An Intimate History* (New York: Norton, 1974).

Domestic Life: Randolph, Sarah Nicholas (TDLTJ). *The Domestic Life of Thomas Jefferson* (New York: Harper & Brothers, 1871).

EOL: Gordon S. Wood, *Empire of Liberty: A History of the Early Republic, 1789–1815.*

Family Letters: Edwin Morris Betts and James Adam Bear Jr., eds., *The Family Letters of Thomas Jefferson* (Charlottesville: University Press of Virginia, 1995).

FB: *Thomas Jefferson's Farm Book: With Commentary and Relevant Extracts from Other Writings*, ed. Edwin Morris Betts (Charlottesville, Va.: Thomas Jefferson Memorial Foundation, 1999).

FLP: Family Letters Project, Thomas Jefferson Foundation, *The Papers of Thomas Jefferson: Retirement Series*, at www.monticello.org/papers/index .html.

Free Some Day: Lucia C. Stanton, *Free Some Day: The African-American Families of Monticello* (Charlottesville, Va.: Thomas Jefferson Foundation, 2000).

GB: *Thomas Jefferson's Garden Book: 1766–1824, With Relevant Extracts from His Other Writings*, ed. Edwin Morris Betts (Philadelphia: American Philosophical Society, 1944).

Hemingses: Annette Gordon-Reed, *The Hemingses of Monticello: An American Family* (New York: Norton, 2008).

Henry Adams, History: *Henry Adams, History of the United States of America during the Administrations of Thomas Jefferson.*

ICJS: International Center for Jefferson Studies

Jefferson, Writings: *Thomas Jefferson, Writings*, ed. Merrill D. Peterson (Library of America).

JHT, I–VI: Dumas Malone, *Jefferson and His Time.*

Kern: Susan Kern, "The Jeffersons at Shadwell: The Social and Material World of a Virginia Family" (Ph.D. diss., College of William and Mary, 2005).

LOC: Library of Congress

MB, I–II: *Jefferson's Memorandum Books: Accounts, with Legal Records and Miscellany, 1767–1826*, ed. James A. Bear Jr. and Lucia C. Stanton.

Parton, Life: James Parton, *Life of Thomas Jefferson.*

PTJ, I–XXXIX: *The Papers of Thomas Jefferson.*

PTJRS, I–VIII: *The Papers of Thomas Jefferson. Retirement Series.*

Randall, Jefferson, I–III: Henry S. Randall, *The Life of Thomas Jefferson.*

TDLTJ: Sarah N. Randolph, *The Domestic Life of Thomas Jefferson.*

TJ: Thomas Jefferson

TJF: The Thomas Jefferson Foundation

VMHB: *Virginia Magazine of History and Biography*

VTM: Merrill D. Peterson, *Visitors to Monticello.*

WMQ: *William and Mary Quarterly*

LIST OF
HISTORICAL NAMES

EDMUND BACON: Jefferson's overseer at Monticello from 1806 to 1823.

JAMES CALLENDER: Journalist. First published allegation that Jefferson had fathered the children of Sally Hemings.

PETER CARR: Nephew of Thomas Jefferson. Alleged lover of Sally Hemings and alleged father of her children. Born 1770, died 1815.

SAMUEL CARR: Nephew of Thomas Jefferson. Brother of Peter. Alleged lover of Sally Hemings and alleged father of her children. Born 1771, died 1855.

ELLEN RANDOLPH COOLIDGE: Granddaughter of Thomas Jefferson. Daughter of Martha Jefferson Randolph and Thomas Mann Randolph Jr. Wrote letter to her husband saying that Samuel Carr was the father of Sally Hemings's children.

MARIA COSWAY: Recipient of Jefferson's love letter "Dialogue between My Head and My Heart." It was thought the relationship was intense but platonic.

MARY JEFFERSON EPPES: Youngest surviving daughter of Jefferson and Martha Wayles Jefferson. Also called "Maria" and "Polly." Born 1778, died 1804. Sally Hemings accompanied her to France in 1787. Married John Eppes.

BEVERLY HEMINGS: Full name William Beverly Hemings. Born in 1798. Son of Sally Hemings. Alleged son of Thomas Jefferson or Peter or Samuel Carr. Ran away from Monticello in 1822.

CRITTA HEMINGS: Sister of Sally Hemings. Daughter of Elizabeth "Betty" Hemings.

ELIZABETH "BETTY" HEMINGS: Mother of Sally Hemings. Alleged mistress of John Wayles, Martha Jefferson's father.

ESTON HEMINGS: Full name Thomas Eston Hemings. Born 1808. Son of Sally Hemings. Alleged son of Thomas Jefferson or Peter or Samuel Carr.

MADISON HEMINGS: Full name James Madison Hemings. Born 1805, died 1877. Son of Sally Hemings. Alleged son of Thomas Jefferson or Peter or Samuel Carr. Interview printed in *Pike County* (Ohio) *Republican* in 1873, in which he said he was the son of Thomas Jefferson.

SALLY HEMINGS: Probable given name Sarah. Alleged mistress of Jefferson. Born 1773, died 1835. Daughter of Elizabeth Hemings.

ISAAC JEFFERSON: Former slave from Monticello. Gave a statement to the *Pike County* (Ohio) *Republican* affirming Madison Hemings's assertion that Jefferson had a sexual relationship with Sally Hemings.

MARTHA WAYLES SKELTON JEFFERSON: Wife of ten years to Thomas Jefferson. Born 1748, died 1782. Daughter of John Wayles. Mother of two children who survived to adulthood, Martha "Patsy" and Mary "Polly."

RANDOLPH JEFFERSON: Thomas Jefferson's younger brother and probable candidate for the paternity of Eston Hemings, as well as Sally Hemings's other children.

GEORGE WYTHE RANDOLPH: Youngest grandson of Thomas Jefferson. Son of Martha Jefferson Randolph and Thomas Mann Randolph Jr. His mother attempted to prove to him and his older brother that Jefferson could not have been the father of Sally Hemings's children.

MARTHA JEFFERSON RANDOLPH: Oldest daughter of Thomas Jefferson. Also called "Patsy." Married to Thomas Mann Randolph Jr. Mother of twelve children, including Thomas Jefferson Randolph, Ellen Randolph Coolidge, and George Wyeth Randolph.

THOMAS JEFFERSON RANDOLPH: Oldest grandson of Thomas Jefferson. Son of Martha Jefferson Randolph. Told his grandfather's biographer that Peter Carr had admitted to being the father of Sally Hemings's children. Told his sister Ellen Randolph Coolidge that he overheard Peter Carr saying that he and his brother were the fathers of Sally Hemings's children.

BATHURST SKELTON: Martha Jefferson's first husband, who died suddenly in 1768.

JOHN SKELTON: Martha's firstborn child, who died at four years of age, before she married Jefferson.

JOHN WAYLES: Father of Thomas Jefferson's wife, Martha Wayles Jefferson.

S. F. WETMORE: Editor of the *Pike County* (Ohio) *Republican*. He was a census taker for Pike County. Wrote down and published Madison Hemings's memoir in 1873.

PROLOGUE

. . . .

We live, my dear soul, in an age of trial. What will be the consequence, I know not.[1]

— JOHN ADAMS, 1774

A YEAR AFTER the bloody Revolutionary War ended in 1782, Martha Jefferson lay near death. She feebly held up three petite fingers to her adoring husband, Thomas Jefferson. Jefferson's face was set as he stared into the red-rimmed eyes of the woman he affectionately called Patty. She whispered the names of their children and clutched Jefferson's long, slender hand. Martha held his gaze, then asked him for a sacred promise—to never marry again. An edge of almost manic desperation permeated her tone. The words had an ominous double meaning for both Martha and her husband. The memory of her own harsh stepmothers colored Martha's protective thoughts for her young daughters, Patsy, Polly, and Lucy.

Outside, the encroaching dusk cast ominous, jagged shadows over Martha's pale face. Jefferson wiped away a single tear. He bent forward and kissed her chastely on the forehead. In a tender moment of complicity, he stroked Martha's hair and lovingly agreed to her dying plea. An aura of calm and serenity infused Martha as the frail, dainty true love of Jefferson's life quietly slipped away in death, closing her hazel eyes forever. Jefferson's attempted words came out as a terrible cry of anguish. He was overcome with emotion and gasped for air, taking in long deep breaths. As he rose, the six foot three Virginian buried his haggard face in his hands and literally fainted. He crumpled at Martha's deathbed, caught

1

from striking the floor by his sister-in-law and by faithful house servants, Betty and Nance Hemings, who sobbed their hearts out. All three bent over Jefferson, blasted by circumstances, trying to revive him.

Grief-stricken and nearly suicidal, Jefferson concealed himself in his study for the next three weeks. His face was a frozen mask of grief. He thought nothing could ever wound him so deeply or jolt his mind so near to the boundaries of insanity. If not for his ten-year-old daughter, Patsy, his lifeline in a torrential sea of pain, there is no doubt Thomas Jefferson, age thirty-nine, author, statesman, scientist, politician, patriot, and beloved husband and father of three would have died from his own hand or a broken heart.

Who was Martha Wayles Skelton Jefferson, and how did she influence and affect arguably one of the most famous Americans in history? What was Martha's life like with Jefferson at their mountainside home of Monticello during the darkest days of the bloody Revolutionary War—enduring six pregnancies and the death of four children while running a household and plantation full of slaves and servants? What was her relationship with her trusted house servants, the Hemingses of Monticello? And the infamous Sally Hemings? What did Martha look like? Was she a kind and loving mother, or a jealous and cold matriarch, as were her two stepmothers? What was her relationship with her famous mother-in-law, Jane Randolph Jefferson, Jefferson's controlling and somewhat eccentric mother?

Martha Jefferson is a little-known and elusive figure in history. She has been all but lost to history—until now. The goal of this biography is to create a fresh portrait of Martha, one that will make her real and charismatic in the same way that she was perceived by her family. By gleaning anecdotes and quotes from a myriad of sources, I have tried to present Martha as a vivid person, rather than merely the dutiful wife of Thomas Jefferson. My goal is to produce a cradle-to-grave narrative that is both dramatic and authoritative, encompassing the explosion of research in recent years that has enriched our understanding of both Jeffersons. Instead of having a frosty respect for Martha as a woman who endured seven difficult and life-threatening pregnancies, I hope the reader will experience a visceral appreciation of this woman who helped her husband every step of the way to reach the zenith of political greatness. Martha's resolve, courage, judgment, sterling character, and steadfast patriotism—these exemplary virtues were forged through a lifetime of hard work and emotional distress but, most importantly, through a deep and abiding love of family.

In the pages to follow, a portrait of Martha emerges as a woman who maintained her charm, sophistication, grace, education, and a profound sense of family while enduring a bloody Revolutionary War. Martha would have been an exceptional woman in any era, but for her to do what she did in eighteenth-century America, given the current attitudes about women, was truly remarkable. Yet Martha has been overshadowed by the other elemental women of the Revolution: Martha Washington, Abigail Adams, and Dolley Madison. Martha was no less a fervent patriot and passionate woman whose tireless pursuits on behalf of her family and her country proved just as crucial to the forging of a new nation as the rebellion that established it. Martha endured the Revolution as valiantly as some men, defending her very doorstep from raiding British troops, notably the flinty British dragoon "Bloody" Banastre Tarleton.

I have attempted a meticulous historical recovery of Martha, even though her "founding husband" seems larger than life and possessed political and intellectual capacities well beyond our own. The awe that most historians feel when we look back at Jefferson is now mingled with an acute sense of loss for Martha, devoted wife, beloved mother, and fiercely loyal daughter. She was probably the Revolutionary woman most taken with the age's liberal prescriptions for enlightenment, gentility, and refinement, due in large part to her father's and husband's profound influences.

"To become a natural aristocrat," offers historian Gordon Wood, "one had to acquire the attributes of a natural aristocrat: enlightenment, gentility, and taste." We shall never understand the young Martha Jefferson until we appreciate the intensity and earnestness of her desire to become cosmopolitan, genteel, and a most enlightened "lady." Whether Martha had that desire from childhood, fostered by her father and accelerated by her famous husband, we shall never know. Yet the desire blossomed from a young age, at times forced by circumstances beyond her control.[2]

"Thomas Jefferson still survives," were the dying words of John Adams, and they are as true today as they were in 1826. But Martha

Jefferson also survives, in spite of Jefferson's attempt to erase her from prying eyes, the "sacred intimacies of a lover," by burning all of their personal and passionate correspondence. Martha's ghost haunts the scenes of her life with as lively a passion as when Maria Cosway wrote to Jefferson years later, querying whether his future at Monticello would be haunted by the "shadow of a woman."

Indeed, Martha is everywhere on the mountain, in Williamsburg, Charles City, at the Shirley and Berkeley plantations, at Bermuda Hundred, The Forest, and at Eppington in Chesterfield. She survives in the commentaries of friends and neighbors, of her daughters and granddaughters, and in the material goods left behind, from wedding salt cellars to the lock of her hair Jefferson wore in a mourning ring. We know about the "other" famous women in Jefferson's life—Sally Hemings, his alleged 14-year-old slave mistress; Jane Randolph, his controlling mother; and Maria Cosway, his flirtatious paramour in Paris years after Martha's death. Yet we know virtually nothing of Martha Jefferson. Daughter, wife, mother of six, Martha was Jefferson's greatest love, his only wife, and his true kindred spirit. Tragically, she was torn from Jefferson by her own deep, overwhelming desire to give him a family. Martha's fragile body, wracked by seven dangerous pregnancies, died at the tender age of thirty-three from complications of childbirth, probably exacerbated by an early form of diabetes and tuberculosis.

Emotionally, Jefferson never recovered from Martha's death. He never married again, true to his promise. Referring to the burning of his correspondence with his beloved Martha, Jefferson's foremost biographer, Dumas Malone, remarked, "Because of this impenetrable silence on his part, probably we shall never know much about Martha Wayles Jefferson and her life with him." Following this assumption, most Jefferson biographers have settled for the usual sketchy descriptions of Martha: beautiful but slight, a devoted mother, genteel, charming in her behavior, and musically gifted. A Hessian officer who was a guest at Monticello wrote that Martha was "in all respects a very agreeable, sensible & accomplished Lady."[3]

But this clichéd and constrained image of Martha as mere refined gentry and an elegant hostess is now unraveled. Martha, while raising three daughters, was also an industrious manager of the myriad demanding requirements of two large estates, Monticello and her father's plantation, The Forest. New research discovers little-known facts about Martha's life, her childhood, her first marriage, the tragic loss of four children, and her domestic life with Jefferson and the Hemings servants at Monticello.

Had some artist been able to capture Martha's lively temperament on canvas, however, deep and tragic shadows might have brooded in the background. For all her vivacity, death seemed to stalk both Martha and Thomas Jefferson. Her father outlived three wives, including Martha's own natural mother, who died a week after Martha was born. But Martha was an emotionally strong woman who endured one tragedy after another before she finally met Jefferson. He later described their ten-year marriage as "unchequered happiness."

And what of Martha's alleged half-sister, the infamous Sally Hemings, the youngest of a family of slaves she inherited from her father, John Wayles? Wayles himself was the victim of a toxic rumor that he had an affair with Sally's mother, Betty Hemings. Was the rumor true? I have attempted to take a fresh look at the historical evidence and make a painstaking investigation into John Wayles, perhaps the most influential man in Martha's life, while investigating Martha's relationships with the men in her life from Wayles; to her first husband, Bathurst Skelton; to Jack Skelton, her young son who died at the age of four; to Jefferson himself. I have attempted to re-create Martha and Thomas Jefferson's relationship in meticulous detail, from the food they ate, the music they enjoyed, the books they read, and the clothes they wore, to the savage war they endured as wife and husband. But for all of their life experiences, in the end, their relationship embodied an American love story for the ages.

I hope to give the reader an exclusive look at the character of Martha, who some historians have called bland, if she has been mentioned at all. Here, Martha is shown to be a passionate, sensitive, capable, well-read girl who matured into a tender and accomplished, sometimes willful, woman. Martha was no milksop, nor was she docile (she lost, by Jefferson's own letters, more than a hundred pounds sterling at cards at the Coles's house, Enniscorthy, in January of 1773, although Jefferson himself abhorred cards and gambling). Martha's temper and vivacity are attested to by her daughter Patsy and her granddaughters, as are her strong opinions about childrearing. Patsy related one incident in which she had been scolded not once but twice by Martha, whereupon Jefferson intervened with some gentle words. Martha's granddaughter, Ellen Randolph Coolidge, cele-brated "her wit, her vivacity and her agreeable person and manners," while her great granddaughter, Sarah Nicholas Randolph, added that Martha was "a person of great intelligence and strength of character" with "a mind of no ordinary caliber. She was well-educated for her day, and a constant reader; she inherited from her father his method and industry."[4]

This paragon of white southern womanhood was not, however, all sweetness—as even her most devoted descendants admitted. "My grand-mother Jefferson," wrote Ellen Randolph Coolidge, drawing on her own mother's memories, "had a vivacity of temper which might sometimes border on tartness." But Martha was tender, too. Jefferson told his sensi-tive daughter Polly (Maria) that Martha had once remarked on being ill-treated by a neighbor, yet she "had rather endure two such insults as to offer one."[5]

Thomas Jefferson did not sit for a portrait until after his wife's death, and no likeness of Martha was ever put to canvas, as far as we know. According to family tradition, Martha was auburn-haired and hazel-eyed, "with a lithe and exquisitely formed figure . . . a model of graceful and queenlike carriage." "Mrs. Jefferson was small," recalled the Monticello slave Isaac Jefferson, and "a pretty lady." Family members described her as "distinguished for her beauty, her accomplishments, and her solid merit . . . a little above medium height" and "slightly but exquisitely formed." "Her complexion was brilliant," and "her large expressive eyes [were] the richest shade of hazel." To judge from traditional family descriptions, Martha bore a striking resemblance to the Medici Venus, a portrait and sculpture that Jefferson owned. Like the captivating statue, Martha was reportedly distinguished for her rare beauty. Physically, Martha's com-plexion was famous for being the finest in the family. Her skin, although described as fair, was free of the red freckles that Jefferson owned.[6]

Martha was also vivacious, musically gifted, well read, intelligent, and otherwise favorably endowed in many practical ways to be Jefferson's spiritual consort on their ideal but remote summit at Monticello. She had a sparkle about her that radiated to everyone she met. Her sister Tabitha's husband, Robert Skipwith, knew her well and praised Martha as pos-sessor of "the greatest fund of good nature [and] sprightliness and sensi-bility." She moved with grace when she walked, danced, or rode a horse, and there was a distinctly musical lilt to her charm. Martha sang beautifully and played the spinet piano and the harpsichord "with uncommon skill." Genial in conversation, she exhibited both "excellent sense and a lively play of fancy." Her personality exhibited a "frank, warmhearted, and somewhat impulsive disposition." She was "a favorite with her husband's sisters, with his family generally, and with her neighbours."[7]

It is these fascinating details that breathe life into Martha Jefferson, the most famous woman in American history that no one knows. She was a woman of her time, with all its graces and vanities. Can we blame her if she spent a little too freely at the dressmaker's shop in Williamsburg (as instanced by a bill called for long after her death by Jane Charlton) or fretted over being replaced in her husband's affections too soon?

In the following pages, it is my hope to bring Martha's character to life for the reader with new and revealing details. The historical period in which Martha matured as a woman, wife, and mother was, quite simply, the greatest and perhaps most tumultuous in American history. She knew and loved Jefferson during the time in which he produced his greatest political writings, and there is new evidence of her influence on these historical documents. She was witness to the creation of the Declaration of Independence, his governorship of Virginia, and the brutal Revolutionary War, in which her own home was invaded by British troops, with Martha barely avoiding capture.

And finally new evidence has emerged as to the probable cause of Martha's death, previously thought to be complications from childbirth. Although properly cautious about such a long-range diagnosis, diabetes combined with tuberculosis were the likely sources of Martha's childbirth woes and complications. Martha's babies grew larger with each birth—a common symptom of a life-threatening case of diabetes—with her final baby weighing an amazing 16 pounds.

Finally, Martha played the most essential role in the life of Thomas Jefferson, that of lover, friend, and partner in fame, a woman who confronted the late eighteenth century's dangers of frequent childbearing and searing anxiety about infant mortality. It is beyond coincidence that Martha died from complications following labor, as did her own daughter, Polly, as did Martha's own mother, Mary Eppes. Death and tragedy seemed to follow Martha Jefferson. All the more remarkable, then, that

Martha looms so large in life and death, and, in her case, in the formation of a fledgling nation.

As one historian has noted, there is an added benefit to knowing Martha Jefferson: understanding the women in the Founding Fathers' lives adds pathos and depth to the public dimensions of their political journeys. "We do them no dishonor when we explore how often public greatness emerged in spite of personal pain and secret disappointment. Far from diminishing these men and women, an examination of their intimate lives will enlarge them for our time. In their loves and losses, their hopes and fears, they are more like us than we have dared to imagine. When we explore [their] influence on these famous lives, we discover evidence so strong, it can easily be asserted that the great man would never have earned their place on fame's ladder without the woman at his side."[8]

Martha Jefferson's pleasures and tragedies, and even the personal charms that her family treasured, were typical enough of Chesapeake women of her time and status. But her crowning achievement was to provide an interlude of simple private happiness to one of the most brilliant and complex individuals in the nation's history. Although Jefferson preserved more than 25,000 letters from others and kept copies of 18,000 of his own, he destroyed Martha's correspondence, going so far as to collect her letters from friends for that purpose. As biographer Dumas Malone succinctly put it, "His wife did not belong to posterity; she belonged to him."[9]

In the end, there is only one picture that lasts: that of a woman who deeply loved Thomas Jefferson. Martha's laughter still rings in the south pavilion, and the trills of her harpsichord echo in the parlor; her step sounds in the beer room and her directing voice in the kitchen. Martha's spirit breathed life into Monticello, so much so that Jefferson could not bear to face it without her and changed it radically in an attempt to mute Martha's strong image.

He never did.

ONE

INFLUENCES

Whatever turns the soul inward on itself, tends to concenter its forces, and to fit it for greater and stronger flights.[1]

— EDMUND BURKE, *A Philosophical Inquiry*

MARTHA was born on October 19, 1748, in Charles City County, Virginia, not far from Williamsburg. One week later, her mother, Martha Eppes Wayles, died from complications in giving birth to her firstborn daughter. Martha would never know her mother, and this deep psychological scar would affect her for the rest of her short natural life.

So little is known about Martha's birth, family, and upbringing that one finds only a rare mention of her in varying accounts, with one source even placing her birth incorrectly in Lancaster, England. By the age of seventeen, Martha began to look for a husband among the young men she met in the plantation drawing rooms, ballrooms, and parlors of Richmond and Williamsburg. She would have been as good a match as her mother had been or even better: her wealthy father, John Wayles, having no male heir, would settle his property on his daughters. But Martha possessed attractions of her own: as well as intelligence and a work ethic, she was a stunningly beautiful young woman, auburn-haired and hazel-eyed, with an exquisitely formed figure.

In fact, Martha and her half-sisters grew up privileged, although not in a strictly secure environment. Their father, John Wayles, made a fortune but in the process fell into the same sort of debt he castigated his neighbors for. Still, there were profits to be made from high prices for tobacco and slaves bought and sold on credit. Martha moved in the most elevated circles, visiting and hosting friends and relations, Eppeses and Skeltons, Bollings and Harrises and Cockes. When traveling, these wealthy familes took along slaves to light their fires, iron their linens, and fetch their tea. Martha had fine goods as well as skilled servants who looked after her expensive dresses, hair powder, and jewels.

But who really influenced the young Martha? Who were her role models, mentors, and people in her young life? From what can be cobbled together from various historical sources, it is clear that, among the many characters in Martha's life, the three most important and influential were her father; her surrogate mother/servant, Betty Hemings (mother of Sally); and her future husband, Thomas Jefferson.

Martha's commanding father held no famous office and died just prior to the Revolution. He is best remembered by historians as the father-in-law of Thomas Jefferson, but he was much more than that to his oldest, adoring daughter, Martha.

Wayles was a planter and a lawyer, a man of business and charm. In the notes listed in the Jefferson family's prayer book, the entry for John Wayles indicates his birth in England in "Lancaster" in 1715. He grew up poor but possessed talent, ambition, and a work ethic second to none, traits that he would pass on to Martha. Sometime in the 1730s, he crossed the Atlantic as a "Servant Boy" and, within ten years, he had acquired a thriving law practice and thousands of acres of land. Wayles inherited nothing in the New World, coming alone to Virginia. He did not arrive as an explorer of the vast wilderness, but rather he acquired accounting and legal skills, settling into the populated areas of the Tidewater in Virginia. The lands along the James River had been taken, so although he bought or built his home inland, he did not settle too far into the wilds.

It is beyond sad and tragic that Martha never knew her mother, but she did know and was raised by her loving, trusted slave, and, for all intents and purposes, surrogate mother—Betty Hemings. Betty was the one constant maternal presence in Martha's life, a life shadowed by the tragic death of a mother she never knew and two stepmothers.

Betty Hemings was a beloved house servant for Martha's father and for thirty-three years—until Martha's own death—acted as a surrogate mother to Martha. In fact, Betty had been part of Martha's life since birth. When Martha's own mother died so young, Martha's guiding principle in her relationship with the Hemingses was to accept responsibility for their welfare. Martha wished to give the Hemingses her fullest protection, and, years later, she placed them in the safest environment she knew, Monticello.

In her authoritative slave biography *The Hemingses of Monticello*, historian Annette Gordon-Reed chronicled Betty Hemings's life and upbringing. In 1735, a man named Hemings, the white English captain of a trading ship, fathered a daughter with a "full-blooded African" woman. The African woman's child was named Elizabeth, also known as Betty. The details come from the account of Madison Hemings, a grandson of Betty Hemings. By 1746—the year Wayles married Martha Eppes—Betty Hemings, then about eleven years old, moved to Wayles's plantation (aptly named The Forest) in Charles City County, near Williamsburg. There, beginning at age eighteen, she gave birth to several children. Not long after John Wayles's death in 1773, Betty was brought to Monticello with her ten children, six of whom were, according to Madison Hemings, fathered by Wayles (Robert, James, Thenia, Critta, Peter, and Sally). Two more children were born to Betty at Monticello (Lucy and John). More than seventy-five of Betty's descendants lived at least some part of their lives in bondage at Monticello.[2]

Betty Hemings was a valued domestic servant whose children and grandchildren occupied the most important household and trades positions on the mountaintop. Three of her sons and six of her grandchildren were freed, or allowed to go free, by Jefferson in his lifetime or in his will—the only slaves to whom he granted freedom.

The only physical description we have of Betty Hemings is that she was a "bright mulatto" woman. But descriptions of several of her daughters and granddaughter refer to them as having been extremely attractive women. According to one historian, "Betty herself was able to attract males of both colors well into her forties, when by the standards of that day she would have been considered relatively old."[3] All of these factors would touch the lives of various members of the Hemings family for more than a century. But one event, the marriage of John Wayles to Martha Eppes, would turn out to be the single most important occurrence in the life of young Betty Hemings, the girl who was to become the Hemings family's matriarch and a surrogate mother to Martha Jefferson.[4]

And then one day, Martha met Thomas Jefferson.

As Martha was growing up at her father's plantation The Forest, young Thomas Jefferson was not far away at his home in Shadwell. The popular mythology of Jefferson's youth was that his father, Peter Jefferson, was a backwoodsman, a native of the frontier, and that Jane Randolph Jefferson, his mother, brought her gentry standards to the Jefferson household. The Jeffersons were a successful planter family, yet, the story goes, the young Jefferson left his Shadwell and Tuckahoe homes and his boyhood schoolmasters and went to the city where he learned his manners and tastes for finer things, first in Williamsburg, then in Philadelphia.[5]

Contrasting popular historical perception, historian Susan Kern concluded that "Peter Jefferson had nearly the status his wife had. He was a county surveyor, after all, a county justice, a burgess, and an acquaintance of many important players in mid-century Virginia. The material world of Shadwell shows, however, that young Jefferson and his siblings did not have to seek refinement elsewhere. They grew up with it and carried it with them. Shadwell was full of the proper tools for entertaining and for teaching children manners. Their expectations, moreover, were not dictated by their location, for Albemarle indeed was still a frontier. Instead, the Jeffersons acquired fine goods and impeccable manners that allowed entry into the gentry world."[6]

In fact, Peter Jefferson studied as a surveyor under one of the most famous land surveyors of the eighteenth century—William Mayo, who surveyed the Potomac River for King George III and Lord Fairfax. Mayo was a neighbor and friend of William Byrd II, arguably one of the most distinguished Virginians of the time. In addition to being a planter and a writer of great wit, Byrd was an ardent politician who served for many years on the Virginia Council. In 1728, Mayo served under Byrd as one of the surveyors of the Virginia and North Carolina boundary line. When Goochland County was formed that year, Mayo became its first surveyor and member of its first court, positions he held until he died. In 1737, Mayo surveyed the towns of Richmond and Petersburg and also campaigned unsuccessfully to develop a map of Virginia. That effort was delayed until 1751, when Joshua Fry and Peter Jefferson made their famous map of the colony. Peter Jefferson was Mayo's neighbor and friend and most probably was tutored by Mayo in his surveying skills.[7]

The Jeffersons also occupied the upper end of the social strata through participation in the church vestry and county government. The heights to which Thomas Jefferson rose were beyond exceptional, historian Kern argues, yet he neither grew up in economic distress nor lived in a world of material aristocracy. Rather, he grew up within a plantation life, where his and his father's responsibilities included public service, as well as the professional tasks of hiring overseers, slaves, and road crews. Yet Jefferson's overriding culture was within a family that valued educating children and instilling social etiquette. It is against this family upbringing that Jefferson first met and chose his future and only wife, his true love, Martha Wayles.[8]

TWO

THE FOREST

···

Her father, John Wayles, had been born in England, the
home of "Royal Forests" so a Lancaster man would be
proud to describe his own land in the New World as "The
Forest."[1]

— Historians REBECCA and JAMES MCMURRAY

O NE HISTORIAN described the state of Virginia in "the
last half-century before the Revolution . . . a land of scattered
plantations where tidewater barons harvested their money crop,
tobacco, with slave labor and vast amounts of land. It is not an under-
statement to concede that the tobacco industry singularly shaped the
whole history of the Virginia colony and set the patterns for all political,
economic, and cultural life. The plantation system did not encourage the
growth of cities, for business centers could not flourish when each of the
river estates had its own docks to handle tobacco exports and imports
from England."[2]

In fact, Williamsburg, the eighteenth-century colonial capital, could
count only a few hundred residents even in the bustling spring and fall
season when planters arrived to attend the court sessions. The typical
planter, one such as John Wayles, "could see a play or hear the Beggar's
Opera during the season in Williamsburg, but the orchestra would be
nothing more than a harpsichord and possibly a violin. One might join
the seventy-five or eighty other guests in minuets, reels, and country
dances when the Lees gave a ball that would last for three days, but he
would have to step to the tune of a French horn and two violins. A tutor
would provide a musical education for the gentry's sons and daughters,

but to make a living the teacher would also have to deal in dancing, drawing, or fencing."[3]

It is against this backdrop that Martha began her childhood in Charles City County, near Williamsburg, at The Forest plantation. Located north of Westover Plantation and about five miles north of Shirley Plantation, The Forest most probably was built above an east-west portico, across the James River from another plantation, Bermuda Hundred. Wayles chose to build his home among the hardwood trees just inland from the banks of the James. Wayles's original house was apparently burned about 1862, and no pictures or archaeological studies have pinpointed its location, although oral tradition still speaks of familiarity with the spot. These facts suggest that the house was a frame building with brick foundation or basement rather than one built entirely of brick like the grand plantation houses at Westover or Shirley along the James River.[4]

Most prominent planters in Wayles's region built their homes as close to the river as they could, for very good reasons, observed slave historian Annette Gordon-Reed. The James River, with its numerous tributaries, empties into the Chesapeake Bay, which gives it a link to the Atlantic Ocean and the world beyond. In fact, the first settlement in the colony, Jamestown, lay forty miles upriver from the Chesapeake Bay. The people who lived in the area and knew the river before the white settlers arrived named it after Powhatan, the leader of the powerful Indian tribe and father of the famed Pocahontas. As the years passed, Gordon-Reed notes, "other settlements and Tidewater plantations stretched out along the river to take advantage of its connection to the bay and Atlantic markets. A similar process unfolded along the Potomac, York, and Rappahannock, three of the other major waterways in Virginia. The waters of all these rivers carried indentured servants, African slaves, and consumer goods into the colony and transported its life-defining staple crop, tobacco, out to foreign markets, namely England. Wayles was intimately familiar with all aspects of life on the James. He lived and worked as a lawyer in the area, and it was from Bermuda Hundred that he sometimes carried out one of the most important parts of his life as a businessman—selling slaves."[5]

The origin of the name of Martha's girlhood home, The Forest, is also historically interesting. It was common in those days for owners of estates to combine their names with words that seemed to them picturesque and harmonious. A variety of combinations is seen in the estates surrounding The Forest, such as Brooke's Bank, Carter's Creek, Carter's Grove, and Swann's Point. In addition, there was Eppington, home of the Eppes family; Wyncove, the home of the Wynnes; Lochaven, the home of the Lockwoods; and Harwick, the home of the Harrises. In devising names like these, Virginians were not creating new patterns but using familiar ones long known in England.

One of the most popular sources of names for Tidewater houses—including The Forest—and the source probably most revered, was found in the settlers' English heritage. Houses and plantations had English names such as Arlington, Berkeley, Brandon, Claremont, Hampstead, Stratford, Wakefield, and Windsor.

Martha's father no doubt was familiar with the practice of naming new homes in America for old ones in England, a widespread custom in the first few years of our history. George Mason, the author of the Bill of Rights, is one who followed this practice in naming his Potomac River home Gunston Hall. His grandmother was Mary Fowke of Gunston Hall, in Charles County, Maryland, and she was the granddaughter of Gerard Fowke of Gunston Hall, Staffordshire, who emigrated to Virginia. When Mason gave a portion of his estate to his son Thomas, he called it Hollin Hall, the name of his mother's family home near Ripon in the north of England. Later, however, when in 1775 he gave another portion to his son George, he did not hesitate to depart from his practice and call it Lexington to commemorate the then very recent first battle of the Revolution.

Others in Tidewater Virginia likewise made use of the names of their family homes in England; for example, the Taliaferros and the Throckmortons in Gloucester County and the Lees in Northumberland County called their homes Dunham Massie, Hail Western, and Ditchley, respectively, for the English homes of their forebears. Descriptive names have always been popular, and Tidewater Virginia offers a variety in the landscape that has been the source of names for many places. For example, the numerous streams and inlets cutting into the land have prompted such names as Haven's Edge, River's Edge, and Water's Edge, as well as Bay Bank, Claybank, Shellbank, and Sunnybank.[6]

As described by slave historian Annette Gordon-Reed, the prestigious family of Martha Eppes, Martha's mother, were among the earliest arrivals to Virginia from their native England. The founding settler, Francis, served on the Council of Virginia in the 1630s. The family took up residence along the James and Appomattox Rivers in Henrico County, which would later be divided in two, creating a new county called Chesterfield. Like other arriving families of the day, the Eppeses acquired large landholdings through the "headright" system, a scheme designed to stimulate immigration to Virginia.[7] Throughout the seventeenth century and into the beginning of the eighteenth, anyone who paid for the passage of other immigrants to Virginia received fifty acres of land for each person, hence the term "headright." For a time, people received headrights for bringing in African slaves.[8]

Francis Eppes, Martha's maternal grandfather, obtained 1,700 acres of land under this system, giving his family a valuable start in the emerging colony. As the years passed, members of the Eppes family married into other prominent families and sometimes even their own cousins. These marriages concentrated landownership within the small planter gentry. With more land came the need for slaves to work the fields of tobacco that emerged as the colony's lifeblood.[9]

Martha's mother, Martha Eppes, together with her servant, Betty Hemings, left her childhood home at Bermuda Hundred in 1746, when Martha married the prosperous English immigrant John Wayles. As a woman of the eighteenth century, Eppes became a "feme covert" when she married—a wife under the cover of her husband who then gained the right to control her property, among other things, in return for his protection. Gentry families often had concerns about losing family property simply because of one marriage. Marriage settlements, essentially eighteenth-century versions of prenuptial agreements, were agreed upon before the marriage to protect the bride's specific property. In exchange, the bride often gave up the right to her dower, which would have given her one-third of her husband's estate upon his death.[10]

Betty Hemings came into the Wayles household as part of the property that Martha Eppes wanted to keep in her family line after she married. One historian opined whether Wayles's lower-class origins played any role in the decision to have a premarital agreement keeping certain Eppes property in the Eppeses' hands. Although he was already wealthy by the time of his marriage and had strong connections to an extremely well-regarded patron, Wayles had no family ties in a colony that thrived on family connections. "Given their relative positions in society," Annette Gordon-Reed argues, "Wayles had more to gain through his alliance with an old Virginia family than he lost by giving up what would be, in the absence of a contract, his property rights as a husband."[11]

As it turned out, Betty Hemings's move away from the Eppes family was not permanent. Over the next five decades, she, her children, and even some of her grandchildren returned to them periodically as servants passing between and among the extended families of the Eppeses, Randolphs, and Jeffersons. Actually, Betty did not have far to go. Her new home, The Forest, John Wayles's plantation, was in Charles City County, across the James River from Bermuda Hundred.[12]

The Eppes family seat became Eppington, a mansion built by Francis Eppes VI in 1766. That residence would play a recurring role in the lives of Martha Jefferson and her children, as they lived there off and on even after the family moved permanently to Monticello. We do not have physical evidence of what young Martha's immediate surroundings were like, but, given her mother's wealth and prominence in their status-conscious environment, her parents would have built a home suitable to persons of their station.[13]

By his thirties, John Wayles was solidly established in Virginia as a planter, slave trader, and lawyer. He was not steeped in legal studies, but he had "great industry, punctuality, and practical readiness," and his business grew rapidly. At the same time, Wayles was a man of large gusto, a generous host and entertainer, "a most agreeable companion, full of pleasantry, good humor, and welcomed in every society."[14]

Wayles, thrice married, loved his daughter Martha but nevertheless exposed her to two apparently loveless and cold stepmothers. By January 1760, Wayles had found himself a third wife and a second stepmother for Martha. This time he chose the widow Elizabeth Lomax Skelton who had inherited property from her late husband, Reuben Skelton. Scarcely more than a year after the wedding, she, too, was dead. Burying a third wife was enough for John Wayles. He never married again.

As a motherless girl, Martha's domestic education would have occurred at an accelerated pace. As was customary at the time, young Martha would have found herself thrust into the role of mistress of the home at a tender age, until her father remarried, and she would be again forced into this role after the death of both her stepmothers. It was common among Wayles's contemporaries for widowers to seek the assistance of female relatives in raising infant daughters or, if the family could afford it, for them to employ tutors. We are unsure which of these scenarios describes Martha's early years, but the poise, domestic skills, and education attributed to Martha as a young woman would point to the likelihood that John Wayles had help raising his daughter. Patty, as she was nicknamed, was taught to make soap, candles, beer, butter, and other household staples of the eighteenth century, and she could cook, sew, and treat illnesses with homemade remedies.

As a young woman, Martha appears to have attended—and would have been expected to have done so, given her father's wealth and close proximity to the capital—social events in Williamsburg. Because her father buried three wives and lived for many years as a widower after the death of his third spouse, Martha most assuredly would have attended these social functions on his arm and would have been responsible for helping to host social affairs at The Forest.

It is clear that, growing up, Martha knew how to manage a large household. Eventually running a bustling plantation with its vast estate, mansion, farms, large slave population, attendant overseers, and frequent guests and visitors (for both Wayles and, later, Jefferson) required considerable skill, work, and energy. Several sources note that, in addition to organizing the family affairs and ordering home supplies, Martha assisted her father in managing the plantation and home business accounts.

Indeed, young Martha was fully engaged in business matters for her father. She was the de facto overseer of two working farms (The Forest and later Monticello). Martha was trained to business by her father. In the land rolls and deeds of Charles City County, there are a half dozen surviving documents franked by "Mrs. Martha Skelton," as witness to a legal transaction between her father and a client. The last one is dated in

November 1771, a mere six weeks before her marriage to Jefferson: it was the probate of the will of her late husband, Bathurst Skelton.

Martha tried to be all business, and she once complained years later that some instance of Jefferson's generosity had gone unappreciated by its recipient. "But it was always so with him," Martha is said to have remarked. "He is so good himself, that he cannot understand how bad other people may be."[15] Smart and strong-willed in business affairs, Martha also liked having her own way. Years later, Jefferson once gently rebuked her for reminding their eldest daughter, Patsy, of an old childhood crime. "My dear, a fault in so young a child once punished should be forgotten," Jefferson said to Martha. Patsy recalled feeling a "warm gush of gratitude" for her father's support.[16]

Out of necessity, Martha was not a woman of retiring nature or quiet views. She had a mind of her own and could be assertive. "My grandmother Jefferson had a vivacity of temper which might sometimes border on tartness, but which, in her intercourse with her husband, was completely subdued by her exceeding affection for him," said Ellen Randolph Coolidge, a Jefferson granddaughter.[17]

At The Forest, Martha continued to enter inventories of food and clothing in her account book. Later, as mistress of Monticello, all of Martha's purchases were reviewed by her sharp-eyed husband, and if she was charged too much for an item he informed her, gently, no doubt. Indeed, she may have been guilty of paying too much for the very first item purchased after her marriage. On January 30, 1772, she noted: "sent to buy cyder 10/," and Jefferson, in copying it into his pocket memorandum book, noted for posterity "which was 6/3 too much."[18]

Martha quickly picked up Jefferson's habits, however—habits that supported those first instilled in her by her own father's work ethic. It was not long before some of the entries in her own household account book could have been written by Jefferson. For example, on May 16, 1774, she jotted down in precisely the same language Jefferson used in his garden book, "first patch of peas come to table." As subsequent servings of her husband's favorite vegetable were picked from the garden, Martha noted the date. She even tried one of Jefferson's characteristic experiments to determine the most efficient way to measure and brew coffee. And she did not stop at just brewing coffee. Martha's father had been fond of good beer, and Martha inherited a thorough knowledge of how to make it. She recorded in her account book the brewing of a fifteen-gallon cask of "small beer." This was the equivalent of twenty-five "six-packs" in today's common measure; yet, before the year's end, Martha had brewed ten more casks.

In her youth, Martha also quickly established herself as manager of her father's household slaves at The Forest. This continued years later at Monticello. In June 1774, she recorded the clothes given to the Monticello house servants. Ursula, Orange, Mary Hemings, and Scilla each received "2 suits of clothes." In fact, when Martha later moved to Monticello, only the dining room wing of the house was completed, and there were more than a hundred slaves to take care of in a very small completed shelter. Running a plantation household was labor-intensive. Like other colonial women of the day, she would have been in charge of the close division of labor among the household servants because their skills were often highly specialized (i.e., seamstress, carpenter, gardener). Like many plantation owners, the Jeffersons were slave rich, having inherited 135 slaves on the death of Martha's father, John Wayles (including the famous Hemings family).

"Whereas Great George's wife Ursula reigned supreme during her lifetime in the kitchen, smokehouse and wash house," describes historian Lucia Stanton, "Betty Hemings and her children took charge inside the house." Their duties, not specifically described, ranged from cleaning and sewing, to personal maids and valets, to assisting Martha in supervising the entire domestic staff. Betty Brown, Betty Hemings's second daughter, and her sister, Critta, were also housemaids. As Jefferson himself recorded in 1793, Critta Hemings was "oftenest wanted about the house," and she was probably Monticello's parlor maid. Sally Hemings was also described by her son as a chambermaid and seamstress.[19]

From descriptions of her, we know that young Martha was not only literate but was well read for a young woman of her time, and she enjoyed poetry and fiction. Families of comfortable means often employed traveling tutors to educate their daughters because young girls were not formally educated at schools. Their basic education at home focused on the domestic arts, a curriculum supplemented by teachers in such areas as literature, music, dancing, Bible study, and even French. Because Martha grew up to be an accomplished musician, it appears likely she received many lessons as a child.

At the center of Martha's civilized world at The Forest was the idea of becoming a "lady," her father's ambition for all of his daughters. A lady would be a woman of good behavior, well bred, amiable, high-minded, who knew how to act in any society, especially in the company of any man. No word in the English language came to denote better the finest qualities of the ideal woman than a lady, and it was the enlightened eighteenth century above all that gave it that significance.[20]

On the flip side of this social coin, notes historian Gordon Wood, "to be a gentleman was to think and act like a gentleman. It meant being reasonable, tolerant, honest, and 'candid,' an important eighteenth-century characteristic that connoted being unbiased and just as well as frank and sincere"—terms that would describe Martha's future husband, Thomas Jefferson. In fact, being a gentleman was the prerequisite to becoming a political leader, argues Wood. It signified being cosmopolitan, standing on elevated ground in order to have a larger view of human affairs. "This age-old distinction between gentlemen and commoners," Wood concludes, "had a vital meaning for the revolutionary generation that we today have totally lost. It marked a horizontal cleavage that divided the social hierarchy into two unequal parts. This enlightened age emphasized new criteria of aristocracy and gentility—politeness, grace, taste, learning, and character."[21] All these words aptly describe Martha and Thomas Jefferson.

Against this social backdrop and in keeping with her demure young lady persona, Martha apparently was not a physically strong woman. She was small in stature and delicately featured. There is no known portrait of her, but family tradition described her as "slightly but exquisitely formed," with a "brilliant" complexion, "expressive eyes of the richest shade of hazel," and "luxuriant hair of the finest tinge of auburn." She walked, rode, and danced "with admirable grace and spirit" and was "frank, warmhearted, and somewhat impulsive."[22] In his memoir, the slave Isaac Jefferson confirmed her small stature and her beauty. In comparing the two Jefferson daughters, Martha (Patsy) and Maria (Polly), years later, Isaac declared, "Patsy Jefferson was tall like her father. Polly low like her mother and longways the handsomest, pretty lady jist like her mother."[23]

❧

Martha had a strict, if not emotionally distressing childhood, imposed on her by two cold stepmothers. One family story held that Martha would stand in the bedroom she shared with her stepsister, Lisbet, as a little girl. Mary Cocke, her stepmother, stood before Martha, her fair face ruddy with emotion, scolding Martha roundly for her stubbornness. Cocke would shake Martha by the shoulders until her teeth rattled.[24]

Many years later, Thomas Jefferson took care to mark the births, marriages, and deaths of Martha's immediate family members into his own records, information Jefferson gleaned from Martha herself. But, interestingly, Jefferson entered no given names for either of Martha's stepmothers, a telling slight. Most probably, Martha did not speak of those women, and, if she did, it was not in kind terms for their names to lodge in Jefferson's legendary memory. In fact, Martha's silence may have been a way to quell the bad memories of a scorched heart.

Martha's two stepsisters were born in this period between 1752 and 1756, a time when her father's disposition and industry, described years later by Jefferson, had finally paid off. From all accounts, Wayles worked hard, and the court records are evidence of this fact. But tragedy would soon strike again.

When Martha's youngest sister was four, the second Mrs. Wayles died. Almost immediately, Wayles married a third time to provide a mother to his four daughters. On January 23, 1760, Wayles married Elizabeth Lomax Skelton, the widow of Reuben Skelton of Goochland County. Elizabeth was sixteen years younger than her new husband. She had no children, and they had no known children together. In the year of his marriage to Elizabeth, Wayles wrote his will, suggesting that he feared death shortly after their wedding. In this document, he requests that two of Martha's slaves from the old tripartite agreement, "Betty Hemings and Jenny the cook," be allowed to remain with his "Dear Wife to continue with her during her natural life and after her death to my said Daughter Martha."

Ironically, Wayles recovered his health, but his young wife died, leaving Martha again motherless. From these painful and emotional experiences, Martha was taught from an early age to prize self-reliance as she grew up and prepared to take on the tasks of an industrious plantation with her father. At barely the age of fourteen, motherless again, Martha assumed the duties of woman of the house. While her servants performed the hardest jobs, Martha learned the ways of butchering hogs, cattle, and fowl; rendering lard to mix with lye and ashes for soap; brewing beer; counting out the linens and spoons; and dispensing clothing and food to slaves. She saw to these duties at The Forest and took part in running John Wayles's other plantations, such as Elk Hill.

As Martha stood in for her mother and stepmothers, she completed her training in housewifery under the supportive and loving eyes of her beloved house servant, Betty Hemings. Yet, whatever Betty could teach Martha about housekeeping, she could not train Martha in everything she needed to know. Other women, female relations and friends, would have initiated Martha into plantation society, the fine art of mingling politeness into genteel conversation, or setting a stitch in fancy sewing. Her father not only taught her to keep household accounts, but also showed her how to ride a horse with expertise. This trait she would later share with Jefferson— they both loved to ride. Teachers and tutors came to The Forest to instruct the young Martha in music and dancing, and Martha became known for her musical gifts, her skill on the spinet and harpsichord, and her sweet singing voice. In fact, Martha played not only the harpsichord, but also the guitar as well. Many references in Jefferson's accounts reference the purchase of "guitar strings for Mrs. J." Historian Helen Cripe in her book *Thomas Jefferson and Music* details the guitars at Monticello, beginning with those owned by "Patty" before she was married to Jefferson.

All these qualities combined would provide a monumental attraction to Thomas Jefferson.

Martha must have had her share of suitors, even though she entered the marriage market at a time of family turmoil. Her father had made a fortune but soon fell into the debt he deplored in his neighbors. Risk was inherent in his business, yet there were profits to be made from tobacco and from slaves bought and sold with credit. No doubt Martha and her sisters traveled in the most elevated circles, visiting and hosting friends all attended to by their family slaves, which begs the historical question: how did Martha feel about the institution of slavery?

There is no known recording of Martha's views on slavery, either as an institution or a moral debate. Servants, both enslaved and indentured, probably found their final resting place near The Forest because Martha's father owned many slaves. Among the ruins of The Forest in Charles City County many graves give silent testimony to that lost world. That Martha grew up with slavery was a fact. Historians simply do not know how Martha felt about her father's ventures into the slave trade. She may have been ignorant of the financial and legal aspects; and, although she was certainly steeped in the daily regimes of slavery, she may never have attended a slave auction herself. But even if Martha did not personally witness the buying and selling of people, she, as almost all of eighteenth-century southern society, may have taken for granted her right to slaves.

In later years, specifically January 1777, at Martha's behest, Thomas Jefferson attended a slave sale. He went to a plantation called Maiden's Adventure, where he spent £10 (on twelve months' credit) to purchase three slaves: Ursula Granger; her fourteen-year-old son, George; and her five-year-old son, Bagwell. Martha wanted Jefferson to buy Ursula, a large woman who could do everything from laundry to smoking hams. To obtain Ursula, who would become a "favorite housewoman," Martha insisted on taking Ursula's children, too, for both Martha and Thomas Jefferson agreed that enslaved families should be kept together. Jefferson would shortly buy Ursula's husband, George Granger, from another planter, and the Grangers were soon central and trusted members of the Jefferson household at Monticello in later years.

Isaac Jefferson, Ursula's youngest son, recalled the way that "Mrs. Jefferson would come out there with a cookery book in her hand and read out of it to Isaac's mother how to make cakes, tarts, and so on."[25] But the relationship between the mistress and her slave woman was more intimate than cakes and tarts. After her marriage to Jefferson, Martha had trouble nursing, as she had anticipated, and her first daughter, Patsy, continued to be small and sickly. The Jeffersons asked Ursula to wet-nurse Patsy, providing what Jefferson called "a good breast of milk."[26] Patsy began to thrive, although Ursula's own baby, Archy, tragically died in 1774.

Thomas Jefferson himself was a consistent opponent of slavery. A strong historical case can be made that Martha not only directly influenced, but may also have accelerated Jefferson's viewpoint that slavery was a moral abomination that needed a solution. It is not merely historical coincidence that, in the twelve years that Martha and Jefferson courted and then married, Jefferson's opposition to slavery increased every year.

In historical records from between the years 1769 and 1782 (his courtship and marriage to Martha), Jefferson expressed the following opposition to slavery. In a letter to the Reverend David Barrow, who founded the Kentucky abolition society, Jefferson wrote:

> Where the disease [slavery] is most deeply seated, there it will be slower in eradication. In the Northern states, it was merely superficial and easily corrected. In the southern, it is incorporated with the whole system, and requires time, patience and perseverance in the curative process.[27]

When Jefferson first met Martha in 1769 or 1770, at the age of twenty-six, he began his political career as a member of the Virginia legislature. Shortly after election, he approached senior legislator Richard Bland and proposed that the two of them undertake an "effort in that body for the permission of the emancipation of slaves." Colonel Bland offered the motion and Jefferson seconded it, but it was resoundingly defeated. In fact, for even proposing that measure, Bland was "denounced as an enemy of his country . . . and was treated with the grossest indecorum." Jefferson lamented that as long as Virginia remained a British colony, no emancipation proposal "could expect success," a condition that he hoped would change.[28]

Jefferson would soon literally practice what he preached. In 1770, he represented a slave in court, arguing for his freedom. Jefferson explained:

> Under the law of nature, all men are born free. Everyone comes into the world with a right to his own person, which includes the liberty of moving and using it at his own will. This is what is called personal liberty, and is given him by the Author of Nature.[29]

Jefferson lost the case, but, in 1772, he argued a similar case. In 1773 and 1774, a number of American colonies, including Rhode Island, Connecticut, and Pennsylvania, passed antislavery laws, all of which were struck down by the king in 1774. That year, Jefferson penned "A Summary View of the Rights of British America." His purpose was to remind the British that legitimate American concerns were being ignored, specifically the king's veto of American antislavery laws:

> The abolition of domestic slavery is the great object of desire in those colonies where it was unhappily introduced in their infant state [by Britain]. But previous to the enfranchisement of the slaves we have, it is necessary to exclude all further importations from Africa. Yet our repeated attempts to effect this . . . have been hitherto defeated by His Majesty's negative [veto].[30]

In 1776, Jefferson wrote a draft of the original state constitution for Virginia and included a provision that "[n]o person hereafter coming into this country [Virginia] shall be held in slavery under any pretext whatever." That provision was rejected by the state convention. Later, in 1776, as a member of the Continental Congress, Jefferson drafted the Declaration of Independence. Among the grievances impelling America's separation from Great Britain, Jefferson listed the fact that the king would not allow individual colonies to end slavery or the slave trade, even when they wished to do so:

> He [King George III] has waged cruel war against human nature itself, violating its most sacred rights of life and liberty in the persons of a distant people which never offended him, captivating & carrying them into slavery in another hemisphere, or to incur miserable death in their transportation thither. . . . He has . . . determin[ed] to keep open a market where men should be bought and sold.[31]

Unfortunately, Jefferson's antislavery clause was deleted from the Declaration "in complaisance to South Carolina and Georgia, who had never attempted to restrain the importation of slaves, and who, on the contrary, still wished to continue it."[32]

In 1778, Jefferson drafted a Virginia law that prohibited the importation of enslaved Africans. In 1784, he proposed an ordinance that would ban slavery in the Northwest territories. But Jefferson always maintained that the decision to emancipate slaves would have to be part of a democratic process; abolition would be stymied until slave owners consented to free their human property together in a large-scale act of emancipation. To Jefferson, it was antidemocratic and contrary to the principles of the American Revolution for the federal government to enact abolition or for only a few planters to free their slaves.[33]

One can make a reasonable historical case that Martha shared, if not directly influenced, Jefferson's views and opposition to slavery. Calling it a "moral depravity" and a "hideous blot," the Jeffersons believed that slavery presented the greatest threat to the survival of the new American nation. Jefferson also thought that slavery was contrary to the laws of nature, which decreed that everyone had a right to personal liberty. These views were radical in a world where slave labor was the norm.

At the time of the American Revolution, and after his marriage to Martha, Jefferson was actively involved in legislation that he hoped would result in slavery's abolition. Did Martha influence his controversial views on abolishing or limiting slavery? A case can be made that Martha's own close relationship with the Hemings family and especially with the woman she considered a surrogate mother, Betty Hemings, may have been the catalyst for Jefferson's opposition to slavery. He could personally see the loving, maternal relationship that a black slave had for a white woman, and this no doubt had a profound influence on Martha, as well as Jefferson and his views on human bondage.

Some historians castigate Jefferson as a hypocrite for not freeing his slaves upon his death: if Thomas Jefferson was indeed so antislavery, then why did he not release his own slaves? George Washington allowed for the freeing of his slaves on his death in 1799, so why did Jefferson not do the same at his death in 1826? The historical record finds a simple answer to this complicated question: Virginia law. In 1799, Virginia allowed owners to emancipate their slaves on their death; in 1826, state laws had been changed to prohibit that practice. But, in 1782, for a very short time, Virginia began to move in a new direction. An emancipation law was passed, declaring:

> [T]hose persons who are disposed to emancipate their slaves may be empowered so to do and . . . it shall hereafter be lawful for any person, by his or her last will and testament, . . . to emancipate and set free his or her slaves.[34]

It was as a result of this law that George Washington was able to free his slaves in 1799. But in 1806 Virginia repealed much of that law. It was under these laws that Jefferson was required to operate. In 1814 he lamented to an abolitionist minister friend in Illinois that in Virginia "[t] he laws do not permit us to turn them loose." And even if Jefferson had done so, he certainly did not have the finances required by law to provide a livelihood and support for each of his freed slaves.[35]

Yet, ultimately, psychological and social considerations, politics, and economics truly explain Jefferson's reticence on this issue. Noted Jefferson scholar Merrill Peterson writes that "neither he nor any other prominent Virginian was ever willing to risk friends, position, and influence to fight for it."[36] Historian Jack Greene found Jefferson to be restrained in his approach to abolish slavery by overriding doubts that differences in color, culture, and possibly intellectual ability precluded freed slaves from ever "achieving full civic competence or being satisfactorily incorporated into the polity as a whole."[37] Historian Joseph Ellis commented on the relevance of "ideology" to Jefferson, noting that he "harbored a set of attractive ideals . . . that he mistakenly believed could be implemented in this world merely because they existed in his head."[38]

Although the Jeffersons continued to advocate for abolition, the reality was that slavery was only becoming more entrenched in Virginia. Beginning in the early nineteenth century, the rich soil in the Shenandoah Valley attracted an increasing number of slaveholders. Between 1800 and 1830, the slave population in the Valley grew by 92 percent, while the white population grew at a rate of just 26.8 percent. In fact, the slave population in Virginia swelled from 292,627 in 1790 to 469,757 in 1830, four years after Jefferson's death.[39]

THREE

JOHN WAYLES

John Wayles of Virginia, a planter and a lawyer, was a man
of business and charm.[1]

— Historian VIRGINIA SCHARFF

Until now, John Wayles was best known in history as Thomas Jefferson's father-in-law. He has been curtly described by previous historians as a wealthy slave dealer who may have had a
sexual relationship with one of his slaves, Betty Hemings, mother of
Sally Hemings. But the most verifiable historical evidence on this much-
maligned man has demonstrated a much different person and casts severe
doubts on some clichéd assumptions about Wayles.

Little is known about Wayles's birth or family in Lancaster, England. Both the town of Lancaster and the county (now Lancashire) were
described at the time simply as "Lancaster." Wayles was born into a culture still divided from the effects of the interregnum period of Oliver
Cromwell and the Stuart restoration to the throne of King Charles II.
The Jacobite War exploded the very year Wayles was born. He was five
years old when the infamous "South Sea Bubble" burst, considered by
some to be the result of "a general immorality." Letters written by Wayles
later in life reflect a sense of England during that time, when "luxury and
lavish living" were counted as the potential causes of terrible misfortunes.
Those were turbulent times in England, and John Wayles seems to have
taken to heart the moral lessons learned from youthful observation.[2]

Jefferson noted in a family Bible that John Wayles was born in Lancaster, England, on January 31, 1715, but gave no additional information about Wayles's parents or family. Little is known of his early life in England or Virginia. The loss of the official records of Charles City County, along with the loss of Wayles's papers, which were taken to Eppington with his daughter Elizabeth, helps explain the lack of personal details about him.

Some historians have defined Wayles solely by what he accomplished in America, as if he had had no life before he arrived, no family, and no parents. If the boy is father to the man, nothing of the boy's life has appeared in print to shed much light on what sort of man Wayles really was. The people who would have known what Wayles's early life in England was like—his daughters Martha, Elizabeth, Tabitha, and Anne—apparently did not write of their father's early beginnings, or, if they did, those writings are not extant or have not been included in historians' writings about the Wayles and Jefferson families. When the issue was addressed at all, the assumption was that Wayles had been trained as a lawyer before he arrived in America. That bit of information, which would tend to point toward an upper- or at least middle-class birth, appears inaccurate.

On August 14, 1715, "John, son of Edward Wales of Lancaster," was christened in St. Mary's parish. As no other child named John Wales (or John Wayles, as he became known) was baptized between 1712 and 1724 in Lancaster, this record of baptism almost certainly referred to John Wayles of Virginia and confirms Jefferson's notation about his father-in-law's date of birth. Following the pattern common in those days, the record listed only the father's name. In the year before Wayles's baptism, however, the parish records noted the November 11 marriage of "Edward Wales of Lancaster and Ellen Ashburner of Bulk," a small town north of Lancaster. Ellen was about seven months pregnant with John when she married Edward, but in those days the betrothal began the union of the couple. The marriage sealed it. If Ellen was born in Lancaster, there is no record of her baptism. Ellen Wales would be memorialized in the names of two of her son John's great-granddaughters. Edward and Ellen Wales apparently had only one other child in Lancaster, a daughter, Mary, whose baptism took place in November of 1718. No other records of children born to Edward are noted in the parish records.[3]

Whatever the town may be like today, one has the sense that Lancaster was a desolate place to live during John Wayles's early life. The noted author Daniel Defoe visited in 1726, when Wayles was eleven years old. He characterized it as a "country town . . . situated near the River Lone or Lune. The town is ancient; it lies, as it were, in its own ruins and has little to recommend it but a decayed castle, and a more decayed port (for no ships of any considerable burthen); the bridge is handsome and strong, but, as before, there is little or no trade and few people."[4]

A town with "little or no trade and few people" held no real prospects for a person as ambitious as John Wayles. This is especially true given that Liverpool, which Defoe also visited and accurately described as having "an opulent, flourishing, and increasing trade to Virginia and English colonies in America," lay just to the south. Liverpool, a thriving port at the beginning of the eighteenth century, was booming because of the trade that would help Wayles make his fortune: the transport and sale of African slaves. Even farther south, London beckoned young people from all over the country. Slavery had created a truly global economy, tying together European, North American, and African villages in the slavery trade. Although Lancaster may not have been an economic powerhouse during Wayles's boyhood, it did have a long-standing connection to Virginia through its tobacco trade with the colony, which started in the late seventeenth century. Tobacco did not bring prosperity to Lancaster. It was, instead, the slave trade that transformed the place from the sleepy village that Defoe described in 1726 into a smaller version of neighboring Liverpool. It was not until 1736, when Wayles was twenty-one, that Lancaster began its involvement in the slave trade.[5]

In that year, the *Prince Frederick* sailed to the coast of Guinea, thus beginning a trade that lasted until the first decade of the nineteenth century and during which period Lancaster became the fourth most prosperous slave-trading port in England. Although Wayles was in Virginia by the time the Lancaster slave trade was at its peak, he probably knew before he came to America about its ability to make merchants rich. "Away from his native Lancaster,"[6] offers one historian, "John Wayles, as did many Virginia plantation owners, would eventually grow wealthy off the slave trade."[7]

Nothing in the record suggests that the Wayleses were a prosperous family in England, however. The name, spelled with or without a "y," was not common, and it is very likely that people who shared that last name in tiny Lancaster were related in some fashion. The Wayles who appear in the public records around the time of Wayles's early life were definitely working class, and, in some instances they were struggling economically. In 1719, Elizabeth Wayles of Lancaster, described as a widow with several unnamed children, was sent to debtor's prison for two years. John Wayles's father's profession is unknown, but his probable grandfather, also named Edward Wayles, was a butcher who died in 1686. His wife, Elizabeth, handled the letter of administration concerning his property on behalf of their four children: John, Thomas, Edward, and Anne. Neither Edward nor Elizabeth could write, and both signed the testamentary documents with their marks as signatures. Edward Wayles wanted more for his children. In a rare move for his time, he left a bond with instructions to his wife to make sure that his children received as much education as the money would provide.

"That John Wayles's life was a version of a rags-to-riches story," commented one historian, "is further supported by a note appended to an 1839 copy of a Lee family memoir transcribed from a document that William Lee wrote in 1771."[8] Lee, who died in 1795, chronicled the family history, discussing individual members' lives, fortunes, and contributions to society. The note states that Wayles came to Virginia as a "Servant Boy" brought over by a Lee family ancestor, Philip Ludwell, a name famous in early Virginia history. However, other historical accounts have Wayles arriving in Virginia already trained in the law.[9]

There were three Philip Ludwells of note in Virginia's colonial period: father, son, and grandson. The Philip Ludwell referred to in the Lee papers was Philip Ludwell III, who was born in 1716 and died in England in 1767. Like his father and grandfather, Ludwell III ranked high in Virginia's political and social culture, and his father had been the rector of the College of William and Mary. Ludwell III, who attended the college and was also on the board of visitors, furthered Wayles's education. In later years, one of Jefferson's slaves, Isaac Jefferson, mentioned Wayles in connection with Archibald Cary, a graduate of the College of William and Mary, in a way that suggested that the two men had gone to school together: "he went to school to old Mr. Wayles."[10]

Philip Ludwell had married Governor Berkeley's widow, Frances Culpeper, bringing the well-known plantation Green Spring, about five miles from Williamsburg, into the family. Ludwell III brought John Wayles to Green Spring in the late 1730s. The *Virginia Gazette* noted that he had traveled there in 1738, and Wayles referred to one of his earliest memories as having taken place there in 1740. Ironically, in the connected world of Virginia's family life, the Ludwell connection continued into the next generation when Ludwell's daughter Lucy and her husband, John Paradise, became friends with Thomas Jefferson while he was in Paris.[11]

The date when Wayles broke off from Ludwell's influence and started his career is murky, but he made reference in a letter to traveling to other estates in the Williamsburg area in 1740. By this time, Williamsburg had been the seat of colonial government for forty-two years. About five miles from Jamestown, situated between the James and York Rivers, Williamsburg was originally called Middle Plantation. In its earliest days, it served mainly as an outpost that settlers retreated to whenever they were attacked by Native Americans. As early as 1677, the year after participants in Bacon's Rebellion had laid waste to "the state house and all other buildings at Jamestown," Middle Plantation was proposed as an alternative to Jamestown as the seat of government. In the intervening years, work began on the establishment of the "free school and college" that became the College of William and Mary.[12]

The Williamsburg that Wayles encountered in the 1740s would certainly have been primitive by the standards of London. Even when Jefferson arrived there in the 1760s, the dirt roads tended toward muddiness, depending on the season. Most of the housing stock in the town was made of wood and painted white, although numerous buildings—the courthouse, prison, and some churches, as well as the residences of a few prominent people—were made of brick. Yet the town was said to have made a "handsome appearance" and was considered a good place to live. It boasted a vibrant commercial district, and a number of gentry families made their homes there.[13] And, true to its role as the seat of government, Williamsburg thrived on the presence of government officials and lawyers.[14]

It is not known when exactly Wayles emigrated to Virginia, although it was likely at some time in the 1730s. He established his home at The Forest, in Charles City County, becoming a planter and a lawyer, a man of business and underestimated charm. Within ten years, he had acquired a thriving law practice and thousands of acres of land. He dealt in real estate and tobacco and in slaves by the hundreds. As one historian commented, "as slavery thrust millions into misery, it lifted John Wayles higher."[15]

It appears that Wayles was not well educated in a formal sense but was a man of great energy and charisma. One historian, for example, describes him as "unusual" (in a complimentary sense), possessing "large gusto" and that he was a "generous host." Wayles did not hold any significant office in colonial Virginia. Yet he did live in Virginia for thirty-three years; he made his own small contributions to the daily life of his times, and he formed the very character of his beloved daughter, Martha. Thomas Jefferson described his father-in-law as successful:

> Mr. Wayles was a lawyer of much practice, to which he was introduced more by his great industry, punctuality, and practical readiness, than by eminence in the science of his profession. He was a most agreeable companion, full of pleasantry and good humor, and welcomed in every society. He acquired a handsome fortune, and died in May, 1773, leaving three daughters: the portion which came on that event to Mrs. Jefferson, after the debts should be paid, which were very considerable, was about equal to my own patrimony, and consequently doubled the ease of our circumstances.[16]

Until Martha met Jefferson, Wayles was her greatest influence and teacher, instilling within her a sense of family, legacy, and land. Through his influence, Martha learned music and how to sit a horse.

John Wayles had no known family in Virginia when he met and courted a young widow, Martha Eppes, in 1746. He was thirty-one when he finally married, the same age as Peter Jefferson, Jefferson's father, when he married. Both men evidently wanted to establish themselves before they took on the important role of husband. Wayles was already a member of the establishment by the time he married, having been admitted to practice in the county courts in April 1741, just a few years after his arrival in the colony.

Martha Eppes, the daughter of Colonel Francis Eppes of Henrico County (now Chesterfield), had first married Lewellyn Eppes "jr." Some ancestors of Lewellyn Eppes were from Wales. The young Lewellyn died after a year or so of marriage and left his father and brother various items of clothing, his horse, and a "Negro man named Hampton," whereas the remainder was left to Martha, who was named as his executrix. She presented his will at the March court in 1743.

Martha Eppes had inherited some land and a house on Swan's Creek in Goochland County from her father. Also from her father's will, she shared with her sister, Anne, certain slaves: Argulas, Will, Parthena, and their future children. Martha's older brother, Francis Eppes, the son of Colonel Francis Eppes, also died a short time later (1737), and her own inheritance increased. From this brother, Francis Eppes, Martha received "two Negro Girles named Kate and Bettey also one hundred fifty pounds Current Money and One Set of Silver Castors to her and her heirs forever."[17] This "Bettey" was later known as Betty Hemings, the mother of the infamous Sally Hemings.

Because Wayles had no known family in Virginia, Martha's family insisted on taking some precautions before consenting to the marriage. An elaborate document defined as "This Indenture Tripartite" was developed as a prenuptial agreement in 1746 for the couple. The agreement was signed by three parties: John Wayles, Martha Eppes Eppes, and her brother Richard Eppes, along with brother-in-law Benjamin Harris. The terms of this agreement placed the ownership of slaves, which accrued to Martha from the wills of her father, Colonel Francis Eppes, and her brother, Francis Eppes, in the trust of Richard Eppes and Benjamin Harris. Richard Eppes and Benjamin Harris were to provide money from the lease of these slaves (and their future children) to Martha and John, but title was to go to the future children of Martha Eppes Wayles, "whereas a marriage by God's Permission is intended shortly to be had and Solemnized between the said John Wayles & Martha Eppes." The agreement also noted that if Wayles died, then Martha, as a widow, could revoke the agreement at that time. The names of slaves specifically mentioned are, "Jenny, Agy, Sarah, Dinah, Judah, Kate, Parthenia, Betty & Ben, a Boy."

Seven and a half months after they married, Martha Eppes Wayles gave birth, prematurely, to twins, a boy and a girl. Her daughter was born dead. Her son lived only a few hours. In colonial Virginia, "til death do us part" could be a real proposition. Martha had already lost one husband, and, even among the most privileged Virginians, wives had a tendency to die young, leaving their children at the mercy of future stepmothers. Childbirth was then a bloody business in Virginia in the middle of the eighteenth century, and having a baby was often a lethal experience for the mother, the child, or both.

A year later, Martha was pregnant again, and this time the baby survived, but the medical ordeal killed Martha. She delivered a daughter on October 31, 1748, lay hemorrhaging for five days, and then died at the age of twenty-seven. The baby, named Martha after her mother and called Patty by her family, never knew the woman who gave her life at the cost of her own.

Upon receiving his license to practice law in Virginia, Wayles was given some cases to try as the prosecuting attorney in Henrico County. He also dealt in real estate and tobacco. Thomas Jefferson described Wayles as an amiable man who worked hard and had an appealing personality. However, having Philip Ludwell as his benefactor was a huge advantage for Wayles over other planters. We see how Wayles gained acceptance in his surrounding community in the letters of Maria Byrd to William Byrd III, in which she refers to Wayles's efforts to find suitable speakers for their church. In a 1760 letter, Byrd wrote, "Mr. Wayles is extremely kind in doing what he can in that respect, he has engaged Parson Masson already and designs likewise to get Parson Duglish, he says to make us laugh." Byrd also noted that attendance at church had been falling off and that Wayles and "Co. Harrison" and "Will Randolph" were making efforts to get "Parson Kenney" to come to preach. Wayles's and Byrd's interactions at church were apparently commonplace. In the preceding year, she reported that during the "very last Sermon Sunday Wayles comes to our pew before Church began & says Madam I give you joy of Mr. Byrd's being made Governor of Pittsburgh."

"With the support of a prominent mentor and the sheer force of his personal will," one historian noted, "Wayles made a place for himself in Virginian society that he could never have made in Lancaster."[18] Wayles's appointment as Farrell & Jones's agent (a London agency) in February 1763 further cemented his place in his adopted society. To say that he was merely an agent[19] does not adequately convey a sense of the breadth of his position. No doubt, an agent arranged deals between eager planters and willing British houses, yet that was only part of his duties. Wayles had another more important financial duty for his London agency: debt collector. "Over the course of Wayles's career in the colony," one historian observed, "planter indebtedness to British merchants grew to such heights that some scholars have suggested it as a chief reason for Virginia's decision to break away from England."[20]

John Wayles was at the center of this commercial endeavor. It was his job to make sure that planters paid their debts, in full and on time. In accomplishing this task, Wayles did not just sit idly by issuing demand letters. He went out to meet the planters at their homes or caught them during court. In a letter to Farrell & Jones, his London agency, he describes his efforts on their behalf and lists names of debtors, one by one, at times offering comments on their character. For example, Thomas Mann Randolph, whose son would one day marry one of Wayles's granddaughters, had "gone to some Springs on the Frontiers to spend the Summer," thus escaping a Wayles visit. Wayles did not give up easily. He wrote: "But as he [Randolph] has altered his Port, I shall endevor to make Lidderdale pay the Debt." Of Carter Harrison, Wayles wrote that "next month I shall go up Country and make it my business to settle Carter Harrisons Affair as you desire. You are not to be Surprized at his selling his tobacco this Year & disapointing the Ships, because the Man is Acting in Character."[21]

The estate of Benjamin Harrison also owed a debt to Wayles's agency. When a family member promised to "discharge it soon," Wayles showed patience, writing, "I shall Apply to him Differently." Another member of the Harrison family proved more difficult: "As to Nat. Harrison, I have wrote more Letters & made more Personal Applications for so small a Sum, then I ever did to any other Gentleman. This family is somehow or other so connected with your other Friends, that, where the debt is not in danger, indulgences are unavoidable. They require more then other People, & therefore on that Score are less desirable correspondents."[22]

This was not a job for a meek individual. Wayles had to be aggressive, no doubt provoking the resentment of the gentry, many of whom were drowning in debt. Some of these men were from the oldest and most powerful families in Virginia. "Perhaps," argued one historian, "they viewed John Wayles as not of their 'kind.'"[23]

❧

Although later in life his friend and legal colleague Edmund Pendleton became famous for his practice of law and his literary efforts on behalf of the American Revolution, John Wayles held no famous office and died just prior to the Revolution.

Some historians have depicted Wayles as nothing more than a wealthy Tidewater Virginia "grandee"—perhaps similar to Colonel William Byrd III or Benjamin Harrison, who were his neighbors in Charles City County. But those men had inherited noble mansions along the James River, and their fathers had plantation lands of 30,000–100,000 acres. In contrast, Wayles inherited nothing in the New World, coming alone to Virginia and settling into the populated area of Tidewater. He did not arrive as an explorer of the vast wilderness, but came with accounting and legal skills, as well as letters of introduction, to make his living. With no mention of education as a barrister in London at the Inns of Court, it may be presumed that he trained as a simple attorney by serving as an apprentice or reading law with a Lancaster attorney. Training in the law in both England and Virginia typically followed one of these two paths, although very few Virginians traveled to London and the Inns of Court. Edmund Pendleton, who requested a license from the Council of Virginia on the same day as Wayles, had been apprenticed in that manner.

According to one historian, "Wayles moved among the gentry of Virginia's famous families, cultivating fine manners and a winning personality. Yet he perpetually walked the line between coldhearted commerce and the customs of the country, between the English merchants he often represented and the Virginia gentlemen who were his friends, and soon to be his relations. He stood just a little outside their ranks, not simply because he was a self-made man, but also because he had chosen one path to fortune that put him at odds with those he sought to please."[24]

But, familiar as he was with the avalanche of debt that threatened to bury some of his friends, Martha's father was leery of extravagance for its own sake. Wayles had seen planters borrow more and more from British merchants. He observed in 1766 that, in his younger years, a planter's debt of 1,000 English pounds "due to a Merchant was looked upon as a Sum imense and never to be got over." But times had changed:

> Ten times that sum is now spoke of with Indifference & thought no great burthen on some Estates. . . . Luxury & expensive living have gone hand in hand with the increase of wealth. In 1'(40 I don't remember to have seen such a thing as a turkey Carpet in the Country except a small thing in a bed chamber. Now nothing are so common as Turkey or Wilton Carpets, the whole Furniture of the Roomes Elegant & every appearance of Opulence. All this is in great measure owing to the Credit which the Planters have had from England . . . tho many are ignorant of the true Cause.[25]

But happier times now befell Wayles. His beloved first daughter, Martha, married Bathurst Skelton, the brother-in-law of Wayles's late wife, Elizabeth. Wayles now had a surrogate son in his small family, and business obligations increased. Daughter Martha was now a new bride, and she and Bathurst set up housekeeping in nearby Goochland County, on land bordering the James River. After a year of marriage, a son, John Skelton, was born, but, a short time later, Bathurst Skelton himself died. The young widow and her infant son were soon back home, under the protection of her father at The Forest. Little John Skelton had been named for his grandfather and had been placed by his own father under the guardianship of John Wayles. Martha was again found witnessing deeds with her father, as she had before her marriage when she had traveled with him. In fact, Wayles had spent years on horseback making a living from debt collection and the preparation of legal documents for men of property. After thirty years of long journeys, he had bought or patented lands of his own, amassing several thousand acres. The last decade of his life, however, was dedicated to accumulating dowries for his daughters so they would marry well.

Wayles had no sons to carry on his name when he suddenly became gravely ill in February 1773. He immediately added a codicil to his original will. When he died on May 28, 1773, he left substantial property—and a debt that took years for Thomas Jefferson and the other co-executors of Wayles's estate to deal with. The majority of Wayles's papers and financial records did not survive, having disappeared from Eppington in the mid-nineteenth century.

His estate was divided between his three surviving daughters, known to him as "Patty" (Martha) Jefferson, "Betsey" Eppes, and "Nancy," who was engaged to Henry Skipwith. Their husbands, Thomas Jefferson, Francis Eppes, and Henry Skipwith, respectively, became his executors. One of the codicils to Wayles's will made a bequest of £200 to Robert Skipwith, husband of "Tibby," and there was no further mention of Tabitha, who apparently had died by February 1773.

Wayles left an estate of roughly 4,000–4,800 acres of Virginia land, mostly patents, but some of it—including some swampy land on the James River—had been purchased. A disastrous flood two years before his death had cost him nearly £4,000. A loan from Bristol merchants Farrell & Jones in the amount of about £5,368 was also left, although modest amounts were also owing to three other accounts. Young Frank Eppes, now living at The Forest with Betsey, did much of the local legwork in settling accounts.

A precise accounting of the Wayles estate is impossible. The loss of records from Charles City County attesting to the settlement of his estate has left only fragments of evidence for review. In a letter to Farrell & Jones from Thomas Jefferson in July 1773, it was noted that the Wayles executors believed the assets of the estate were worth £30,000 and that it was subject to the following debts, beyond those of Farrell & Jones:

Cary and Co., London	£1,000
Thomas Waller, London bookseller	£200
Mr. Flood of Virginia	£6006

After the death of his third wife, some historians believe John Wayles took his slave Elizabeth "Betty" Hemings as his mistress.[26] According to several sources, he was the father of her children Robert, James, Peter,

Critta, Thenia, and the infamous Sally Hemings. Until now, Wayles's involvement in the Sally Hemings controversy was a footnote to the history of Thomas Jefferson. In fact, Wayles has been simply a footnote to a footnote. Yet, Wayles should be prominently placed in the Sally-Jefferson historical debate. If Wayles were indeed the father of Sally Hemings, then Sally was the half-sister of Martha Jefferson. This notion of the half-sister relationship between the two women led to speculation about the relationship of Jefferson and Sally Hemings.

However, as discussed in detail in the epilogue, the verifiable historical record is devoid of evidence of Wayles being involved in such a relationship with Betty Hemings (or any slave for that matter), and strong, although not incontrovertible, evidence exists against it.

F O U R

THE YOUNG WIDOW

As a young widow already possessed of some estate and
with the prospect of more from her father, Martha Wayles
Skelton attracted many suitors.[1]

— Historian JON KUKLA

A MONTH AFTER celebrating her eighteenth birthday, Martha Wayles married twenty-two-year-old Bathurst Skelton on November 20, 1766. The couple had known each other for years. In the convoluted manner of Virginia planter families, Martha's new husband was in actuality her stepuncle, the youngest brother of her stepmother's first husband, Reuben Skelton.

Skelton was described as "bold and dark of look and grim of the habitual set of his mouth, yet pleasant enough."[2] The couple apparently wed at the Wayles's family home, The Forest. Given the fact that Elizabeth Lomax Skelton, the third wife of Martha's father, had formerly been married to Bathurst Skelton's older brother Reuben, it is likely that the Wayles family had known the Skelton family for some time.

Bathurst Skelton was born in June 1744, making him four years Martha's senior. The Skelton family was, by all accounts, reasonably prosperous, and Bathurst attended the College of William and Mary in Williamsburg. Unfortunately, little is known about the marriage of Bathurst and Martha or their lives together except that a son, John ("little Jack"), was born on November 7, 1767.

Bathurst was just two years out of the College of William and Mary when he married Martha. Skelton was a student at the College of William and Mary from March 1, 1763 to December 16, 1764, and was a

45

friend of Jefferson and his inner circle. Bathurst was the fifth child of James Skelton and Jane Meriwether. Large grants of land in Henrico County had been made to his father in the 1720s, and the elder Skelton also patented land on Elk Island (which ultimately came to Martha). He also served as sheriff of Hanover County for two terms and as justice of the peace. In 1751, he was engaged to remodel the Capitol in Williamsburg, as evidenced by the diary of John Blair.[3]

The small library that Bathhurst Skelton would bequeath to his widow, Martha, included volumes on mathematics, algebra, mechanics, astronomy, French, and geography, thus offering an inkling of Skelton's interests—or at least his College of William and Mary curriculum. He also owned two translations of Virgil, Addison and Steele's *Spectator*, and a sampling of the essentials of English literature: Milton's *Paradise Lost*, eight volumes of Swift, ten of Pope, and Dr. Johnson's *Dictionary*. Thus, it is more than mere social coincidence that Martha married not one but two literary intellectuals who possessed a vast amount of books, both of them passionate readers and collectors.

When she married Skelton, Martha had property of her own, but no marriage indenture was recorded for Martha and Bathurst Skelton. Instead, John Wayles relied on the contract he had made with Martha's mother twenty years earlier, reinforced in his own will, which guaranteed that Martha, the eldest daughter, would inherit money, land, and slaves, including the trusted servant Betty Hemings and her children. One way or another, however, the law would transfer Martha's property to her young husband, who would promise to protect and provide for her, as she in turn would pledge to honor and obey him so long as they both lived.

Who was Bathurst Skelton, and what drew Martha to marry this man?

To begin with, some historians have surmised that the "Skelton" family of England and Virginia has for centuries lived under a misapprehension as to the proper spelling and pronunciation of the family name. One historian claims that the proper spelling is "Shelton" or Chilton (pronounced alike) and not Skelton:

> I found several branches of my own family hanging on the Skelton tree, where they have been for many generations, owing to the poorly written record of the first Susannah, who married Thomas

Meriwether. . . . The wife of Thomas Jefferson has been published repeatedly as Martha Skelton whereas she was the widow of Bathurst Shelton, as is correctly stated in Clark's Colonial Churches of the Original Colony of Virginia. . . . There were no Skeltons in Virginia at this time. . . . In Land Grants the name is spelled Skelton, Shelton, Chilton, etc., all for the same piece of land. . . . Many errors may be attributed to the similarity of the old fashioned "h" and "k."[4]

However, there is a plethora of historical evidence that "Skeltons" were present in Virginia. For example, in the Richmond *Standard* there is recorded: "V. Bathurst Skelton, b. June 1744, d. 1771, 43 married Martha, dau. of John and Martha (Eppes) Wayles. On the death of Bathurst, she married January 1st., 1772, Thomas Jefferson." Moreover, documentary evidence established the marriage bond of Jefferson and Martha Skelton in *The Domestic Life of Thomas Jefferson*, written by his great-granddaughter, Sarah N. Randolph. Albert Jay Nock, one of Jefferson's first biographers, concludes in his biography, *Life of Jefferson*, that "this bond is wholly in the handwriting of Mr. Jefferson." If this is true, it is hardly probable that his intended would have been written by as Skelton, if her name had been Shelton.[5]

More importantly, Bathurst Skelton's name appears in the records of Cumberland County as witness to the will of Colonel John Fleming of New Kent, in 1756. Moreover, the will of Bathurst Skelton, dated September 10, 1768, in Charles City County, gives his "faton" (phaeton) and horses, his slaves, and other property to his wife, Martha, and to his son, John, and it appoints his father-in-law, John Wayles, guardian. This will is found in the State Library, Charles City Records, dated 1771. Bathurst's board bill at the College of William and Mary is also found in the bursar's book 1754–1769, with his surname spelled "Skelton."

The earliest biographer of Jefferson, historian Henry Randall, in his *Life of Thomas Jefferson*, also recorded that "Bathurst Skelton" had a son, John, who died in infancy. In preparing his work, Randall had access to the original correspondence of Thomas Jefferson, and it is unlikely that he would have spelled the name with a "k" in his work if Jefferson had not so spelled it in his private correspondence.

Other historians who had access to original documents in which the name appears spell it with "k." The only spelling to the contrary is contained in a single article by Mrs. Mary Morris Tyler of Sturgeon Point, Virginia, in Westover Parish, and she is a lone authority for this statement: "At 'The Forest' Thomas Jefferson married the widow Shelton."[6] This sentence is the whole evidence upon which one historian hangs Thomas Jefferson on the "Shelton" family tree. Yet, the historical evidence is unmistakable that the name Skelton is correctly spelled with a "k." The evidence is also unmistakable that there exists a different "Shelton" family in America, one that is not the same family under a different spelling of the name.

Meriwether Skelton, Bathurst's brother, was the eldest of the Skelton children. He was appointed by the Convention of 1775 as a member of the Committee of Safety for Hanover County. He owned land in Albemarle County in 1775, conveyed to him by Edward Smith and his wife. Meriwether never married, and he was the elder brother mentioned in the will of Reuben Skelton. Meriwether left a will dated March 13, 1778, recorded in Hanover, Virginia. He left his property to his sisters, Lucy and Sally, with the Hanover lands going to Sally only, and the Goochland and Fluvanna lands to both sisters, and giving Lucy the legal power to dispose of the whole by her will.

Reuben Skelton, Bathurst's second brother, was clerk of St. Paul's Parish Hanover and member of the House of Burgesses in 1758–1759. A will of his, apparently unexecuted but dated May 15, 1759, is found pasted in the back of the parish register of St. James Northam, Goochland County. In this will, he instructs that, in the case of the death of his wife, he wishes his estate to descend to his younger brother, Bathurst. Reuben married Elizabeth, daughter of Lunsford Lomax, on July 9, 1751. In an ironic historical twist, his widow, Elizabeth Lomax, married John Wayles, Martha's father, on July 23, 1760.

When Martha married Bathurst, the Skeltons set up housekeeping at Elk Hill, a Goochland County plantation that John Wayles had purchased in 1746, a beautiful place that both of them knew well. They occupied a bluff-top brick house overlooking Byrd Creek at its confluence with the James River. The newlyweds could gaze out over the lush bottomland of Elk Island, where Bathurst owned a thousand-acre plantation and John Wayles leased land and grew tobacco. Elk Hill must have seemed an obvious place for the young couple to make their home. Here, they had a comfortable house with a gorgeous view, land offering an abundance of game, and access to the Elk Island plantation. There, they would host hunting parties and family gatherings as the warm and vivacious Martha began her life as Mrs. Bathurst Skelton.

A Virginia plantation wife's principal duty was to provide her husband with an heir, and Martha fulfilled that expectation. On November 7, 1767, not quite a year after their wedding, Martha gave birth to their first and only child, a boy they named John after his grandfather, John Wayles. But whatever joy they felt at the birth of their son was cut short. Ten months later, on September 30, 1768, Bathurst Skelton died suddenly. The exact date and cause of Skelton's death has been historically confusing and has been variously reported as 1768 and 1771. The bursar's book of the College of William and Mary notes his death in 1769, stating that "he is since dead."[7] Henry Randall, Jefferson's earliest biographer, gave Skelton's death date as 1768, stating that "we glean these details from records, lying before us in the handwriting of Thomas Jefferson, and furnished by his family." But Skelton's will was not proved until September 4, 1771. Definitively, however, Jefferson historian Dumas Malone makes reference to Skelton's death notice in the *Virginia Gazette* by the funeral home of Purdie & Dixon on October 6, 1768.[8]

Skelton made his will on his deathbed, too weak to sign the document himself. In extremis, Skelton was aware of Martha's legacy from her mother, the foundation of her fortune, currently in his hands. Knowing that Martha was likely to remarry, he made sure to provide for his son in the chief form of wealth he possessed—his slaves:

> Whereas my wife Martha will be entitled to sundry slaves at the death of her father, by virtue of a marriage settlement made betwixt him and her mother, all which slaves I give to her and her heirs forever in case my son dies under age, or unmarried. But if he attains to lawful age or marriage, then the said slaves to be equally divided betwixt them, my wife and son.[9]

Skelton named Martha and John Wayles as guardians for little Jack and as his own executors, and he added a note bequeathing his phaeton, a light, doorless, two-wheeled carriage, and horses to Martha.

At the age of nineteen, Martha must have been deeply stunned and saddened by her unexpected widowhood. As an infant, she had endured the death of her natural mother; later she faced the loss of two stepmothers and a sister; now, she mourned her own young husband. And, more profoundly, she was a widow and the mother of an infant who had not yet reached his first birthday. She left Elk Hill, although years later, in happier times with Jefferson, she found a way to reclaim her first bridal home.

Martha returned to the comfort and safety of her father and The Forest, where Wayles and Martha's beloved and loyal house servant, Betty Hemings, would provide her and little Jack with sympathetic shelter.

Not yet twenty, Martha had endured the profound emotional loss of her young husband and three mothers. How did she cope with this emotional distress? Many people seek solace in faith, but whether religion provided some comfort to her, we cannot say. Her father was a churchgoing man after the fashion of elite Virginians of the time, more given to the social than spiritual aspects of their observances. He was an active member of his Episcopal church.

Perhaps Martha's optimistic outlook on life and capacity to laugh sustained her through these deeply depressing times, too. "Despite so many emotional blows," wrote historian Virginia Scharff, "she somehow managed to retain the spark that those who knew her best remarked on so often. Her ability to move forward with grace and purpose, to seek and find joy, bespeaks an impressive and resilient young woman."[10] When Martha returned to The Forest in late 1768, she found a household full of servants, mostly Hemingses. Betty Hemings had borne two sons and a daughter: Robert (born 1762), James (born 1765), and Thenia, born the same year as little John Skelton. Hemings's oldest children, Mary (fifteen), Martin (thirteen), Betty (nine) and Nance (seven), were now old enough to take on household duties.

Not much is known about Martha's first child with Bathurst, John "little Jack" Skelton. The only mention Jefferson made of him was in an account of the estate of John Wayles on February 26, 1772, in reference to an item "of goods imported for Mrs. Jefferson & J. Skelton from Cary & Co. $ 20-14-0 (pounds)." Yet Jefferson set up an account for John Skelton in his fee book, with himself as guardian on behalf of Martha, his wife. "Little Jack" Skelton died before Martha was formally married to Jefferson, and one can only imagine her profound grief following her husband's death and then her child's death soon after, on the morning of June 9 or 10, 1771, at The Forest. One historical fictional account attempted to re-create how Martha most probably would have reacted to these events, confiding her feelings in a typical eighteenth-century journal:

> I am undone. The early light falls gray on my table, gray on my paper, and gray on the raggedy crooked quill which is gray from his own tiny fingers upon it. Now he lies forever in the ground. I had thought, for a time, I would die of my grief, I never had imagined I would want my journal, yet here I sit, wondering how to begin, knowing only that I must unburden myself so I can be strong when Thomas comes.[11]

From historical accounts made during that year, in all probability little Jack was suffering from a severe ear infection and high fever, and even laudanum could not ease his pain. His fever would have grown to such a height that he would have shook in Martha's arms and burned with fever. Betty Hemings may have feared to have her own children near John, so she would have sent them to the slave quarters.

It is likely that Martha's father would have ridden for the doctor at Charles City Courthouse, but the child apparently died before help could arrive. The doctor most likely would have diagnosed a malignant brain fever as the cause of a painful death.

Although no historical accounts exist to depict the actual death of "Little Jack," novelist Roberta Grimes attempted to re-create, within a reasonable degree of historical accuracy, the most probable death scene, common to eighteenth-century death rites:

What can I say about that day. Betty washed and dressed him [Jack]. I could not do that, I wept until there was nothing left in me, no feeling left, not even pain, and then near evening I went to lie beside him where Betty had laid him on my bed. He looked so like his father lying there. I had always pretended he took after me, but there was Bathurst's sleeping face, his own dark hair and long, dark lashes, his nose that was broad from base to tip and his mouth small and pursed with no lip to it. Poor Bathurst had left but this one child. This felt like his second and final death.[12]

And, indeed, this was very much like Bathurst Skelton's death all over again, the surprise of it no doubt cutting through Martha, with grief mingled with shock. One can imagine Martha lying there spent beside her child, thinking of Bathurst because she could not bear to think of her Little Jack. The next morning, she and Wayles probably buried Jack in the graveyard near the creek where Martha's mother was buried, and the young widow would have been comforted to see Jack laid beside his grandmother.

Although we have little historical record of the days that followed, it is not unreasonable to believe that Martha wandered through those days in near insensible grief. She would have wept, sanded floors, and scrubbed bedsteads to keep her mind off her sorrow. She may have brewed small beer and walked by the mill pond and grieved. In the eighteenth century, mothers tried to keep their natural affection for their infants damped down until their children reached the age of three, since mortality was rampant. Jack Skelton was three when he died. Psychologically, it may have been this deep sorrow, the loss of a first and only child, that prompted Martha to yearn for a large family and go on to have six more children with Thomas Jefferson. Martha longed to hold another baby in her arms.

But Martha Wayles Skelton was a now a widow, and her child was dead. Her future looked bleak.

Slowly but surely, Martha emerged from this period of deep grief with the support of her father, her stepsisters, and, of course, her loyal servant, Betty Hemings. After this grieving time, the young widow appears to have attracted many suitors. Wealthy, beautiful, and accomplished,

Martha would have been a very attractive candidate for wife to any Virginia gentleman. Her personal and physical attractions lent an extra incentive to her father's ample fortune.

Martha no doubt found some solace and distraction in running her father's plantation and witnessing deeds, as she had before her marriage when she traveled with him. She settled in at The Forest, taking care of her father and acting as hostess for his dinner parties, overseeing domestic affairs (including the care and management of slaves), and, it seems, dealing as she saw fit with the numerous men seeking her attention.

With time and loving support from her family, the shock of Bathurst's and John's deaths inevitably ebbed, and Martha looked ahead again. Slowly, she began to enjoy society and, it seems, to entertain suitors. One such admirer arrived at The Forest for a brief visit in early October 1770.

Thomas Jefferson.

FIVE

THOMAS JEFFERSON

It is the strong in body who are both the strong and free in mind.[1]

— PETER JEFFERSON

When traveling in Virginia, you must be prepared to hear the name of Randolph frequently mentioned . . . it is also one of the most numerous and wealthiest.[2]

—THE MARQUIS DE CHASTELLUX, in 1782

IT IS MORE than mere coincidence that Thomas Jefferson and Martha Wayles had extremely similar upbringings, and this similarity may account for their strong attraction to each other. The correspondence between their social circumstances and the influence of their fathers is not only uncanny, but it is also a historical anomaly otherwise overlooked until now. Both Jefferson and Martha were very much a product of their class. As one historian noted, Martha "was bred to be a plantation mistress, and during her years of married life with her illustrious husband, she worked hard at being a successful one."[3]

Jefferson, as well as his siblings, married into distinguished Tidewater families (Bolling and Wayles, respectively). Jefferson's sister Martha married Dabney Carr, his best friend who lived in Louisa County just east of Albemarle County. Carr served colony-wide interests as a burgess. Jefferson's sister and brother, Lucy and Randolph Jefferson, married their

55

Albemarle-based Lewis cousins (siblings Charles and Anna) whose family held local office. Anna Scott married Hastings Marks, a small planter in Albemarle County.

Just as Martha grew up on a plantation of increasing fame—The Forest—so, too, did Jefferson. On no topic is Jefferson scholarship more mixed in historical interpretation than on Jefferson's youth at Shadwell, his birthplace, in what is now Albemarle County. A long, gently sloping hill five miles east of Charlottesville, Virginia, marks the spot where Jefferson was born, April 13, 1743. Only a few aged locust trees are still left to mark the place, and two or three sycamores stretch out their long majestic arms over the greensward beneath, once the scene of young Jefferson's boyish games but now a silent pasture where sheep browse.

The history that Jefferson's mother, Jane Jefferson, wrote for her family in her prayer book confirms details of Jefferson's early years. Biographers of Jefferson have known from his own autobiography that he was born at Shadwell, yet the birthplaces of Jefferson's two older sisters and when the family moved to Shadwell (and later to Tuckahoe) have been long-standing questions. When Jefferson's earliest biographer, Henry Randall, cited Jefferson's prayer book, he was silent on the birthplaces of Jefferson's sisters. The University of Virginia acquired Jane's Bible with her inscriptions in 1954, so it was not available to Randall or to Marie Kimball for their influential biographies of Jefferson. They, too, cited Jefferson's prayer book. In Jefferson's *Autobiography*, he wrote of his father: "He was the third or fourth settler, about the year 1737, of the part of the country in which I live." Famed Jefferson biographer Dumas Malone dismissed this date out of hand as being too early. According to historian Susan Kern, "Jane's inscription tells us that she and Peter indeed had moved to Shadwell by June 27, 1740, when Jane [Thomas's sister] was born there, and probably moved some months before June to avoid traveling late in Jane's pregnancy. The family moved to Tuckahoe in time for Jane to give birth to Martha there on May 29, 1746. They returned to Shadwell following the birth of Lucy in October 1752. The activities in Peter Jefferson's account book suggest that August 1753 marked their return home."[4]

In the fall of 1765, the whole family was thrown into mourning by the death of Jefferson's older sister, Jane Jefferson, 28, "so long the pride and ornament of her house." The eldest of her family, Jane's death was a great emotional blow and was felt more deeply by Jefferson himself. His grief for her was profound and constant. They were very close, and he cherished her memory to his last days. Years later, Jefferson wrote plans for a graveyard at the back of his memorandum book. In an emotional essay, he composed an epitaph for Jane. Memories of his sister colored his perceptions of his world, and women, for decades to come. He recalled Jane's singing even in "extreme old age" and said that "often in church some sacred air which her sweet voice had made familiar to him in youth recalled to him sweet visions of his sister."[5] Jefferson passed on stories about Jane to Martha, his daughters, and his grandchildren. In a revealing fact, Jefferson composed only three epitaphs of deep, emotional grief: for his sister Jane; for his boyhood friend and brother-in-law, Dabney Carr; and for his own wife, Martha Jefferson.

As a country boy, Jefferson "was thin-skinned and rather shy, and he feared rebuffs," posits historian Thomas Fleming. "He concealed his inclination to be sociable behind a facade of studiousness. He used to be seen with his Greek grammar in his hand while his comrades were enjoying relaxation," one friend recalled.[6] Family legend has Jefferson studying fifteen hours a day, but he also ventured out into social settings. He joined the Flat Hat Club at the College of William and Mary, a college society that recorded its antics in mock-Latin verse. He also made lifelong friends with Virginia notables such as John Page, a descendant of "King" Carter, who invited him to Rosewell, the magnificent three-story mansion where Page had grown up.[7]

There and in other great estates to which his Randolph family kinship opened doors, Jefferson discovered the fascinations of the opposite sex. Their names still twinkle in his youthful letters: Rebecca Burwell, Susanna Porter, Alice Corbin, Nancy Randolph. At nineteen, when he was studying law under George Wythe, Jefferson fell deeply in love with Rebecca Burwell, a fetching sixteen-year-old with excellent family connections. "Jefferson confided his love for her," wrote historian Jack McLaughlin, to his friend John Page in letters that have served to remind his biographers that even the most respected statesmen were once young. Rebecca is referred to by the code names "Belinda, Adnileb (Belinda spelled backward), Compana in die (Bell-in-da), rendered in English and Greek, lest his friends should learn of his suit."[8]

Jefferson spent the years between nineteen and twenty-three adoring Rebecca, his first "crush," who was an heiress from Yorktown.

"'Enthusiasm' was the 18th-century word used to describe Rebecca," notes historian Tom Fleming, "implying a strong, emotional personality. For two years, the romance percolated while Jefferson struggled to bring himself to ask for her hand in marriage. He rhapsodized in letters about 'Belinda'—the playful nickname he gave Rebecca."[9]

But something about her intimidated Jefferson and tied his tongue. Perhaps it was the simple knowledge that marriage meant the end of youth or farewell to his bachelor's freedom. Jefferson spent hours before a ball at the Raleigh Tavern composing a series of romantic compliments for Rebecca. "I was prepared to say a great deal," he told his friend John Page. "I had dressed up in my own mind such thoughts as occurred to me in as moving a language as I knew how, and expected to have performed in a tolerably creditable manner." But when Jefferson came face to face with Rebecca, he wilted. "Good God! . . . a few broken sentences uttered in great disorder and interrupted with pauses of uncommon length were the too visible marks of my strange confusion!"[10]

His awkward marriage proposal failed miserably.[11]

Jefferson's father, Peter Jefferson, like Martha's father, was a commanding and strong presence in his son's life. "Peter Jefferson was a wealthy Virginia planter and surveyor," writes historian Gordon Wood, "who married successfully into the prestigious Randolph family. But he was not a refined and liberally educated gentleman. He did not read Latin, he did not know French, he did not play the violin, and as far as we know, he never once questioned the idea of a religious establishment or the owning of slaves. His son Thomas was very different. Indeed, all the revolutionaries knew things that their fathers had not known, and they were eager to prove themselves by what they believed and valued."[12]

Yet, it is historical myth that Peter Jefferson was merely a backwoodsman, a settler of frontier Virginia. "His father worked in his study on the first floor of the house," according to Jefferson biographer Jon Meacham. "It was one of four rooms on that level—at a cherry desk. Peter Jefferson's library included Shakespeare, Jonathan Swift, Joseph Addison, and Paul de Rapin-Thoyras's history of England. 'When young, I was passionately fond of reading books of history, and travels,' Thomas Jefferson wrote.

Of note were George Anson's *Voyage Round the World* and John Ogilby's *America*, both books that offered the young Jefferson literary passage to larger worlds. A grandson recalled Jefferson saying that 'from the time when, as a boy, he had turned off wearied from play and first found pleasure in books, he had never sat down in idleness.'"[13]

Jefferson's mother, Jane Randolph Jefferson, however, did bring gentry standards to the household, although her influence was not as strong as that of Jefferson's father. The Jeffersons, like the Wayleses, were a successful planter family, and, in the end, it was this socially upward influence that was the catalyst for young Thomas to leave his Shadwell and Tuckahoe homes and his boyhood tutors. Jefferson ventured into Williamsburg where he could practice his cultivated manners and tastes instilled by his refined mother.[14]

Most scholars acknowledge that Peter Jefferson did not possess the social status of his wife, Jane. Some historians argue that Jefferson was an aristocrat on his mother's side but a yeoman on his father's. Yet the foremost Jefferson scholar, Dumas Malone, "never accepted any such simplistic explanation. My studies showed me that Peter Jefferson had achieved a position of recognized distinction and was a fully accredited member of the gentry . . . the fact was that Peter Jefferson gave his son an assured place in society and the means to maintain it."[15] Malone could have written these words about Martha's father, John Wayles, because both fathers had similar goals for their children.

Some historians have overlooked the fact that Peter was, among other things, a county surveyor, a county justice, a burgess, and an acquaintance of many important figures in colonial Virginia. Peter Jefferson was also a strapping pioneer who had found time to serve in the House of Burgesses. The son inherited his father's height, with Jefferson growing to almost six foot three inches in height. Years later, Jefferson would dangle his long legs out of bed and plunge his feet into a basin of cold water at dawn—a lifelong habit he believed good for his health. At Monticello, his plantation in the Southwest Mountains near the Blue Ridge Mountains of Virginia, it was said that the metal bucket brought to him every morning wore a groove on the floor next to the alcove where he slept.[16]

Jefferson also inherited an interest in politics from his father. From his mother, a woman proud enough of her English heritage to boast of a family crest, the young revolutionary inherited his more delicate facial features. His height and countenance combined with an engaging personality that allowed Jefferson to connect with almost any audience. Jefferson's charisma enabled him to enclose acquaintances "with a sanguine warmth, intellect, and humor that earned him countless friends."[17]

Young Jefferson developed many appealing qualities due to his parents' influence, character traits that would put him in good stead in his future political career. "He was never blunt or assertive as John Adams could be," wrote historian David McCullough, "but subtle, serene by all appearances, always polite, soft-spoken, and diplomatic, if somewhat remote. With Adams there was seldom a doubt about what he meant by what he said. With Jefferson there was nearly always a slight air of ambiguity. In private conversation Jefferson sparkled. 'Never contradict anybody,' he was advised by Franklin, whom he admired above all men, though it was advice he hardly needed. He abhorred dispute. Jefferson would one day advise a grandson, 'When I hear another express an opinion which is not mine, I say to myself, he has a right to his opinion, as I to mine. Why should I question it. His error does me no injury, and shall I become a Don Quixote, to bring all men by force of argument to one opinion? . . . Be a listener only, keep within yourself, and endeavor to establish with yourself the habit of silence, especially in politics.'"[18]

In fact, Jefferson had all any young man would need for success in life. According to historian Susan Kern in her authoritative book *The Jeffersons at Shadwell*, "young Thomas and his siblings did not have to seek refinement outside of the material world of Shadwell—he had most everything he needed right there." Similar to Martha's surroundings at The Forest, Jefferson grew up with a modicum of wealth. Shadwell was full of the proper tools for entertaining and for teaching children manners. "Their expectations, moreover, were not dictated by their location," argued Kern, "for Albemarle indeed was still a frontier in many ways. Instead, the Jeffersons acquired fine goods and the manners that allowed participation in the colonial gentry world wherever they could find, or make it."[19]

Jefferson's life at Shadwell illustrates that his family occupied the high end of the social spectrum, one that molded leaders through participation in the militia, the church vestry, and county government. "Of course the heights to which Thomas Jefferson rose were exceptional," according to Kern's research, "yet he neither struggled against excessive economic hardship nor lived the exclusive life of a wealthy aristocrat. Rather, he grew up within a culture of plantation owners whose responsibilities included public service and the professional tasks of overseeing workers, slaves, road crews, and militia, as well as the social tasks of educating family members and perpetuating civic culture."[20] In recent years, archaeological and documentary research at Shadwell reveals a picture of a well-adorned gentry house at the center of a busy plantation landscape still undergoing settlement. Historian Susan Kern chronicled that the Jeffersons accommodated, in their house, landscape, and material goods, "the most up-to-date social expectations of Virginia's elite tidewater culture."[21]

Shadwell seems to have extended the boundaries of Tidewater culture for the Jeffersons, which often included a five-day ride to the colonial capital, Williamsburg. In this remote region where there were no store displays with the latest English goods, Jane Jefferson actively pursued finery and culture because she could not come by them easily.[22]

Jefferson's father, Peter Jefferson, partner to Joshua Fry in making the famed 1751 "Map of the Inhabited part of Virginia," may have first seen this land on the Rivanna River during one of his surveying ventures. Peter Jefferson acquired land in this region in 1734 and obtained the initial two hundred acres for the home site from his friend William Randolph for the price of "Henry Weatherburn's biggest bowl of Arrack punch"[23] in 1736 at a tavern in Williamsburg. Peter may have moved to Shadwell as early as 1737, from Fine Creek, also in Goochland County. Jane joined him after their marriage in 1739, and they named their home Shadwell after the London parish where Jane was born. Their daughter, also named Jane, the first of their ten children, was born at Shadwell in 1740.

Before his death in 1757, Peter Jefferson accumulated a vast amount of land, more than 1,500 acres along the Rivanna River, including the mountain that his son later named Monticello. He also amassed other land in the Piedmont, for a total of more than 7,200 acres. Although Thomas Jefferson called his father's education "quite neglected," Peter was an accomplished surveyor and a respected public official, a keeper of accounts who had fine penmanship and a decent library. The husband of the literate Jane Randolph, he was also a father concerned with the education of his sons and daughters to high standards of propriety.

According to historian Susan Kern's research and recent excavations at Shadwell, the house and other material goods had explicit social functions. The property arranged the people who lived and worked there according to the divisions of plantation society, separating master from servant, planter from laborer, and white from black. "Slaves left the main quarter site via a small gate in a split-rail, or Virginia fence and passed by the kitchen and up a slight rise to arrive at the south porch of the main house, where they would receive work assignments or finish domestic tasks. The slaves who lived and worked in the plantation kitchen building occupied a physical space between the Jeffersons in their house and the site farther east that served as a center of slave life at Shadwell. Family stories remembered by Jefferson's granddaughters recounted how the slaves summoned their grandfather on the night Shadwell burned: they had not rescued Jefferson's beloved books, but a slave saved his violin. In fact, Isaac Jefferson, a slave of Jefferson's at Monticello years later, recalled Jefferson's younger brother, Randolph Jefferson, as 'a mighty simple man [who] used to come out among black people, play the fiddle and dance half the night' at Monticello."[24]

Peter Jefferson's estate inventory of Shadwell describes a house "a story and a half in height [with] four spacious ground [floor] rooms and hall[way], with garret chambers above." The first house may have been as small as 600 square feet on the ground floor, if it occupied only the space of the surviving brick cellar. However, evidence of rebuilding of the west wall of the cellar suggests that the house may have been larger than its cellar footprint. The upstairs had two heated bedchambers, both of which held bed furniture and case furniture.[25]

There is no record that Peter Jefferson traveled overseas, but he traveled widely in the colonies. He surveyed Virginia at least from the Virginia-North Carolina line to the headwaters of the Potomac, to the branches of the Mississippi. He did, however, spend time with many people who traveled abroad, such as his wife, Jane, who was born in London to her ocean-crossing father, Isham Randolph, and English mother, Jane Rogers. In fact, Peter's older brother, Thomas, died aboard the ship *Waynesburg* en route to Virginia from England.[26]

Among Peter's friends was the Reverend James Maury. Maury was one of forty investors, along with Thomas Walker, Peter Jefferson, and Joshua Fry, in a landholding company. Maury had a place among surveyors and was considered by Jefferson as a family friend, fellow investor, and professional. Maury later became one of Thomas Jefferson's first teachers, in 1758. His students also included Dabney Carr, John Walker, James Junior, and Matthew Maury. Jefferson admired Maury's library and called him a "correct classical scholar." Their friendship concluded with the young Thomas Jefferson standing as a baptismal sponsor for Maury's son, Abraham.[27]

Before his death, Peter Jefferson gave a prayer book to his son, then ten years old. Later in life, Thomas Jefferson used this prayer book to record his family's important dates and events. For example, twenty years later, when his own daughter Martha was born in 1772, Jefferson began using this same prayer book to register the important events of his own family. With Martha's birth, Jefferson started a record of his family on blank leaves in the book.

When Peter Jefferson died, by his own request, his family buried him at Shadwell. Thomas Jefferson's granddaughter, Septima Anne Randolph Meikleham, later wrote: "After Mr. Jefferson's death the grave was lost sight of and now it cannot be found."[28] Samuel Cobbs, a local carpenter, built a coffin for Jefferson for which he was paid ten shillings. Cobbs worked on Jefferson's mill at Shadwell in previous years and also witnessed Jefferson's will when it was registered. The Reverend James Maury, later to become the tutor of young Jefferson, received two pounds for speaking at the funeral. Captain Charles Lewis, Jane and Peter's brother-in-law, procured sugar for the funeral at the expense of two pounds. "Someone in the household, probably the slave cook or housekeepers," observed historian Susan Kern, "followed Jane's orders and used the sugar to produce between thirty-five and one hundred gallons punch for the drinks of the guests to attend the funeral. Among Peter Jefferson's friends and mourners were officeholders and educated professionals, planters, surveyors, doctors and clergy."[29]

In the final analysis, Jefferson's father gave his son an enthusiasm for knowledge and the confidence in the human mind that characterized his entire life. An anecdote was told by his granddaughter Sarah Randolph that gives one an idea of Thomas Jefferson's thirst for knowledge. On one occasion, while traveling, Jefferson stopped at a country inn. A stranger who did not know Jefferson entered into conversation with him. The stranger introduced one subject after another and found Jefferson acquainted with each. Impressed, the stranger asked the landlord who his guest was, saying that, when he spoke of law, he thought he was a lawyer; when on medicine, felt sure he was a doctor; and having touched on theology, became convinced that he was a priest. "Oh," replied the landlord, "why I thought you knew the Squire." The stranger was astonished to hear that the traveler whom he had found so affable in his manners was Thomas Jefferson.[30]

In short, education was valued by both of Jefferson's parents, and this ideal was instilled within Jefferson. "It was said," wrote one historian, "that Jefferson studied fifteen hours a day, rising at dawn and reading until two o'clock each morning. At twilight in Williamsburg he exercised by running to a stone a mile from town; at Shadwell, he rowed a small canoe of his own across the Rivanna River and climbed the mountain he was to call Monticello. For Jefferson laziness was a sin. 'Of all the cankers of human happiness, none corrodes it with so silent, yet so baneful, a tooth, as indolence,' he told one of his daughters. Time spent at study was never wasted. 'Knowledge,' Jefferson said, 'indeed is a desirable, a lovely possession.'"[31]

Like his father, he believed in the virtues of riding and of walking, believing that a healthy body helped create a vigorous mind.[32] His father also left Jefferson with the notion that he should enter public life in recognition of his social responsibilities. In fact, for the next twenty years, Jefferson appeared not as a politician in the modern sense, but as a public servant, due in large measure to his father's influence.[33]

The one glaring difference between Martha Wayles's childhood and her future husband's was simple: Jefferson had a steady, if not somewhat domineering, mother throughout his life. Martha, tragically, did not.

Born in London, Jefferson's mother, Jane Randolph Jefferson, grew up in the household of the well-established London merchant and agent for the colony, Isham Randolph, and his English wife, Jane Rogers. They were aristocrats, and privilege was common to the family name. For example, when John Bartram planned a visit to the Randolphs at their

Goochland County home, Dungeness, in 1738, it prompted his sponsor Peter Collinson to forewarn him to "make up that Druggett Clothes, to go to Virginia In," and he added, "these Virginians are a very gentle, Well Dress'd people, & look phaps More at a Man's Outside than his Inside, for these and other Reasons pray go very Clean, neat & handsomely Dressed to Virginia." Bartram reported being treated with "all ye expressions of kindness & Civility."[34]

As historian Susan Kern concludes, "Jane Jefferson paid attention to and invested in teaching her children and surrounding them with fine goods."[35] She was born February 9, 1721 (O.S.)[36] in Shadwell parish, Tower Hamlets, London. The parish register of St. Paul's, Upper Shadwell, notes her baptism on February 25, 1721, as the daughter of Isham Randolph, "mariner" of Shakespeare's Walk (literally around the corner from the church), and Jane Rogers. The Randolphs left London for Virginia shortly thereafter and were in the colony by October 1725, when Jane's sister, Mary, was born in Williamsburg.[37]

Jane was first Jane Randolph of Dungeness, and her first cousin, Mary Isham Randolph of Tuckahoe, was the grandmother of Chief Justice John Marshall. Thus, both these commanding figures in American history trace their ancestry back to the same Randolph, William Randolph of Turkey Island, the founder of the family in Virginia, who was likewise the ancestor of General Robert E. Lee.[38]

Thomas Jefferson writes in his memoir "that his mother's family trace their ancestry back into the early mists of Scottish and English history." Jefferson himself, according to historian Jefferson Randolph Anderson, took very little interest in such matters, but the family traditions to which he refers go back in Scotland to Thomas Randolph, the Earl of Moray, who became the Lord Regent of Scotland. He was a nephew of Robert Bruce, Earl of Carrick, and later King of Scotland. Randolph makes his first appearance in history at the fatal battle of Methven, and later, in 1312, he took by a desperate assault Edinburgh Castle, supposedly impregnable. The next year, he was advanced to the command of the center of the Scottish Army at the decisive battle of Bannockburn and distinguished himself by the defeat of Sir Robert Clifford, "who had been detached by the English King to turn the flank of the Scottish army and relieve the siege of Stirling Castle; which, if successful, would have put an end to the war."[39]

"The first record of Jane's presence in Virginia," according to author and historian Susan Kern, "is her marriage to Peter Jefferson on October 3, 1739 in Goochland County, probably at Isham's home on the James River, called Dungeness. There is no evidence that Jane brought any land or servants to the marriage. Isham provided her a dowry of £200 but it was not paid until his death, three years later, from the proceeds of his estate. During her marriage, Jane had an amazing ten children with Peter. Her children included: Jane, the oldest (1740), Mary (1741), Thomas (1743), Elizabeth (1744), Martha (1746), Peter Field (1748), an unnamed son (1750), Lucy (1752), and a set of twins, Anna Scott and Randolph (1755)."[40]

Jane was a "notable housekeeper," wrote a great-granddaughter. "She possessed a most amiable and affectionate disposition, a lively, cheerful temper, and a great fund of humor. She was fond of writing, particularly letters, and wrote readily and well."[41] When her husband, Peter, was away, Jane was left to oversee the plantations at both Tuckahoe, and later, Shadwell. That Jane was an indefatigable woman is evidenced by the fact that she rebuilt Shadwell after it burned in 1770 rather than moving. "It was her world in the way Monticello became her son's," historian Jon Meacham concluded, "and she sought to arrange reality as she wanted it to be."[42]

Unfortunately, for young Thomas Jefferson, after his father died, there would be no more evenings spent in the first-floor study, looking over maps, listening to tales of brave expeditions, tinkering with the tools of surveying, discussing Shakespeare or *The Spectator*. Those hours with his father were now to live only in memory, with the image of his father both inspiring and daunting. "Shadwell was now to be dominated by Jefferson's mother, Jane," according to biographer Jon Meacham. Jane "almost certainly exerted as great an influence on her eldest son as the legend of Peter Jefferson did—but in subtler ways. Jane ran things as she deemed. Literate, social, fond of cultivated things—from fancy china to well-made furniture to fine clothing—she was to endure the death of a husband, cope with the deaths of children, and remain in control to the end, immersed in the plantation around her and in the lives of those she loved."[43]

Perhaps Jefferson chafed under his mother's direction or even unconsciously resented her as a replacement for his influential father. It may be of some historical note that in extant correspondence, Jefferson seldom mentioned his mother. In an autobiographical sketch he began when he was seventy-seven, Jefferson talked of his mother only in relation to his father. Of Peter Jefferson, Jefferson wrote: "He was born February 29th, 1708, and intermarried 1739 with Jane Randolph, of the age of 19, daughter of Isham Randolph, one of the seven sons of that name and family settled at [. . .]."[44]

According to historian Dumas Malone, Jefferson's foremost biographer, there was an "almost complete failure to mention her name" outside of his financial records. Jane, therefore, "remains a shadowy figure."[45] A reference to her in Jefferson's correspondence can be found in a June 1776 letter from him to his uncle William (Jane's brother), a merchant in Bristol, England. Among other issues, Jefferson, almost casually, writes William about Jane's death. "The death of my mother you have probably not heard of. This happened on the last day of March after an illness of not more than an hour. We suppose it to have been apoplectic."[46]

The paucity of sources leaves a number of outstanding questions about Jane, such as whether she died at Monticello rather than at Shadwell (her late-nineteenth-century tombstone states the former). Certainly, any attempt to recover the real Jane Jefferson has been concealed by fanciful assumptions about the kind of person she was. Observed historian Susan Kern, "the family accounts reveal that she oversaw her family's resources with a level of care, skill, and prudence that may have chafed her oldest son's spending habits, yet which also kept the family out of debt, an achievement in eighteenth-century Virginia."[47]

Jane's refined tastes, however, were revealed in her material goods. The Jeffersons invested money to entertain and also to teach their children the social rituals required to enter an elevated status in Virginia. The Shadwell house is living, historical evidence that demonstrates that the Jeffersons wished to participate in upper social culture, even if they lived on a frontier.[48]

The Jefferson children set the tables with knives, forks, spoons, and napkins, in an era when many people still ate with only a spoon or their hands. From the recent excavations at Shadwell, "it was evident that the family had silver soupspoons, tablespoons, teaspoons, and ladled punch with silver. They served two courses on silver-plated or white salt-glazed stoneware plates, and a soup course in silver-plated soup plates. Both the silver-plated and the white salt-glazed plates were new to the consumer market in the 1740s. Chafing dishes show that the food served at Shadwell demanded tools for finer detail than the large kitchen fireplace, spits, and pots and pans offered. A lacquered plate oven by the fire warmed the dishes that waited for the table, and a cruet stand and 'silver salts' held spices to adjust seasonings in the food."[49]

Jane Jefferson served tea, coffee, and punch in her hall using equipment that elevated these luxuries to the status of ritual. She had a tea service of silver, a "China teapot," and a "Black teapot" to put on their three tea tables. Clearly, the physical and social standards at Jane Jefferson's Shadwell, as was Martha's at The Forest, "did not suggest the Jeffersons thought of themselves as removed from society. In fact their social world included tidewater and Piedmont families."[50]

The Jeffersons also obtained a modicum of wealth through the cash crop of Virginia—tobacco. "The tobacco economy extended into this part of Virginia," suggested one historian, "and with it, tobacco culture. The Jeffersons built at the head of navigation on the North Branch of the James, later called the Rivanna River, and thus shipped tobacco to market via the same water as other great planters."[51] For people of moderate wealth, such as the Jeffersons and Wayleses, the connection to the markets was direct. At Shadwell, building materials such as glass, lead, and nails suggest that the Jeffersons operated a store for neighbors. Historical evidence reveals that the Jeffersons placed orders directly with ship captains for leather gloves, coffee, salt, and nails from Bristol, England.

Peter Jefferson died in 1757, leaving his house and plantation on the Rivanna River to his wife, Jane. A young Thomas Jefferson, just home from the College of William and Mary, complained about the isolation of Shadwell in letters; he was targeting the lack of companionship other than his sisters and brother.[52] And although much of the main house at Shadwell burned in 1770, Jane continued to live there until her death on March 31, 1776. Jane was buried in the family graveyard at Monticello. But, like Martha Wayles's childhood home, The Forest, scholars agree that Peter and Jane Jefferson built a home that prepared their family for the social status and responsibility of their class. The location on a ridge signaled to all that Shadwell was an important estate.

SIX

TRUE LOVE

....

Martha Wayles was beautiful, talented and wealthy, but Jefferson also found her status as a widow attractive.[1]

— Historian JON KUKLA

IT IS NOT exactly known when or where Martha first met Thomas Jefferson. But, in all likelihood, she met him through Bathurst Skelton because her young and ill-fated first husband had been part of the college social set Jefferson moved in at Williamsburg during the early 1760s. Bathurst Skelton had been a year younger than Jefferson and had also studied at the College of William and Mary. (His marriage to Martha lasted only twenty-two months, from their wedding on November 20, 1766, to Skelton's death on September 30, 1768, after a sudden illness.) Even though Martha was six years younger than the members of the college social group, she may have heard of or met Jefferson in this social circle. It is also possible that Jefferson met his future wife as early as October 1768, when he accepted her father as a legal client just a few weeks prior to Bathurst's death.

As a young widow, Martha already possessed some property, and, with the prospect of more acquired from her father, she undoubtedly attracted many suitors in a society that never frowned on an advantageous marriage. Jefferson wrote in his autobiography that Martha's portion of her father's estate "was about equal to my own patrimony, and consequently doubled the ease of our circumstances."[2]

Jefferson made his first recorded visit to The Forest in the autumn of 1770, when Martha was a widow with a three-year-old son. As a romantic gesture, the twenty-seven-year-old Thomas Jefferson—lawyer, planter, and member of the Virginia House of Burgesses—probably brought mockingbirds, his favorite birds, with him as a gift to Martha.[3] She must have encouraged his attentions, since he soon returned. It was a busy time for Jefferson even before he began to woo Martha. His family home at Shadwell had burned to the ground early in 1770, with the flames consuming not only the house but nearly all of his books and papers as well. Painful as this was for him, it was relieved by the fact that Jefferson's plans for his permanent home on the mountain were well under way. Now he had a reason to complete Monticello: a potential wife, Martha Wayles Skelton.

Martha was beautiful, musical, well read—and Jefferson adored her. She was also striking looking. "Her complexion was brilliant—her large expressive eyes of the richest shade of hazel—her luxuriant hair of the finest tinge of auburn,"[4] Jefferson's earliest biographer Henry Randall wrote after interviewing her descendants. No doubt Jefferson was physically attracted to Martha from the start. She had an arresting face, pointed of chin, square of jaw. Her eyes were pale blue and starred with bristly black lashes. Her impeccable manners had been imposed on her by her stepmother's stern admonitions and the gentle discipline of her mammy, Betty Hemings. Martha's magnolia white skin was guarded with bonnets, veils, and mittens against both the sun and the chafing Virginia cold.

She was, a contemporary said, a woman of "good sense and good nature."[5] Her granddaughter Sarah Randolph described Martha as "so lavish with her charms for her, to great personal attractions, added a mind of no ordinary calibre. She was well educated for her day, and a constant reader; she inherited from her father his method and industry, as the accounts, kept in her clear handwriting, and still in the hands of her descendants, testify. Her well-cultivated talent for music served to enhance her charms not a little in the eyes of such a musical devotee as Jefferson."[6] Such contemporary comments by others, wrote historian Dumas Malone, "leave no doubt that she was musical and a few of them suggest gaiety of spirit, but the last ones refer to her gentleness, even to her saintliness."[7]

Martha and Thomas Jefferson shared tastes in literature and wide-ranging conversation. One kinsman, Robert Skipwith, who later married Martha's sister, thought the Jeffersons "a couple ... well calculated and disposed to communicate knowledge and pleasure." Martha had "the beginnings of knowledge," suggesting an interest in education similar to Jefferson's own.[8] In Martha, Jefferson found the most congenial of companions. The fast-fading bachelor was singing love songs: Jefferson had finally found a woman who supplanted his cynical nature with a yearning for romantic love. A fragile, delicately boned beauty of twenty-two, Martha had an abundance of the virtue that Jefferson valued above all other female attributes: sweetness of temper. Perhaps this was a virtue that his mother, Jane Randolph Jefferson, may have lacked and that Jefferson needed to find in a mate. Two other qualities were attractive to Jefferson: "spriteliness and sensibility." "The latter had become especially important to Virginians," historian Thomas Fleming proclaimed. "It, too, was an offshoot of the growing fondness for emotion in poetry and novels. A woman, especially, felt inferior if she was deficient in such sensibilities."[9]

At some point, Jefferson emerged as the leading contender among Martha's numerous suitors. Some five years her senior, six feet two inches tall, brilliant and agreeable, he was tall and lean, with reddish hair, hazel eyes, and a fair complexion. He usually wore his copper-colored hair unpowdered and in a queue. "Jefferson's eyes," one historian observed, "gazed forthrightly at his viewer with a crystalline intelligence. Any attempt to penetrate beyond them to the inner man is reduced to conjecture, for the eyes are reflections rather than portals. The nose is patrician, the mouth firmly set, the facial muscles in perfect tune beneath the skin."[10] Jefferson, who was slightly taller than George Washington but long limbed and loose jointed, "was a reserved man whose tight lips bespoke a secretive personality," historian Ron Chernow wrote. "Jefferson had calm eyes that seemed to comprehend everything. Shrinking from open confrontations, he often resorted to indirect methods of dealing with disagreements. He could show a courtly charm in conversation and was especially seductive in small groups, where he became a persuasive advocate. At the same time, his mild manner belied his fierce convictions."[11] Biographer Henry Randall agreed and offered an appealing picture of the young man:

Mr. Jefferson was generally . . . rather a favorite with the other sex, and not without reason. His appearance was engaging. His face, though angular, and far from beautiful, beamed with intelligence, with benevolence, and with the cheerful vivacity of a happy, hopeful spirit. . . . He was an expert musician, a fine dancer; a dashing rider.[12]

Historian David McCullough agreed, describing Jefferson as customarily standing "with his arms folded tightly across his chest. When taking his seat, it was as if he folded into a chair, all knees and elbows and abnormally large hands and feet. Where [John] Adams was nearly bald, Jefferson had a full head of thick coppery hair. His freckled face was lean like his body, the eyes hazel, the mouth a thin line, the chin sharp. Jefferson was a superb horseman, beautiful to see. He sang, he played the violin. He was as accomplished in the classics as Adams, but also in mathematics, horticulture, architecture, and in his interest in and knowledge of science he far exceeded Adams. Jefferson dabbled in 'improvements' in agriculture and mechanical devices. His was the more inventive mind. He adored designing and redesigning things of all kinds. Jefferson, who may never have actually put his own hand to a plow, as Adams had, would devise an improved plow based on mathematical principles, 'a moldboard of least resistance.'"[13]

Martha Skelton and Thomas Jefferson shared much more than a love of music. Although she was almost six years Jefferson's junior, Martha's life as a wife and mother had given her a maturity and capacity for intimacy that Jefferson had still to learn. Martha taught her children and her nieces and nephews what tradition calls "the beginnings of knowledge," suggesting a deep interest in knowledge and education similar to Jefferson's. Skipwith wrote to Jefferson that "My sister Skelton, Jefferson I wish it were, with the greatest fund of good nature has all that sprightliness and sensibility which promises to ensure you the greatest happiness mortals are capable of enjoying."[14]

Although their courtship was undoubtedly filled with music, wine, and talk, Jefferson surely confided in Martha his view of politics. A granddaughter recalled Martha Wayles Skelton's "passionate attachment" to Jefferson and her "exalted opinion of him." For his part, Jefferson's "conduct as a husband had been admirable in its ensemble, charming in its detail."[15] Jefferson needed a woman who shared his passion for music and all that music represented—sophistication and the life of the imagination and the heart. Martha "Patty" Wayles Skelton was such a woman. Jefferson became determined to have her and to lavish on her the best of everything.[16]

Two anecdotes about Martha's courtship with Jefferson have been preserved by family tradition. The first recounts the story of two rival suitors who happened to approach the front door of The Forest simultaneously. Ushered into a sitting room, they heard Martha's harpsichord and soprano voice wafting through the house in harmony with Jefferson's violin and tenor. The rivals listened for a few minutes and then "took their hats and retired, to return no more on the same errand."[17]

The second story is recorded in Jefferson's account books, in December 1770. Jefferson decided to buy Martha a small clavichord. He wanted it to be "as light and portable as possible" and veneered with "the finest mahogany." Six months into their courtship, he decided that his fiancée should have a larger and more expensive pianoforte "of fine mahogany, solid, not vineered" and of a quality "worthy [of] the acceptance of a lady for whom I intend it."[18]

Martha was indeed beautiful, multitalented, and wealthy, but Jefferson may also have found her status as a widow attractive. "Intimate emotional engagement with women," historian Winthrop Jordan observed, "seemed to represent for [Jefferson] a gateway into a dangerous, potentially explosive world." It seems that, in private life and in public policy, Jefferson seemed more comfortable with married women than with their undomesticated sisters. Jordan was not the first to notice that "throughout his life after the Burwell affair, Jefferson seemed capable of attachment only to married women."[19] Jefferson's first biographer, who had the unique advantage of direct conversations with his family and contemporaries, hinted at such. "Last [but] not least," Henry S. Randall wrote in his list of Martha's appealing qualities, "she had already proved herself a true daughter of the Old Dominion in the department of house-wifery."[20]

The roles of eighteenth-century husbands and wives were put more clearly by Mary Deverell in an essay she published near Philadelphia in 1792:

To the moment of your marriage it is your reign, your lover is proud to oblige you, watches your smiles, is obedient to your commands, anxious to please you, and careful to avoid everything you disapprove; but you have no sooner pronounced that harsh word obey, than you give up the reins, and it is his turn to rule so long as you live.[21]

~

Little recorded historical evidence is left of the early courtship of Jefferson and Patty Wayles Skelton. Yet, with a reasonable degree of historical probability based on eighteenth-century customs and habits, in addition to what we know of Jefferson's recorded behavior, an amalgam of historical facts can be used to re-create their likely first meeting.

"Mr. Jefferson" would have been invited to dinner at Martha's mansion, The Forest. All of this would have been arranged by Martha's father, John Wayles. The family would have left them alone in the parlor before the meal was served. A maid would have sat by the door, mending linens as chaperone. Perhaps Martha confided to Jefferson her reluctance to marry again with the death of her husband still fresh in her memory. The revelation obviously did not deter Jefferson, and their talk surely turned to his favorite topic—the home he was building on his mountaintop, Monticello. They very likely discussed their mutual interest in Laurence Sterne's *Tristram Shandy*, a popular novel of the time.

It is likely that the two were taken with one another from the start, Jefferson towering over a slight and beautiful Martha, perhaps cozying by the warmth of a parlor fire. What did they first talk about? Most probably what they had in common: music, horses, perhaps of a mare Martha had recently ridden. Perhaps they talked of fine food or wine, and the home farm on the top of a mountain he was building, Monticello. His servants had leveled the highest heights, and there Jefferson was building what he assured Martha was a temporary cottage where he planned to be living this winter.

No doubt, Martha liked Jefferson from the beginning. Unlike his fellow revolutionary John Adams, Jefferson was described as reserved, self-possessed, and chronically optimistic, qualities that Martha apparently possessed herself and found quite attractive. "He disliked personal controversy," noted historian Gordon Wood, "and was always charming in face-to-face relations with both friends and enemies."[22] And Martha surely would have felt a sense of security in his confident presence.

As with so much of the life of Martha, the facts surrounding her meeting of and courting by Thomas Jefferson are frustratingly few. If they did not meet at The Forest, as some historians have surmised, perhaps their first meeting was at a dinner party in Williamsburg at Governor Botetourt's royal ball. If they had met at the Governor's Palace in Williamsburg for the royal ball, in the eighteenth-century tradition, the dinner table would have been set for sixty people. Set upon trestles on the ballroom floor, the tablecloth would have been homespun linen and laden with the fruits of three days of work, quails and sausages, squash-corn salads, kidney-mutton savories, and sweet potato biscuits.

In the eighteenth-century tradition, Martha would have been dressed in that "gay and splendid" style that made Virginia famous, her hair "craped" high with rolls on each side, topped by a cap of gauze and lace. Jefferson would have looked almost as splendid in clockwork silk stockings, lace ruffles, and breeches and waistcoat of blue, green, scarlet, or peach. Some ladies in attendance may have worn homespun dresses—a coming fashion in colonial times, with the nonimportation resolutions in the House of Burgesses imposed upon the colonies. Since the British had resolved to tax the colonists' imports, this affront had so heated Virginia gentlemen that they had been pleased to ban the import of fine goods from England. Thus, when Governor Botetourt gave a holiday ball, every lady there may have been in a homespun gown.[23]

Most probably, there would have been excitement in the air for a royal ball of this magnitude. Martha's custom was to play the harpsichord, perhaps as a reason for avoiding most of the dancing with the gentlemen. One historical fiction account attempted to re-create the scene in Williamsburg and describe Martha's most likely first meeting with Jefferson:

> So I gaily danced with my usual spirit, freeing myself from my chain of beaux, and as I danced I noticed Mr. Jefferson standing tall and quiet by the parlor-door. I had gained my first sight of him only that morning and had my introduction at dinner-time, yet the sight of him was so pleasing to me that I felt from the first a discomfiting connection. I feared that he thoroughly viewed my mind, my rejection of my suitors and my liking for him, so I danced along faster and averted my face

that he not read my thoughts within it. After I had flown from my last failed beau, I took my turn at the harpsichord. This I played on heartily until I had a thought of eyes upon me and I found Mr. Jefferson standing beside me wearing a look most warm. I dropped every finger onto the keys. I recovered, but then all the dancers were off so I hastened the measure to catch them up.[24]

As was the tradition in eighteenth-century Virginia, a ball or dance of this sort called for a great deal of space. If the ball was not held at the Governors' Palace, Martha may have first met Jefferson at a ball at her father's estate, The Forest. John Wayles, a practical man who had four daughters of marrying age, probably would have built onto the eastern end of his house a ballroom larger than the house itself. The smell of curing tobacco would have filled it even during a minuet, but it seems a reasonable surmise that it would have served very well its intended purpose. Wayles would have offered to give balls each year at the spring and fall sittings of the Burgesses, and whether or not these balls were the cause, he had already married off two daughters out of four.

If Martha and Jefferson first met at The Forest, by all historical accounts, Jefferson was considered a fine dancer, schooled at the Governor's Palace, light on his feet despite his height and very loose of limb. The fact that he was a most interesting conversationalist would not have been lost on Martha; and, by this time, Jefferson may have lost his shyness with women.

Jefferson would have seemed to Martha remarkably tall, perhaps the tallest man that she had ever met, with a strong nose and chin and a look about him of sweet good humor and gentle wit. His hair was red-brown, less ruddy than Martha's, but she may have thought their coloring much the same. Martha may have liked his lack of wig or powder.

No doubt, Jefferson would have been a keen prospect for a son-in-law, but there may have been one obstacle: he may not have been John Wayles's first choice for Martha. Wayles may have had higher prospects for Martha, a member of a more prominent Virginia family—a Carter or a

Byrd. Socially, the Jeffersons were relatively unknown compared to other established Virginia families, their Randolph connection having been somewhat diluted. Wayles may have sought acceleration of his rising status by a marital connection with one of Virginia's great families.

On February 20, 1771, Jefferson complained to a friend about how "the unfeeling temper of a parent" could obstruct a marriage. There is another possible, even probable, explanation for John Wayles's hesitancy about Jefferson, according to historian Thomas Fleming: "Like most first-generation English emigrants to America, Wayles may have retained a strong loyalty to the king and Jefferson was already an outspoken advocate of a break with England."[25]

The love-smitten Virginian did not let Wayles's opposition, or anyone's for that matter, deter him. Not two weeks went by without seeing Jefferson and his servant, Jupiter, ride up the hill to The Forest. His romantic pursuits may have been helped by a temporary suspension of transatlantic hostilities that began in 1770 and made some people think that the dispute with England would soon vanish.

Inevitably, Wayles must have realized Martha had no intention of loving anyone but Thomas Jefferson.

SEVEN

MARRIAGE

....

Our friendship as it became in December I can compare
to nothing other than that moment of courtship intensely
sweet when lovers share an intimacy but they have as yet
no sense of a future. This suited my heart for I could not
bear to accept him or to let him go, and it suited him as
well for his shy reserve made him reluctant to press a lady.[1]

— ROBERTA GRIMES, from the novel *My Thomas*

JEFFERSON appears to have been in love from the beginning of
their courtship, writing glowingly about the hazel-eyed beauty. He
was also fond of Martha's son, Jack, and looked forward to serving in
a paternal role. But at least one letter suggests that he worried whether
the feelings were mutual. In a response to Jefferson's concerns to this
end, a mutual friend—a Mrs. Drummond—wrote to the young man:
"Let me recollect your description, which bars all the romantical, poetical
ones I ever read. . . . Thou wonderful man, indeed I shall think spirits of
a higher order inhabit your airy mountains—or rather mountain, which
I may contemplate but can never aspire to." Mrs. Drummond further
advised Jefferson to persevere, saying that Martha has "good sense, and
good nature"; she offers words of encouragement, hoping that the widow
Skelton will not refuse her suitor's love; and she closes by saying that she
suspects Martha's heart is already "engaged."[2]

Why did Martha hesitate to marry Jefferson? Perhaps she thought
it was seemly to do so. Maybe she was considering other offers. Possibly
she was afraid to commit herself again, having lost one husband so young.

And although Jefferson's letter to James Ogilvie suggested that neither his mother nor her father opposed the match, Jefferson had supported the Virginia Burgesses' nonimportation agreements in response to the Townshend Acts, and John Wayles was the agent for British merchants. In 1766, Wayles had declared the uproar over the Stamp Act a "great Licentiousness."[3]

Still, Wayles was an acquaintance to the Randolph clan and doubtless knew Jane Jefferson, Jefferson's mother, as well as her son. And, by the beginning of June, Jefferson had won over his prospective bride. And why did Martha say yes? She had reason enough to choose a husband carefully. As Henry Randall observed, "With rank and wealth (if the last can be supposed to have had any influence on the men of the olden time!) it is not wonderful that Mrs. Skelton was a favorite with the other sex—that her hand was sought by wooers far and near."[4]

Martha stood to inherit more than Jefferson possessed, so she was not marrying for money. As a daughter of the Eppes line, she did not need to marry for social advantage. She might have remained an unmarried widow, as her future sister-in-law, Martha Jefferson Carr, would do and as another future sister-in-law, the childless Anna Jefferson Marks, would do much later. Jefferson's two sisters, left vulnerable by their husbands' deaths, fell back on their brother as provider and protector, but Martha had no brothers. But she did have a small fortune of her own, and if she needed a man to administer her affairs, she had her father.

Martha most likely accepted Jefferson's proposal not out of necessity, but on account of love and desire. She wanted more children, but she could have had those with a richer, more important man. She chose Jefferson because she wanted him. In 1771, she could not have predicted where the course of life would take Jefferson. He was a Virginia planter with good prospects to be a leading man in the colony, but did Martha imagine more? "We have to conclude, in the end," commented historian Thomas Fleming, "that she decided to marry Jefferson because of a mutual attraction, an emotional and physical chemistry between them that meant a great deal to both. Many people they knew married, without such connections or expectations, seeing sustenance, security, and status as good enough causes to make a match. Many were content with less, but Martha wanted more. As we would say now, she loved him, and accepted his proposal because of that, and because he loved her."[5]

But at least one obstacle to their marriage had been removed. "On November 11, 1771," historian Thomas Fleming observed, "the no longer unfeeling [Wayles] gave his permission. The young couple set the wedding date for January 1, 1772—visible proof of their impatience."[6] Whatever Martha's initial hesitation about a second marriage, Jefferson had overcome it. To be an aged spinster was a shameful thing in the eighteenth century, but Martha Skelton was no spinster. She was married at eighteen, widowed at nineteen and her son, "little Jack," was nearly three. Although at first hesitant at the idea of a second marriage, she felt an emotional pang for Jefferson, with his promise of love and nurturance. Stability and love would have been alluring to Martha and her son.

The couple managed to see each other often, sometimes in Williamsburg, and their friends hoped their relationship would succeed. In all likelihood, Martha must have decided that Jefferson was the one for her soon after their initial meeting because, within a year, Martha Wayles Skelton would consent to become Mrs. Thomas Jefferson.

The marriage between Jefferson and Martha would have come after a suitable period of mourning for the late Bathurst Skelton, but it was common in the colonial period for widows and widowers to remarry rather quickly, especially if children were involved through one or both partners, as was the case with Martha and her son, Jack.

But Martha matured quite early. Perhaps it was this maturity that was one of the qualities that attracted Jefferson. She had just turned eighteen when she and Skelton were married in the fall of 1766. While still nineteen she gave birth to a son, and before the boy was a year old his father was dead, ambushed by one of the marauding diseases that caught so many people of the period.

On December 23, 1771, Jefferson traveled to The Forest from Monticello to sign a wedding bond. The bride's brother-in-law, Francis Eppes, served as Jefferson's cosigner, writing:

> Know all men by these presents that we, Thomas Jefferson and Francis Eppes, are held and firmly bound to our Sovereign Lord the King, his heirs and successors, in the sum of L50 current money of Virginia. . . . If

there be no lawful cause to obstruct a marriage intended to be had and solemnized between the above Thomas Jefferson and Martha Skelton of the county of Charles City, widow, for which a license is desired, then this obligation is to be null and void; otherwise, to remain in full force.[7]

Martha and Thomas Jefferson had many things in common when they first married, most especially the gift of music. Jefferson was devoted to his violin, she to her harpsichord, and they both loved to sing. Their children would later record that they could hear their parents humming in the garden and in their bedroom.

What, apart from music, drew Martha and Thomas to marriage? Perhaps Martha's widowhood is more than an incidental detail. "Though younger," historian Jon Meacham argues, "Patty already knew more of marriage and its consolations and demands than Jefferson did—a fact that may have given her more confidence in herself as she embarked on a new life."[8] They were also of similar rank in society, both related to important families through their mothers, with fathers who had succeeded in business by working hard, cultivating friendships with influential people, and marrying well. Each was left with only one parent. They were both products of plantation life and were accustomed to a modicum of wealth and fine imported goods. But they also had similar ideas about the pursuit of happiness. Both were devoted to the novels of Laurence Sterne, a writer who celebrated sentiment. They also discussed the poetry of Ossian (an ancient Scottish poet, translated by the eighteenth-century writer James Macpherson). Martha had a pragmatic father, but she embraced the sentimentalism then popular in the cultured classes of the colonies.[9]

As a young, unmarried lawyer during the 1760s, Jefferson owned Laurence Sterne's books *Tristram Shandy* and *The Sermons of Mr Yorick*. He also acquired *A Sentimental Journey* shortly after it was published in 1768. Later, during the years he spent in Europe as the new nation's minister to France (1784–1789), journeying through the south of France and northern Italy, he approached his London bookseller for pocket-sized editions of Sterne's works. During this same period, he alluded often in correspondence to episodes from Sterne, and, years later, as president, he still sought copies of Sterne's works.[10]

Martha, as well as Jefferson, found in Sterne a confirmation of life's fragility and uncertainty. Jefferson had felt the deep loss of his father before he was old enough to track alongside him in the frontier wilderness that Peter Jefferson had charted. A few years later, he lost his favorite sister, Jane, whose voice, he claimed even in old age, to hear in the "sacred air" of church.[11] He had roamed the mountaintop that was to become Monticello with his best friend and brother-in-law, Dabney Carr, just before Carr died of a virulent fever and became the first to be buried in Monticello's graveyard. The death of Carr, whom people observed to be a "highly-gifted young Virginian, whose early life was so full of promise," took place on May 16, 1773, at the age of thirty. Carr's wife, Jefferson's sister Martha, "was a woman of vigorous understanding and earnest warmth of heart," but Carr's death fell like a blight on her young life. She found Jefferson to be a loving and protecting brother, and a fatherly figure for her six children; later Martha Jefferson Carr's three sons and three daughters were received into Thomas and Martha Jefferson's family as their own. After Jefferson's death years later, the following was found written on a sheet of notepaper:

INSCRIPTION ON MY FRIEND D. CARR'S TOMB

Lamented shade, whom every gift of heaven
Profusely blest; a temper winning mild; Nor pity softer, nor was truth
more bright. Constant in doing well, he neither sought
Nor shunned applause.[12]

It was with this consciousness of death's imminence that Thomas Jefferson, in 1772 or 1773, turned to his literary commonplace book, a scrapbook of significant quotations that he had been keeping since his college days, and made an entry from the ninth volume of *Tristram Shandy*:

Time wastes too fast! every letter I trace tells me with what rapidity life follows my pen. the days & hours of it are flying over our heads like clouds of a windy day never to return more! every thing presses on: and every time I kiss thy hand to bid adieu, every absence which follows it, are preludes to that eternal separation which we are shortly to make![13]

A decade later, Jefferson would identify this passage with the greatest tragedy of his life—the death of his beloved wife, Martha.

$$\mathcal{C}\!\sim$$

By early 1771, Thomas Jefferson had made his marriage intentions clear, although Martha Skelton had not quite accepted his marriage proposal. He wrote to his friend James Ogilvie in February with news of a mutual friend who "is wishing to take himself a wife; and nothing obstructs it but the unfeeling temper of a parent who delays, perhaps refuses to approve her daughter's choice." Like the friend, Jefferson hoped to marry soon. But he was forced to wait not because of parental disapproval, but due to the fire that had destroyed Shadwell a year earlier, robbing him of a proper house to which to bring a bride:

> I too am in that way [of hoping to marry]; and have still greater difficulties to encounter not from the forwardness [sic] of parents, nor perhaps want of feeling in the fair one, but from other causes as unpliable to my wishes as these. Since you left us I was unlucky enough to lose the house in which we lived, and in which all its contents were consumed. A very few books, two or three beds &c. were with difficulty saved from the flames. I have here lately removed to the mountain from whence this is dated, and with which you are not unacquainted. I have here but one room, which, like the cobler's, serves me for parlour for kitchen and hall. I may add, for bed chamber and study too. My friends sometimes take a temperate dinner with me and then retire to look for beds elsewhere. I have hopes however of getting more elbow room this summer.[14]

Jefferson was also a busy man, shuttling back and forth between Williamsburg and Charlottesville with a busy law practice that obliged him to ride around to plantations, county courthouses, and the General Court in Williamsburg. As a member of the House of Burgesses, he was also consumed by the growing conflict between the British government and the colonial legislatures. All of this while he tried hurriedly to build a house for his bride at Monticello and find time to court Martha.

 ℰ ⌒

Jefferson envisioned a summer wedding, although he still had to convince Martha to marry him. A Quaker woman he knew from Williamsburg urged him to "persever thou, good Young Man, persevere. She has good Sence, and good Nature, and I hope will not refuse (the Blessing shal' I say) why not as I think it, of Yr. Hand, if her Hearts, not ingaged already . . . And belive me, that I most sincerely wish You, the full completion, of all Yr. Wishes, both as to the Lady and every thing else."[15]

 ℰ ⌒

"The women of 1776 had high expectations from marriage," wrote one historian. "They wanted not only affection but respect as persons. For a lucky few, these essentials could blend into near adoration."[16] One Virginian began his letters to his wife with "My dearest life" and declared that she "blessed the earth" with her presence. At the same time, essays about unhappy marriages frequently appeared in the newspapers. One correspondent in the *Virginia Gazette* blamed these misfortunes on women who spent too much of a man's money on luxury and on men who, for the sake of beauty or wealth, married "a fury" or an "ideot [*sic*]." "But we now see how strongly the founders, especially those primary political rivals Alexander Hamilton and Thomas Jefferson, stressed the importance of a happy marriage in a man's life," argues historian Tom Fleming. "Thanks to his five years in France as America's ambassador, Jefferson was able to compare American and European marriage customs and found America's far superior."[17]

So, deeply in love, Martha accepted Jefferson's marriage proposal. On December 30, 1771, Jefferson purchased a marriage license in Williamsburg, then traveled back to The Forest. Francis Eppes, who was married to Martha's sister Elizabeth, signed the marriage bond, and Jefferson paid forty shillings for the license. Captivated by visions of their new life together, Jefferson had unconsciously deleted Martha's first husband from her life. In his bond for a marriage license, dated December 30, 1771, Jefferson referred to her as a "spinster." On the document, another hand, most probably Francis Eppes, crossed it out and inserted "Widow."[18]

In all probability, the couple had thought to be married near Christmas Day, but Jefferson was so occupied in constructing Monticello that he did not arrive until the end of that week. Then, they had to wait for additional friends to arrive, and he had to post his marriage bond. At last, they set the wedding day for the first day of the new year.

Martha's first wedding had been a pious rite with only family in attendance, but her marriage to Jefferson would fill her father's parlor with so many friends and family that, when time came for the couple to approach Reverend Coutts, they would have trouble parting the crowd. In the eighteenth-century tradition, Martha most probably would have worn a new-sewn gown in the very latest London fashion, a splendid yellow silk brocade with gold-embroidered stomacher and petticoat. The cloth probably came from the Eppeses at Bermuda Hundred, a family nearly as wealthy as the Carters, or perhaps a dress from her mother. When Martha's mother lay near death, she may have made John Wayles promise that her yellow silk would be saved for her newborn child and made up into her wedding gown. So Wayles may have kept it for Martha so it could be made up by the local seamstress, most probably Mrs. Oglethorpe at Charles City Court House. Her servants were trained at embroidery, so the gold-thread thistles on the stomacher and petticoat were, perhaps, the finest Martha had ever seen.[19]

The wedding day was a joyful holiday for twenty-three-year-old Martha Wayles Skelton and twenty-nine-year-old Thomas Jefferson. The customary holiday festivity provided by Squire John Wayles was joyously crowned by the nuptials of his delightful eldest daughter. On that wintry Wednesday, they were married at the home of Martha's father, who was also one of Jefferson's legal clients and was known as "a most agreeable companion, full of pleasantry and good humor."[20]

Jefferson, as any bridegroom, was probably speechless when he saw Martha in her wedding gown. Perhaps he gazed at Martha with his face gone rapt, then he would give her his deepest bow as Martha gave to him her curtsey. In honor of the occasion, Jefferson would have powdered and tightly curled his hair, something he seldom troubled to do. It is likely that he had as his bridesman Dabney Carr, and Martha had her dearest sister Betsy, who was pregnant with her second child, due to be born within that month, as her bridesmaid.

Was Jefferson nervous, as any man on his impending wedding would have been? Did his soft voice shake when he said his vows? No one knows if the couple would have danced and supped in the Wayles ballroom, where Frances Alberti, a little Italian man with bowed legs and a most ill-fitting wig, would have played the violin so well that Jefferson may have joined him for some of the music. In fact, if Alberti had taught music to both Martha and Jefferson separately.

Jefferson described the wedding in his memoir: "On the first of January 1772 I was married to Martha Skelton widow of Bathurst Skelton, and daughter of John Wayles, then 23 years old." The guest list included the bride's father and the Eppeses, who were then building their house at Eppington in Chesterfield County. Her other sisters, Anne and Tabitha, and the men who would be their husbands, brothers Henry and Robert Skipwith, probably also attended.

The Anglican ceremony was conducted by the Reverend William Coutts, and the celebrations ran for several days. Although Coutts officiated, the minister for the parish, William Davis, was also present. Jefferson paid each clergyman five pounds, five times what the law deemed. He also tipped Betty Hemings—Sally's mother's first appearance in his account books. On January 2, the *Virginia Gazette* reported the marriage: "Thomas Jefferson, Esquire, one of the Representatives for Albemarle, to Mrs. Martha Skelton, Relict of Mr. Bathurst Skelton."[21]

The ceremony began with the three "causes for which matrimony is ordained," the first being for "the procreation of children, to be brought up in the fear and nurture of the Lord, and to the praise of His holy name"; the second, "as a remedy against sin, and to avoid fornication"; and the third, "help and comfort, that the one ought to have of the other, both in prosperity and adversity."[22]

They made their vows, according to the rites of the Church of England, as embodied in "The Form of Solemnization of Matrimony" in the *Book of Common Prayer*. Prayers followed: that the couple be blessed with children and live long enough to give those children a Christian upbringing; that in the marriage, representing "the spiritual marriage and unity between Christ and his church," Jefferson would love his wife and Martha would "be loving and amiable, faithful and obedient to her husband, and in all quietness, sobriety and peace, be a follower of holy and godly matrons."[23]

Reverend Coutts no doubt reminded the couple of Saints Paul and Peter's advice on the duties of husbands and wives, enjoining Jefferson to love his wife even as himself, weaker vessel that she was, and reminding Martha to "submit to your husband as unto the Lord, for the husband is the head of the wife, even as Christ is the head of the church," to be in subjection and obey with a meek and quiet spirit, "as Sarah obeyed Abraham, calling him Lord."[24]

Jefferson promised to love Martha, "honor her, comfort her and keep her in sickness and in health." Martha swore to "obey him, serve him, love, honor and keep him in sickness and in health." John Wayles stepped forward to give his daughter to Jefferson, as he had done once before to Bathurst Skelton. Both vowed to love and cherish one another, and Martha again promised to obey her husband.[25]

Historian Virginia Scharff recorded that "Jefferson's mother, Jane Jefferson, if her health permitted, would have been present at the wedding of her eldest son, along with her daughters Elizabeth and Anna and son Randolph. Jefferson's sister Mary and brother-in-law John Bolling, friends of the Wayles family, would also be invited. We cannot say whether Martha and Dabney Carr would have been in attendance, given their fast-growing family." Surely Jefferson wanted his brother-in-law and best friend, and the sister who had become his closest sibling, to share his joyous wedding day.[26]

Music and feasting would have been the order of the day, as evidenced by Jefferson's generous tips to "a fidler" and two trusted servants from The Forest (including Betty Hemings and her son, Martin) for tending to the guests and their horses.[27] Before the wedding, Jefferson had ordered a new pianoforte from London, "worthy the acceptance of a lady for whom I intend it." And Jefferson no doubt sang, with his bride's accompaniment, at the wedding party, for he had a "fine clear voice," according to his slave Isaac, and was "always singin' when ridin' or walkin.'"[28]

When the supper was well along and some of the guests retired, Jefferson most probably took Martha's hand, and they left together to climb the ladder to their wedding garret. Jefferson may have carried up a featherbed and all of ten or more blankets to ward off the cold. There it was that the newlywed couple slept together for the first two weeks of their married life. Martha doubtless treasured the memory of climbing into their garret and dropping the door, pegging it and being truly alone together as they had never been before.

No doubt it was bitterly cold in the dead of winter; within weeks, a blizzard dropped the greatest snowfall in the middle and lower Potomac River valley and surrounding area since European settlement (more than three feet). In the eighteenth-century tradition, the newlyweds most likely did not fully undress, but hurried into the blankets and talked and kissed until they were warmed and able to remove their clothes. Perhaps they laughed for the shyness of their being naked together for the first time. The intimacy of their first few days together came into their bed even that first night, as evidenced by the birth of their first daughter exactly nine months later.

At that moment Martha was open to Jefferson and united with him, body and soul.

Their honeymoon lasted two and a half weeks. The couple stayed at The Forest in hopes of better weather, but the winter settled in with yet more snow and ever colder winds. Not until January 18 did the newlyweds begin their trip for Monticello. The couple began their winter journey with a stop at nearby Shirley, the James River mansion of Charles Carter. Carter, like Jefferson, had been a student at the College of William and Mary. The plantation house at Shirley had recently been rebuilt by Carter, and it fascinated Jefferson because its exterior was similar to what he was building at Monticello. Historian Jack McLaughlin argued that "the double porticoes at the northeast and southwest ends of the house were similar to the Palladian superimposed orders Jefferson had drawn for his own house, so much so that later historians wondered whether Jefferson had a hand in designing them."[29]

On the way to Monticello, Martha and Jefferson also made a sentimental stop at Tuckahoe, where Jefferson had spent some of his boyhood while his father managed the estate of his friend and in-law, William Randolph. Because they had set out in the dead of winter to reach their home still under construction at Monticello, they were obliged to stay each night at some plantation along the road. By the time they reached Tuckahoe, three days after leaving The Forest, the snow fell in deadly earnest, and their carriage nearly lost a wheel, so they stopped once again and had it mended. After a week or so, they moved on to Elk Hill, a plantation of 669 acres in Goochland County along the James River and Byrd Creek. Elk Hill belonged to Martha—she had lived there with her first husband—and the Jeffersons made much use of the house and the land.[30]

For another two days, the couple made but very little progress, driving swathed in blankets while their horses strained to drag them through the knee-deep snow. By the time they reached Blenheim plantation, they knew the phaeton would not make it up the mountainside, so they left it there and borrowed saddles for two horses from Colonel Carter's overseer. There was but one sidesaddle at Blenheim, and the overseer would not let it go, but Jefferson persuaded him with talk of being a newlywed and eager to be at home.[31]

They set out on horseback to complete their journey to Monticello through the blizzard. At one point, the storm abated enough so that they saw a brilliant orange light that Martha declared to be a fine omen, and Jefferson declared to mean there would be a warm fire laid when they arrived. They had eight more miles to travel, and this through snow more than two feet deep and drifted as high as their horses' breasts. But both Martha and Jefferson were accomplished riders, both having been taught expertly by their fathers.

The snow piled deeper with every mile as they moved into hilly Albemarle County. With only a few miles to go, they were "obliged to quit the carriage and proceed on horseback,"[32] pressing forward as the sun disappeared behind the Blue Ridge Mountains to the west. At sunset, they began their ascent, slowly and miserably taking the mountain's 867 feet. The trees along the path up to Monticello were weighed down by ice and snow. The Jeffersons had to pass through thickets of frozen branches hanging low across the trail.

Jefferson took Martha to their new home, such as it was. He had been sketching plans for Monticello for several years, but, on the eve of his wedding, the only habitable part of the new house was a small one-room brick structure, twenty feet square, that now comprises the South Pavilion of Monticello. Jefferson had moved into this temporary residence after his house at Shadwell was destroyed by fire in February 1770. He had been living there and supervising the construction of the main house throughout the entire period of his romance with Martha.[33]

Finally, after riding for hours "through a mountain track rather than a road, in which the snow lay from eighteen inches to two feet deep," Martha had arrived at what would be her new home for the next ten years.[34] They tied their horses in the kitchen for want of other space. The poor beasts had not even water, so they probably brought them buckets of snow to drink. A blazing hearth, a hot meal, and cozy blankets might have transformed any cottage into a honeymoon sanctuary against the raging snow and sleet, but it was "late at night" and the young bride found "the fires all out and the servants retired to their own houses." Martha's new quarters were little more than a cabin at the edge of a raw and frozen construction site. Her first impression of her husband's architectural project was "the horrible dreariness of such a house, at the end of such a journey." But Martha's first night at Monticello did not stay dreary for long.[35]

"Part of a bottle of wine, found on a shelf behind some books," was made to substitute "for both fire and supper." Then, as the story was told to their children and friends, Martha found "sources of diversion" and the "horrible dreariness was lit up with song, merriment and laughter. As a result, this room has come to be known in present times as the "honeymoon cottage," although it later served as Jefferson's office.[36]

Martha may have discovered her fortepiano, for which she had waited those six months past. She may have opened the cover and touched a chord of it, feeling clumsy in her gloves. The keys shone a cheerful blue in the gloom. With bodies warmed and glasses full, the lovers lolled before the fire, Martha's auburn head bent low, her hazel eyes shining over the latest sketches of the magnificent house in which Jefferson vowed they would grow old together.

It was a night that would become one of Martha's most cherished memories.

EIGHT

MR. & MRS. JEFFERSON

....

Harmony in the marriage state is the very first object to be aimed at.[1]

— THOMAS JEFFERSON

LIFE FOR the newlyweds at Monticello was described as "a warm portrait of a harmonious and happy life on the little mountain, a life of ideas, invention, and the making of music. It was the life Jefferson had long hoped for—the kind of life his father had built and his mother had maintained, and which he now gave his own family at his chosen summit."[2] As Jefferson's granddaughter later recorded, "possessing a estate and being blessed with an accomplished husband, Martha Jefferson seemed launched upon the great ocean of life with every prospect of a prosperous and happy voyage."[3] And prosperous they were becoming. From Jefferson's account books, his income was a handsome one for that day, being three thousand dollars from his practice and two thousand from his farms. This was later to be increased substantially by the receipt of Martha's fortune when her father, John Wayles, died.[4]

No doubt, like any young bride, Martha's thoughts were less focused on money, in which she was adept and frugal, and more on her fledgling new home, Monticello. She surely dreamed of a house and garden of her own making. She had knowledge from her father working on a plantation, but she also depended on Jefferson's gardening expertise. She would have known her husband owned numerous books on gardening and planting, for example, *James on Gardening*, translated from Leblond's manual of the French formal style of gardening, as well as other books that gave examples of English landscape gardens.

When Martha arrived in 1772, Monticello was very much a work in progress. As early as 1767, before he wooed and married Martha, Jefferson had determined to build on the summit of his "little mountain"—his Monticello—rising above his birthplace, Shadwell. Deeply immersed in books on architecture, of which he already owned a number, Jefferson's preferred building style was Palladian, with its appeal to the harmony of mathematical proportions. Making himself master of architectural drawing to a degree quite beyond the skill of any colonial builders of his time, Jefferson designed Monticello with Palladian porticoes that were new in the southern colonies. By a genial adaptation to his mountain site of Palladio's schemes of colonnaded service wings, which he depressed below terraces, he would eventually give Martha's house an uninterrupted view of the magnificent panorama of plain, valley, and mountain range.[5]

In 1772, when Jefferson brought Martha to their mountaintop home, they had no doubt spent many hours going over the drawings of the mansion they intended to build together. Because Martha spent a significant amount of time at her first marital home, Elk Hill, while Jefferson was away and Monticello was under construction, it is likely that Martha's thoughts and architectural ideas influenced Jefferson's ultimate design of Monticello.

Elk Hill was a relatively small plantation, located near Elk Island at the mouth of Byrd Creek in Goochland County. Martha had obtained the land comprising the Elk Hill plantation in three different stages, but the majority of it consisted of 307 acres bounded by Byrd Creek and the James River. Today, Elk Hill is situated one mile south of State Route 6 and the James River. It was part of the Wayles estate, where it was listed as 348 acres by Jefferson in his "Rough estimate of the value of the land to be divided" and "Mr. Wayles's lands."[6]

Elk Hill was impressively situated on a hill overlooking the James River amid the farmlands of Goochland County. During the Revolutionary War, Elk Hill was occupied for a time by Lord Cornwallis and his troops. Jefferson later related that Cornwallis and his troops had done a great deal of damage to the property. The stucco-covered brick dwelling was rebuilt in 1835 and 1839 by Randolph Harrison Jr. on land that formerly belonged to Martha, and it stands as a distinguished example of Greek Revival architecture.

Martha's Elk Hill property was once a part of an early patent issued to a John Woodson in 1714. John Wayles purchased the land from Richard Weatherford by deed dated September 12, 1746. In 1778, Martha set about reassembling the Wayles-Skelton tract at Elk Hill: she and Jefferson purchased 307 acres from Anne Wayles and her husband, Henry Skipwith, of Cumberland County. In January 1782, they also purchased 312 acres "on the Byrd Creek at the Mill Pond" from Edward Smith and his wife, Sally. Jefferson completed his purchase by acquiring fifty adjoining acres from other members of the Smith family in May 1783.[7]

The interior of Elk Hill was sophisticated and followed Richmond precedent. The rather complex division of the main hall into three distinct passages, similar to the Governor's Mansion in Richmond, suggests the work of an urban architect or master builder. Further sophistication was enhanced by fine carving and detailing, with the finely executed marble mantel and plaster ceiling ornamentation in the rear parlor characteristic of the most stylish houses of the capital city.[8]

When Jefferson brought his bride to Monticello in 1772, their future together on his mountaintop was full of promise. They had no doubt spent many hours going over the drawings of the mansion he intended to build for her, and it is likely that Martha took part in its design, and certainly the decisions dealing with the use of space. The two semi-octagonal additions to each wing of the house were added to the original plan at about the time of their marriage, and it is quite probable they were the result of Martha's appeal for more space in the dining room and bedroom wings.

In fact, Martha could not have been too pleased with the distribution of floor space in the various rooms of the house, Jefferson's library being one of the biggest rooms in the house. It is here that she most probably asserted the greatest influence on the design of the house, in particular the living quarters. Jefferson's drawings for the two L-shaped dependency wings underwent many changes, with numerous erasures and redrawings. Although the dependencies were never constructed during Martha's lifetime, their continuing evolution on the drawing board was no doubt a reflection of Martha's influence.

"The functional symmetry of Monticello," writes Mark R. Wenger, architectural historian at the Colonial Williamsburg Foundation, "private and public domains flanking a grand ceremonial core—echoed that of earlier houses like Tuckahoe, Jefferson's boyhood home, where the physical arrangements vividly reflected the growing tension between two diverging spheres of life: "[the] house seems to be built solely to answer the purposes of hospitality. . . . It is in the form of a H, and each wing has two stories, and four large rooms on a floor; in one the family reside, and the other is reserved solely for visitors." Tuckahoe's emphatic segregation of family and guests, explained Wenger, "expressed a growing conflict between the planter's desire for greater privacy and his need to maintain customary forms of hospitality. At Monticello, Jefferson's visibility as a public figure, coupled with his proclivity for strictly enforced periods of private activity, amplified this conflict."[9]

Like many of their peers, Wenger posits, Martha and Thomas Jefferson sought to devise an architectural remedy. Over a period of several years, the Jeffersons persistently explored the architectural implications of how they wished to live. According to Jefferson's designs, the two dependency wings would incorporate all of the outbuildings usually found scattered about the main house of a large Virginia estate. In the southern wing would be a brewing room, smoke room, dairy, laundry, kitchen, pantry, and summer dairy. On the opposite wing would be stables for twenty horses, a chariot house, and a saddle room. Servants' rooms and privies were located in each wing, and a "hosterie," a room apparently to be used for the servants of visiting guests, was in the north wing. Any complaints about inadequate storage were satisfied by several dependency spaces specified as storerooms. Between the house and the kitchen, which was located at the L-turn in the south dependency, a large pantry was planned, and in the same position on the opposite service wing, an even larger "store room." Directly under the parlor a "ware room" was designed to be used for storage.

The first Monticello stood from about 1781 until 1796. After seeing the house in 1782, the Marquis de Chastellux wrote that Thomas Jefferson was "the first American who . . . consulted the fine arts to know how he should shelter himself from the weather." The Duc de la Rochefoucauld Liancourt visited the house in 1796 and later wrote that "Monticello, according to its first plan, was infinitely superior to all other houses in America, in point of taste and convenience." Author John Summerson has expressed a similar opinion about the architectural importance of the house, writing that "Monticello in its first state showed more real thought than any previous American building, possibly excepting those of Harrison."[10]

$\mathcal{C}\sim$

The great world of Virginia courthouses and mansions saw nothing of Martha and Thomas Jefferson for two months after they arrived at Monticello. Jefferson was perfectly content with his new bride, domestic tranquility, and tending to their mansion, farm, and books. One historian described him in these years as "a bookish, unworldly fellow, more at home with intellectual pursuits than in the hurly-burly of politics. Once back at Monticello, he presented himself as a monkish stranger to all political striving, as if it were a youthful folly he had outgrown. 'The little spice of ambition . . . ,' he told Madison some years later, 'has long since evaporated . . . The question is forever closed to me.'"[11] However, during his bitter political rivalry with Jefferson, John Adams would gruffly write about Jefferson's political detachment, declaring the latter's exit from Philadelphia to his beloved Monticello: "A good riddance of bad ware. . . . He is as ambitious as Oliver Cromwell. . . . His soul is poisoned with ambition."[12]

Martha no doubt urged Jefferson to brush off such criticism. In love and content at Monticello, Jefferson took her advice and professed sublime indifference to politics. "I live on my horse from morning to night," he declared to Henry Knox. "I rarely look into a book or take up a pen. I have proscribed newspapers."[13] In fact, the House of Burgesses met in Williamsburg without the twenty-seven-year-old delegate from Albemarle County. The bridegroom did not bother to jot a single note about money or other matters into his usually busy pocket diary. Not until April did the Jeffersons end their honeymoon and descend from their mountain for a journey to Williamsburg. They enjoyed the capital's lively spring season, going to the theater frequently and riding out to visit friends in the vicinity. On the way back, they stopped for a month-long visit with John Wayles at The Forest. By the time they reached Monticello again, it was almost summer. The flowers and fruit trees planted by Martha were blooming, and so was Martha Jefferson.

She was expecting their first child. On September 27, 1772, an hour after midnight, Martha gave birth to a daughter. Jefferson promptly named the child after her mother. The next months were an anxious time, however. The baby, nicknamed Patsy, was underweight, and she did not seem to thrive at Martha's breast. Not until someone, perhaps Jefferson, suggested letting one of the Monticello slaves, Ursula, nurse her did tiny Patsy begin to grow plump and healthy. The ordeal, however, left Martha Jefferson weak and bedridden—a pattern that would follow her through-out her short life.[14]

Jefferson relieved his worries about wife and infant daughter by con-centrating on the mansion he was building for his beloved Martha and their growing family. It was not an ordinary house—he wanted a house that elevated the soul and comforted the body. By now, Monticello's basic structure was visible. It was organized around a spacious central room with an octagonal section facing west that Jefferson called the parlor. This was entered from a hall on the east side, through a classic white-pillared portico. Flanking the parlor was a smaller square dining room to the north, balanced by a second square room to the south, which could also be used as a dining room. Off the hall was to be a large staircase to the roomy library, situated above the parlor. On either side of the library were two bedrooms. The ceilings of the downstairs rooms were eighteen feet high—twice the height of an ordinary plantation house. The decorations on the portico, on the mantels and indoor friezes were carefully selected for variety and beauty from the classic architectural orders: Doric, Ionic, and Corinthian.[15]

Like any housewife of that time and place, Martha undoubtedly spent her time conferring with their cook and other servants, ordering furniture and rugs to decorate the mansion emerging before her delighted eyes. And, in the midst of the chaos of construction and rebuilding, in the summer of 1773, Martha became pregnant again. Theoretically, she must have considered it good news. Like most men, Jefferson wanted a son to continue the family name. But in days when three out of every four babies failed to survive childhood, a woman accepted the need to have many children as a fact of life. But there was an undercurrent of worry in Martha's joy. Her own mother had died giving birth to her, and her father's next two wives seem to have been notably unkind to Martha. This doubled Jefferson's fears—if Martha were to die, it would mean future unhappiness for their infant daughter.

Historian Jack McLaughlin noted that "throughout much of her ten-year marriage to Jefferson, she was either pregnant, nursing, grieving the death of an infant, or sick from the complications of childbirth." Martha bore these pregnancies during "the difficult years of the American Revolution and in an unfinished house, littered with workmen's debris, while simultaneously undergoing the physical and emotional stress of multiple pregnancies and infant death."[16]

Jefferson worked at his law practice, and Martha pushed ahead at Monticello, directing free and enslaved workers as they made thousands of bricks, cleared stumps, and dug out and graded the first of the roundabout roads for carriages. In a sweet moment amid all the heavy work, the couple noted the small delight of harvesting the first peaches on the mountaintop, at the late date of October 8. Patty Jefferson, as Jefferson now lovingly called his wife, became a careful housekeeper, taking steps to ensure that her husband's private world ran smoothly. She saw to fresh supplies of meat, eggs, butter, and fruit. Vegetables, poultry, and eggs produced by slaves were commonly sold to Martha, and later to her daughter Martha Randolph, on a regular basis, providing a small, steady income to the slaves. "As hard as they worked for their masters, enslaved people sometimes managed to raise a little cash by gardening, gathering, raising poultry and trapping small game," noted historian Virginia Scharff.[17]

Martha also oversaw the brewing of immense amounts of beer; the slaughtering of ducks, geese, and hogs; weaving; sewing; soapmaking; and candlemaking. Her accounts record the production of fabrics in a spectrum of quality: "fine linen shirts [for] Jefferson," "fine mixt cloth for the children [her own]," "mixt cloth for the house servants," and, for the "out negroes," "hemp linen" and "coarse linen." She traded bacon to the slaves for their chickens, and she supervised the preparation of meat for her own family: "packed up for our own eating 28 hams of bacon 21 shoulders 27 middlengs. packed up for workmen 40 hams 50 shoulders." In fact, Martha delighted in taking personal direction of the work of the kitchen on more sophisticated foods. Every day, as slave Isaac Granger recalled, she came to the kitchen to give cooking instructions to Ursula. "Mrs. Jefferson would come out there with a cookery book in her hand and read out of it to Isaac's mother how to make cakes, tarts, and so on."[18]

In addition to cooking, Martha took a deep interest in her land at Monticello. An Italian neighbor and good friend, Philip Mazzei (credited with naming Monticello, Italian for "little mountain),[19] had brought Martha several kinds of European seeds when he arrived to stay with the Jeffersons while his own estate was being completed. Martha was pleased, especially at the "fifty-day Indian corn" and the winter wheat. Mazzei explained to Martha that these crops would grow very well on hills like Monticello and that they thrived in the mountainous sections of Italy, near Casentino and Valdarno.

"The wheat pleased the men; the corn, the women," Mazzei wrote in his memoir. "In Virginia, and I think it is also true of other States, the wife is in full charge inside the house; the husband, outside; he does, however, see to the purchase of whatever provisions his wife tells him are needed." In fact, Mazzei's firsthand recollections of Martha and Thomas Jefferson give significant insight into life at Monticello when Martha lived there. He noted that "if the wife needs indoors someone working outdoors, she asks her husband for him; and the husband, his wife if he needs outside someone working indoors. Hostesses just love to have their dinner guests find uncommon fare, especially early fruits or vegetables. Of their nine or ten varieties of Indian corn preferable to our own none mature as early as our fifty-day corn, and over there they make a very appetizing dish with corn that is not fully ripe. That is why the ladies were grateful to me for the fifty-day corn."[20]

Martha was so pleased with the crop that she nicknamed it "Mazzei's corn." In fact, Mazzei taught the Jeffersons a great deal about farming and crops. For example, Mazzei related to Martha that "it is a well-known fact that plants produced by pear or apple seeds always degenerate and generally produce fruit so bad that even hogs will not eat some of it. Sometimes, however, an excellent new species is generated by them. This generally happens where the vastness of the land seeded makes it impossible for its owner to graft more than a small portion of the trees."[21]

Martha saw firsthand that one of Mazzei's ungrafted trees produced a cider apple "superior to the best of Brittany and England . . . it is called Becker's apple because it originated on his land. In New York State the same was true of a winter eating apple, better than any I know, and there it must be known by the name of the man on whose land it originated, but in Virginia and the other States it is called New York apple."[22]

Because New York apples kept well, the Jeffersons, as well as other Virginians, probably bought and sold many quantities of them, shipping them to other states in barrels and butts. Mazzei recorded that he had known them in London, where a "Mr. Allaire, a young New Yorker, had had a buttful sent to him and gave me quite a few. I was thus able to give a taste of them to Marquis Caracciolo, the Minister from Genoa, the Resident from Venice, the Envoy from Portugal, and the Spanish Ambassador, all of whom agreed they were better than any others both for beauty and taste. They are bigger and rounder than the French, of a prettier green and smoother skin."[23]

"When I lived in Virginia," Mazzei remembered, "I would buy many barrels every year. Once I was surprised to find a perfectly sound apple surrounded by rotten and decomposed ones, but a knowledgeable Quaker told me that only the infected or bruised ones rot and that the infection is not communicable because apple skin is thicker than that of any other kind of fruit. I have not had the same experience with other varieties of apples, but I am inclined to think the same thing would happen with any of them."[24]

Martha herself oversaw the planting of as many as forty-eight fruiting cherry trees for Monticello's kitchen. Thomas Jefferson later noted that one beloved variety of his, Carnation, was "so superior to all others that no other deserves the name of cherry." The Jeffersons also enjoyed their ornamental effect in bloom.[25] Eventually, Martha encouraged Mazzei to start a winery on his land near Monticello. "According to what I was told by my men," Mazzei noted to her, "who had roamed through the woods and observed the varieties of wild grapes, there were probably no fewer than two hundred. I observed thirty-six varieties on my land, some good, some fair, some bad, and some that stank. I chose six of the best to make two small casks of wine, one of which I kept for myself, giving the other to my men, who did not drink it because they found they could sell it at one Virginia shilling a bottle. I am of the opinion that when that State is populated in proportion to its area, the best wines in the world will be made there."[26]

The grapes with which Mazzei first made two casks of wine were picked from treetops near Monticello, in very thick woods, from vines which had an immense amount of branches. Three months later, Mazzei observed "their wine caused the cork to fly off as does the sparkling wine of Champagne. I think that in no other country is nature so propitious to the grapevine as there." In fact, Martha and her husband had supervised their own vine cuttings at Monticello of the July grapes, "grapes so juicy that . . . I made wine from them." Mazzei wrote with satisfaction that his "first year, those cuttings that reached me in good condition, no matter of which variety, produced shoots so long that good Vincenzo Rossi remarked: 'Master, Sir, don't write that back home; you know, they wouldn't believe you and you'd be thought a liar.'"[27]

However, the next year, the Jeffersons' venture into a winery was thwarted by nature. During the night of May 4–5, 1774, a frost caused by the northwest wind nipped the wheat crop in the bud, froze young oaks and other saplings, and caused leaves to fall off all other trees. Monticello's trees remained leafless until the following year. The formed clusters of grapes froze along with the grain crops, and even the established grapevines suffered, producing about half of their normal harvest. Mazzei, whose vineyards had suffered the same fate, discussed the matter with a Dr. Bland, who had been in Europe and studied medicine in Edinburgh. Bland assured Mazzei that "in this country only fire can destroy the grapevines."[28]

During this time, Martha would have also overseen, at least in part, some of the stables and construction work at Monticello while Jefferson was away in Williamsburg. Because Martha was herself an accomplished rider, she would have overseen the assemblage of a stable of beautiful saddle mares and draft horses to make long trips in comfort. When she arrived at Monticello, she also would have noticed that mules were greatly valued for heavy work there. But the only jackasses she saw, according to her neighbor Philip Mazzei, "were grey and puny and consequently the mules too were grey, puny, and also very mean." In all probability, she or Jefferson would have purchased the four Maltese mules noted by Mazzei, three male and one female. "In fact," wrote Mazzei, "the sight of those animals caused surprise and they were liked so much that their fame spread throughout the land."[29]

At Monticello, Martha had an abundance of land, encompassing a mountain, dense forest, and streams, and ordinary livestock was customarily turned loose to graze and forage in the woods. Valuable (and often dangerous) breeding bulls and horses were kept penned up, but noncas-trated male animals were allowed to roam through the forest. In fact, a neighbor of the Jeffersons, "a certain Morris, a good but indolent man, overseer of Mr. Richard Carter," was repeatedly warned by both Jeffer-sons and Mazzei "to pen up his mischievous young bull, but to no avail." Mazzei instructed his overseer, "'since you have been so good, have him warned once more, and if he does not heed the warning, have your people kill the bull.' It was just what happened, and my men divided among themselves what money they got for it. That is the reason why my friend was kind enough to castrate my two miserable horses, one of which was known to be five years old and the other nine."[30]

The Jeffersons had many conversations with Mazzei about the culti-vation of the land in and around Monticello. In particular, they discussed the heavy damage caused in Italy by the embanking of rivers, especially in Tuscany after Count de Richecourt, as head of the Regency, allowed mountains to be deforested. "The time does not seem far off," Mazzei warned Jefferson, "when water will reassert its right to open up its most convenient course, to the grave injury of landowners. The descendants of those who cleared the land of forests and enjoyed the benefit of two or three good harvests will have stones where soil and trees had been."[31] Both Jeffersons agreed that the enactment of a law limiting deforestation would be a good thing, "but not before its importance has been brought home, for to deprive a landowner of his right to do with his property as he pleases is too repugnant to the concept of liberty. However, when the heads of families see that the law tends to free their descendants from bad consequences, they themselves will ask for it," Jefferson wrote.[32]

It seems that Mazzei was so fond of Martha Jefferson that he had his stepdaughter stay with her while his own land was cleared and his house built near to Monticello. "When we left home," Mazzei wrote, "my stepdaughter wept; she wept even more when we left Mr. Jefferson's. The girls took after her father in character. I had noticed [Martha] was fond of her."[33]

NINE

SLAVERY AND
DOMESTIC LIFE

....

Under the law of nature all men are born free [and]
everyone comes into the world with the right to his own
person which includes the liberty of moving and using it
as his own.[1]

— THOMAS JEFFERSON, in the Howell slavery case, 1770

B Y 1773, Jefferson returned to the full-time practice of law, which
he later abandoned after seven years, concluding that the law was
"intellectually stultifying." This meant he was away from Monticello for weeks at a time, defending clients in various county courtrooms
around Virginia. By the time Edmund Randolph took over his practice
in 1774, Jefferson had handled more than 900 cases, representing common farmers to the most powerful and wealthy of the colony's planter
elite. Only one of his cases compels attention in this study of Martha
and Thomas Jefferson's private life: a 1770 attempt to free a mulatto
named Samuel Howell. Did Martha encourage or influence Jefferson
to take the case, with her close affiliations to Betty Hemings and their
mulatto slaves?

According to author and lawyer Richard Dixon, Jefferson had mentioned the "natural rights" of all men early in his defense of Howell.[2] A
1705 statute provided that a bastard born of a free white woman by a
negro or mulatto father would be bound by the church wardens to be a
servant "until it be 31 years of age."[3] This was the condition of Howell's
grandmother. A subsequent 1723 statute provided that if a female, while
in such servitude, should have a child, then "such child" shall also "serve

105

the master" for the same amount of time. This was the condition of Howell's mother. Then, while in servitude, this woman gave birth to Howell.

Jefferson sued for Howell's freedom on the basis that the law did not reach "innocent offspring." He argued that Howell was born free, proclaiming, "Under the law of nature, all men are born free." That would require a law to bind him to slavery based on his mother's condition, whereas the "such child" reference in the 1723 statute referred only to Howell's mother, not to Howell himself. Jefferson also argued to the court that Howell's relationship to the master was not one of servitude but "apprenticeship," and this was broken by the death of the master.

The court rejected Jefferson's reasoning, but this incident marks two important points in Jefferson's life and his views on slavery. "First, this was not a slave case," according to Dixon, "and although we do not know the percentage of Howell's white blood, Jefferson applied the doctrine of natural rights to him as a mulatto. Second, the case gives us insight into Jefferson's penchant for the rule of law. The case illustrates his understanding that morality is often trumped by legal considerations. Although Howell ought to be free by natural right, he could not claim freedom because statutory law placed him in servitude. Jefferson unsuccessfully tried to create a legal rationale consistent with the law for Howell to gain his freedom."[4]

More importantly, perhaps, a strong case could be made that Martha influenced Jefferson's views on slavery. When we analyze Martha's background, the closest person to a loving mother that she knew was a slave, Betty Hemings, who cared for and nurtured Martha almost all of her life. This benevolent, if not loving relationship, cannot be overlooked and most probably was recognized by Jefferson after Betty moved to Monticello. All of the Hemingses were treated differently from the other slaves on the plantation, as evidenced by their household duties instead of hard field labor. There can be no historical doubt that this circumstance was due to Martha's relationship with Betty, the patriarch of the Hemingses and surrogate mother figure to Martha Wayles Skelton Jefferson.

The nature of this relationship could not have been lost on a perceptive man like Jefferson, whose life was also linked to a slave at a young age—his body servant, Jupiter. In 1743, both men were born at Shadwell, a newly opened plantation of Virginia's western frontier. "As boys," notes historian Lucia Stanton, "they may have fished in the Rivan[n]a River,

set trap lines along its banks, and shared hunting escapades in the surrounding woods. As young men they traveled the length and breadth
of Virginia together and found wives on the same plantation near Williamsburg."[5] In fact, Jupiter always accompanied Jefferson on his travels
and acted as his personal attendant while he studied law in Williamsburg.
Later, Jefferson described Jupiter's duties: "shave, dress, and follow me on
horseback." In Williamsburg, Jupiter walked down the Duke of Gloucester Street to buy Jefferson's books, fiddlestrings, and wig powder, and to
pay the bills of the baker, shoemaker, and washerwoman. When Jefferson
was short of change, Jupiter lent him money to tip the other slaves, the
domestic servants of his Williamsburg colleagues.[6]

Thus, it is not mere coincidence that both Martha and Thomas Jefferson had a close personal attachment, if not relationship, with two trusted
slaves, Betty Hemings and Jupiter. This semifilial connection undoubtedly influenced their views on slavery. As historian Stanton argues, "Jefferson . . . saw the behavior of Jupiter . . . in terms of their 'fidelity.'"

Perhaps this was the reason why Jefferson represented the slave
Howell without charging a fee. Howell claimed he was a free man, and
Jefferson agreed with him. Under the "law of nature," he told the startled
judge, "we are all born free." Jefferson contended that it was bad enough
that the law required a person born of a slave to remain in servitude for
thirty-one years, and then extended this status to her children. But only a
new law passed by some future legislature, "if any could be found wicked
enough," would inflict this fate on a grandchild.[7]

However, the judge found no merit in Jefferson's argument, and
Howell remained enslaved. The defeated lawyer proceeded to do something highly irregular: he loaned Howell $10. There may have been some
verbal advice included with the money because Howell soon ran away
and was never seen in Virginia again. According to historian Thomas
Fleming, the case not only revealed Jefferson's dislike of slavery (and
probably Martha's, too) but also his sympathy for mulattoes whom he
considered especially victimized by the system.[8]

A few years later, the Virginia Assembly passed two laws regarding
slaves, which the king did not approve. The first prohibited their importation; the second authorized owners to set them free. "The veto of the
first was probably due to the great profit accruing to the London Africa
Company from that inhuman and infamous traffic," wrote Philip Mazzei,

a Jefferson friend and neighbor at Monticello. "As for the second, I would not know what to attribute its veto to."[9]

Mazzei noted in his memoir that "Jefferson declared that he did not go in for palliative remedies but for what was essential; that he would move for abolishing slavery entirely since both humanity and justice demanded it; that to keep in bondage beings born with rights equal to our own and who differed from us only in color was an injustice not only barbarous and cruel but shameful as well while we were risking everything for our own freedom [during the Revolutionary War]. He concluded by saying that it would be preferable to run the risk of having to till the land with our own hands."[10]

John Blair, secretary of the Virginia Assembly, was a man Mazzei remembered as "endowed with talent, a clear mind, and a good heart, and owning many slaves, agreed, saying, Of course, we'd rather work the land with our own hands, although he was patently lacking in physical strength." Mazzei himself "ardently desired to see that come to pass as soon as possible, that is, as soon as circumstances permitted. But in the existing situation such a step seemed too risky to me, there being twice as many blacks as whites. In my opinion the benefit would have a better effect if they were told that their owners were disposed to grant it to all those whose good conduct deserved it and granting it suddenly and universally might lead them to think that we did it out of fear brought about by the circumstances."[11]

According to Mazzei's detailed memoir, written when he was eighty years old, George Mason expressed his views on the necessity of educating slaves before taking such a step and of teaching them how to make good use of their freedom. "We all know," he said, "that blacks consider work as punishment," pointing out that unless previously educated, the first use they would make of their freedom would be to do nothing and that they would become thieves out of necessity. But Mazzei was quick to point out Jefferson's adamant views against slavery. "Beginning with Jefferson, they all were convinced by the reasons advanced by Mr. Mason and myself. Hence it was agreed to propose the two laws vetoed by the present King of England and to begin spreading the word that another would be enacted compelling slave owners to send black children to public schools in every county in order to learn reading, writing, and arithmetic and how to make good use of the freedom that their owners were determined to give all those who would so behave as to deserve it. The two laws were passed as soon as they were proposed."[12]

"Later I learned," Mazzei wrote, "that all the other States had followed suit. Consequently if a landowner of the Sugar Islands, where slaves outnumber free men more greatly than in any of the United States, should wish to go and settle there with his slaves, the latter would become free upon landing. As for the other laws then contemplated, circumstances have prevented me from knowing what became of them. I do know, though, that the number of blacks freed by their masters increased daily."[13]

In fact, in his original draft of the Declaration, "in soaring, damning, fiery prose, Jefferson denounced the slave trade as an 'execrable commerce . . . this assemblage of horrors'" and a "cruel war against human nature itself, violating its most sacred rights of life & liberties.'" As historian John Chester Miller put it, "The inclusion of Jefferson's strictures on slavery and the slave trade would have committed the United States to the abolition of slavery."[14]

There is no historical doubt that Jefferson, as well as Washington, Madison, and other Virginia planters, acknowledged the immorality of slavery while admitting perplexity as to how to abolish it without causing financial ruin. "When denouncing British behavior on the eve of the American Revolution," wrote historian Ron Chernow, "Washington made clear the degrading nature of the system when he said that, if the colonists tolerated abuses, the British 'will make us as tame and abject slaves as the blacks we rule over with such arbitrary sway.'"[15] "To get some historical balance," argues historian Gordon Wood, "it is important to remember that by the time of the American Revolution slavery had existed in Virginia and in America for more than a century without substantial criticism or moral censure. Therefore by condemning slavery and putting the institution morally on the defensive, Jefferson and many of his fellow revolutionaries did confront the slaveholding society in which they had been born and raised. It was an accomplishment of the Revolution that should never be minimized."[16]

Jefferson gave up his law practice on the inheritance he gained upon his father-in-law's death. His decision also revealed something about the

Jefferson marriage. The man who had spent so many hours wrestling with "Old Coke"[17] and worn out horses up and down Virginia's wretched roads to build a thriving law practice abandoned his profession. He sold his client list to a cousin, twenty-one-year-old Edmund Randolph, and henceforth became a man with only two pursuits—husband and farmer. Giving up his law practice may have been a sacrifice Jefferson made to prove to Martha that there was nothing in his life more important to him than his marriage and the children whom she bore.

Upon his return to Martha and Monticello, and throughout their marriage, Martha and Thomas Jefferson shared a love of children and, perhaps most fundamentally, music. He was devoted to his violin, she to her spinet, and they both loved to sing. They rejoiced in playing together.

What, apart from music, made their marriage so happy—as Jefferson later described, "ten years of unchequered happiness"? Primarily, both had similar ideas about the pursuit of physical and emotional happiness. Both were true romantics, devoted to the novels of Laurence Sterne, a writer who celebrated sentiment. They also discussed the poetry of Ossian, an ancient Scottish poet, translated by the eighteenth-century writer James Macpherson. Both spouses had pragmatic fathers, but they both embraced the romanticism then popular in the upper strata of Europe. Jefferson, the most famous disciple of reason in American history, never underestimated the influence of the "head and heart." Years later, Jefferson wrote one of his most famous letters with this very title, "A dialogue between the Head and the Heart." One of his early biographers, James Parton, observed that "the mightiest capacity which this man possessed was the capacity to love. In every other quality and grace of human name he has been often equalled, sometimes excelled; but where has there ever been a lover so tender, so warm, so constant, as he?"[18]

Although countless books and articles have been written about the life and work of Jefferson, none have particularly noted a preoccupation to which both he and Martha devoted much time and interest—their mutual love for clocks and Jefferson's specific fascination with watches. Probably more so than any other notable American statesmen, Jefferson had a special interest in timepieces, and his personal records and correspondence abound with references to them. He was a chronic gadgeteer, and, at his estate at Monticello, many devices are still preserved that he designed and had created for the purpose of making living more gracious and easy for Martha. A devoted student of the arts and sciences, it is not surprising to discover that Jefferson had such an absorbing enthusiasm with timepieces that he designed several of his own, most probably as a present to his beloved Martha.

There are numerous entries in Jefferson's account books relating to the purchase and repair of pocket watches. Over the course of the years, particularly between 1789 and 1809, he purchased many watches from dealers in America, England, and France, with many of the timepieces made to his special order. He frequently presented watches as tokens of his esteem to his friends and members of his family. For instance, as each of his granddaughters reached the age of twelve, Jefferson deemed that she had achieved the status of a young lady. Tradition states that he gave on her birthday to his daughter Patsy (Martha) a personal servant, whom she was required to train, and a gold watch. Jefferson selected each of these watches carefully to fit the personality of the child. A number of these timepieces have survived, and several are displayed at Monticello.

Although it was later in Europe that Jefferson first had the opportunity to indulge in his enjoyment of the arts, no doubt Martha had a keen interest in the arts as well, one that had begun very early in her life, starting with her prolific music lessons. This was the more remarkable since artistic stimuli and artistic opportunities were so scarce in the fledgling colonies, especially in the South, where the scattered plantations were somewhat isolated. An effort to determine how Martha was able to form an appreciation of the arts, as she very notably did, is an interesting historical topic.

It is difficult for modern Americans to understand how very few and inadequate were any works of art in the colonies generally, and in Virginia particularly, at the time of Martha's youth. As late as 1781, Jefferson would write in his *Notes on Virginia*: "The first principles of the art are unknown, and there exists scarcely a model among us sufficiently chaste to give an idea of them."[19] Of sculpture, the first work to come to Virginia was the marble statue of Lord Botetourt voted for by the colony in 1771, executed by Richard Hayward in 1773, and set up in the capitol building at Williamsburg. Of paintings, we know of almost none in Virginia at that time except portraits, the best of them being scarcely more important than those owned by the Knellers at Westover. Painters working in the colony were few and poor enough: John Wollaston, John Hesselius, John Durand. In 1768, the young Charles Willson Peale's full-length portrait of Pitt was sent from London to Richard Henry Lee in Westmoreland, and it is possible that the Jeffersons viewed this ambitious work. But it was not until 1774 that Peale himself first painted in Williamsburg, when Martha had resided there in the Governor's Palace as first lady of Virginia.

As a youth, Jefferson had one opportunity to see something of what other colonies had to offer. In 1766, he went to Philadelphia to be inoculated against smallpox by Dr. John Morgan, to whom he took a letter of introduction from John Page. Jefferson then passed through Annapolis and pressed on to New York. The figure of Pitt and the equestrian statue of the king, ordered that same year by the Assembly of New York, were not received and set up until 1770, but Philadelphia, more than any other colonial town, already had a small group of collectors. Judge William Allen had copies of several Italian works, including a Venus by Titian, *The Concert* by Giorgione, and a Holy Family by Correggio. John Penn's collection was "very great and elegant." Former governor James Hamilton had at Bush Hill what passed for an original by Murillo, a Saint Ignatius taken from a Spanish ship, and copies by West. In his garden were "seven statues of fine Italian marble curiously wrought." As early as 1761, John Morgan had paid tribute to both Allen and Hamilton, "from whom I have received so many favors," and we cannot doubt that he introduced the brilliant and fashionable young Virginian into their society.[20]

"Although as a young man," noted Pulitzer prize-winning historian Gordon Wood, "[Jefferson] had seen very few works of art, he knew from reading and conversation what was considered good, and in 1771 he wrote a list, ranging from the Apollo Belvedere to a Raphael cartoon, of the celebrated paintings, drawings, and sculptures that he hoped to acquire in copies." By 1782, "without having quitted his own country," Jefferson was "an American who . . . is a Musician, Draftsman, Surveyor, Astronomer, Natural Philosopher, Jurist, and Statesman," the French visitor the chevalier de Chastellux noted.[21]

As the years went by, Martha and Thomas Jefferson were full of bliss and contentment with their tranquil family life at Monticello, both of them satisfied with "their farm, family and books." But both death and destruction were on their horizon.

TEN

PATSY AND POLLY

....

While Thomas Jefferson assisted at the birth of his country in Philadelphia, Martha Jefferson fought for her life in Virginia.[1]

— Historian VIRGINIA SCHARFF

WE CANNOT estimate with any precision the rank of Martha Jefferson among the great lovers in history, but throughout her life she proved to be a woman who physically and emotionally loved deeply, and whose actions and ideas were shaped by that love. Existing evidence suggests that her emotional passion for the man who would become her husband was vibrant, lifelong, and deep.

When Martha married Jefferson, elite Virginians had begun to believe that husbands and wives should share "mutual affections." These feelings were different for each, because they were based on a system of reciprocal obligations and emotions. Thomas and Martha both embraced what the age called "sensibility," a development of sensitivity toward others, particularly one's inferiors—the poor and the weak, including females and children.

Like others of their time, each expected different things from one another. Jefferson was a devoted partisan of "domestic tranquility," an ideal that depended on a wife's willingness to put the goal of pleasing her husband above every other need. He took pride in keeping his own temper in check and in presenting a mild face to the world, although he intended to be in charge. He assumed that Martha would play her part as a sweet and sunny helpmate who would defer to his wishes and judgments. "Gentle and sympathetic people always attracted him most, and clearly she was that sort," wrote Jefferson's premier biographer, Dumas Malone.

As with most eighteenth-century married women, Martha's main wifely obligation was to produce children, an obligation that she fulfilled with great ardor, but often without good luck. Martha gave birth six times during the decade of her marriage and had a total of eight pregnancies, despite her husband's unavoidable absence from home for long intervals. Thus, during her childbearing years, Martha was often pregnant every other year (roughly 54 of the 128 months of their married life together). Only two daughters survived to adulthood, Patsy and Polly. Although childbearing was considered to be one of Martha's primary functions, raising and educating their children also took much of her time and energy.

The eighteenth and early nineteenth centuries was a time for large families. In fact, the size of the family of Martha's eldest daughter, Patsy Jefferson Randolph (twelve children), was not uncommon. John Tyler, the tenth president of the United States (born in 1790), fathered fifteen children: eight with his first wife, Letitia, and seven more with his second wife, Julia Gardiner (who was thirty years younger than Tyler). In fact, nearly half of all plantation wives in the late eighteenth century had six or more children, and one of every ten bore twelve or more. Because of the infant mortality rate, however, mothers often buried as many children as they reared to adulthood, as did Martha Jefferson.[2]

Jefferson hated being away from Martha. Although he was a recently elected member of the Virginia legislature, he stayed home at Monticello for more than a month after they set up housekeeping there in January 1772, thus missing a whole session of the House of Burgesses. It may have been this conspicuous absence during the honeymoon period that started what later became a common criticism among his Revolutionary compatriots: that Jefferson was inordinately fond of his domestic life with Martha to the dereliction of his patriotic duties. So annoyed were some of Jefferson's colleagues that they made acerbic remarks in letters to him, trying to goad him back to work. Phrases like "your retreat to the Delights of domestic life" (John Adams), "your pleasure at home" (Edmund Pendleton), and "your darling Pleasures" (John Page) were veiled references to Jefferson's misplaced priorities. Pendleton, having failed to persuade Jefferson to stay longer in Philadelphia in the summer of 1776, put his finger on what he was sure was the problem when he suggested that, at least in Virginia, "having the Pleasure of Mrs. Jefferson's Company, I hope you'll get cured of your wish to retire so early in life from the memory of man, and exercise your talents for the nurture of. Our new Constitution."[3]

But there was no "cure" for Jefferson's desire to be with Martha. Martha was often ill, and the solicitous Jefferson wanted to be at her bedside. He could not forget that Martha's mother had never recovered from bearing her, and his anxiety was heightened whenever she was pregnant—which was almost half of their married life. And yet that awareness of a detrimental cause and effect does not seem to have put much restraint on the happy couple's intimate sexual life.

Whatever the personal details of their marriage may have been, it is clear that there was a persistent conflict between Jefferson's love for Martha and his duty to politics, a conflict that he wrestled with for the next ten years.

Martha Jefferson was very much a product of her class and her time. She was bred to be a plantation mistress, and during ten years of married life, she worked hard at being a successful one. She was, however, apparently physically unequal to the rigors of the task of bearing a child every other year. It weakened and ultimately killed her.

Martha expected her first child to Thomas Jefferson almost immediately after their marriage. Martha "Patsy" Jefferson was born on September 27, 1772, nine months after the wedding at The Forest. The Jeffersons named the child after Martha's mother—also a Martha—but the little girl was nicknamed Patsy, whereas Martha herself was called Patty. Weak and small, like many of Martha's children, Patsy Jefferson would be the only one of Jefferson's children to live a long life, surviving to take tender care of her beloved father—and Monticello—into his old age. She inherited her father's vigorous constitution and died sixty-four years later, in 1836, ten years after Jefferson.

Frail and frequently both ill and pregnant, Martha's pregnancies were challenging physical and emotional ordeals for both wife and husband.

Her recovery from each birth was slow and difficult. In each instance, Jefferson remained as close as possible, helping to nurse her through pregnancy and recovery. Martha's fragility appears to have been a sad legacy handed down from her mother, who died as a result of delivering Martha herself. And so, too, was it passed down to her children. It was often said that Patsy Jefferson resembled her father, even to possessing his formidable intellect, whereas daughter Mary ("Polly"), born on August 1, 1778, shared her mother's petite physical appearance, mannerisms, and fragile health. Tragically, Polly also died from the ordeal of childbirth at the tender age of twenty-six.

The Jeffersons were not spared the loss of older relatives and friends during their early years of marriage. Martha's father, John Wayles, was dead and gone at the age of fifty-eight, just a little over a year after Martha's wedding. Jefferson's mother, Jane, also not yet sixty at her death, never knew of her son's authorship of the famous Declaration of Independence. Dabney Carr, his brother-in-law and the closest friend, was carried off by an intestinal fever while still in his twenties.

Martha and Thomas Jefferson's children were the most obvious evidence of their physical intimacy, but each birth took its toll on Martha's vitality. Any instance of childbirth can be a life-threatening event, but in eighteenth-century America, the pattern of repeated births, commonly spaced about two years apart, sapped many women's strength and often proved fatal. The prospect of repeated pregnancy instilled fear in many women, too. A case could be made that if they lived long enough, many women regarded menopause as a welcome relief from the exhausting years of pregnancy and childbirth.

Unless death intervened, the average eighteenth-century Virginia woman had seven or eight full-term pregnancies during her childbearing years. Patrick Henry's second wife, Dorothea, and the Jeffersons' eldest daughter, Patsy, each raised eleven robust children to adulthood. At the other extreme, couples such as George and Martha Washington had no children.

The Jeffersons' second daughter, Jane Randolph Jefferson, was conceived in July 1773, immediately after the Jeffersons returned from a visit to The Forest and almost ten months after Patsy's birth. Jane was born at Monticello on April 3, 1774, but died seventeen months later in September 1775.

More than two years passed after Jane's birth, a time marked by momentous events of war and independence, before Martha's only son was born. Their male child, sometimes identified as Thomas, was born at Monticello on May 28, 1777, but sadly lived less than two weeks.

The early deaths of Martha's children undoubtedly caused her deep sorrow, but, in those preantibiotic days, were not a great surprise. In the typical eighteenth-century family, it was actually a rare thing for all the children to reach adulthood, as whooping cough, measles, mumps, and scarlet fever took their deadly toll. A strangulating and deadly whooping cough would kill Lucy Jefferson, Jefferson's young daughter, a few years later.

When Mary (Polly) Jefferson was conceived in November 1777—just five months after the birth of their short-lived son—the Jeffersons were in Williamsburg for the autumn session of the General Assembly. Polly was born at Monticello on August 1, 1778 and seems to have inherited her mother's physique, "low like her mother." Polly, also sometimes called Maria, died in 1804 from complications of her second childbirth at the age of twenty-six.

Martha and Thomas Jefferson gave the name Lucy Elizabeth Jefferson, in turn, to their last two children. The first Lucy Elizabeth was conceived at Monticello in March 1780—nineteen months after Polly's birth—and was born there on November 30. She was not yet five months old when she died on April 5, 1778, six weeks before Colonel Banastre Tarleton's troop of British cavalry invaded Monticello, sending the family scrambling to Poplar Forest in Bedford County. The second Lucy Elizabeth was conceived at Poplar Forest in August, eight and a half months after the birth of her namesake, and born at Monticello on May 8, 1782. This was to be Martha's last and fatal pregnancy.

In a marriage that lasted almost eleven years, Martha had been pregnant nearly half the time. Her husband's intermittent absences during the American Revolution most likely occasioned the long intervals between two of her pregnancies. During the 29.5 months from Jane Randolph's birth in April 1774 to their son's conception in September 1776, Jefferson's involvement in state and national affairs caused recurrent absences that must have coincided with Martha's ovulations and fertility. Similarly, the 9.5 months prior to the first Lucy's conception in March 1780 coincide with his tenure as governor of Virginia. The intervals between her other three births and subsequent conceptions averaged only 7–9 months.

Contraceptive techniques were not unknown in eighteenth-century America but seem not to have been much used among married couples. Martha Jefferson's difficulty with breastfeeding denied to her the months of lactation that enabled other mothers to postpone conception and space their children's births at least two years apart. For Martha, as for her mother and her daughter Polly, physical intimacy ultimately proved fatal.

Examining eighteenth-century statistics, one finds that approximately 30 percent of the women in a sample born between 1710 and 1799 (Martha was born in 1748) died before age forty-five. About 10 percent of women in those years were preceded in death by their husbands (men who were, typically, several years older than their wives). The higher female mortality rate may well be related to childbirth and, in particular, to the debilitating effects of malaria. Historians and scientists Darrett and Anita Rutman have hypothesized that Chesapeake women of childbearing age who, like Martha, lived in and around Williamsburg may have been weakened by exposure to malaria.[4]

A preliminary look at the letters and diaries written by hundreds of Virginia gentlewomen between 1760 and 1830 reveals that, after 1790 or 1800, some of them, at least, were becoming ever more articulate and insistent in their complaints about the burdens of repeated pregnancies and childbirths. "Their dialogue with their husbands," observed historian Anita Rutman, "dwelling as it did on their pain and suffering alone, was perhaps not wholly the language of feminine autonomy, let alone rational economic discourse, but it may eventually have been effective."[5]

In the letters of Virginia gentlewomen written between 1760 and 1790, childbirth was regarded as an extremely difficult time for a woman. But what is striking is the stoicism displayed by eighteenth-century Virginia women as they discussed childbirth. Even as late as the 1790s, according to Rutman's research, the entire business of childbirth, including its fears, was discussed in routinized language, evidenced in this letter from Martha Carr (Jefferson's sister) to Lucy Terrell on August 9, 1794: "[Patsy Randolph will have a child soon] How happy should I be could I repeat my attentions to you on the same occasion but I have not a dou[b]t of your being blest with some good female friend that will act the Mother [and] sooth you with her compassion when the painful hour arrives and soften [you] by her tenderness. The necessary time of retirement may God of his mercy grant you a favorable time."[6]

In this letter, the woman's need of companionship can be met by some "female friend" who will fill a standard role by "acting the Mother" in "the painful hour," that is, in "the necessary time of retirement." "This is still largely the standardized language of the stoical eighteenth century," Rutman argues, "in which such conventionalized formulae at once expressed and yet controlled the fear and other emotions which, by the very use of such language, were assumed to be simply the inevitable concomitants of childbirth."[7]

Thus, childbirth was traumatic and frightening but, like all other emotions, it was, in the eyes of eighteenth-century women, nothing "to make a great fuss about." Men similarly recognized pregnancy problems, but with much less empathy. To William Byrd, it was simply "breeding," as in "my wife is breeding again." To David Meade, his daughter's impending delivery of a child was called "being taken to the Chamber for a season." "She will not," he continued, "be without your anxious wishes for her speedy recovery from so critical a state."[8]

By the turn of the eighteenth century, some Virginia women began to discuss childbirth much more frequently, expressing their hesitations and fears. "It was not that they did not love their children," concludes Rutman. "But, if anything, the increasing value that the nineteenth century attached to the individual tended to make a mother more satisfied with a smaller family upon whom she could lavish more affection. Thus, Eleanor Lewis, anticipating the birth of her second child in 1801, could tell a friend, 'You say my Dear Mrs. Pinckney, that you shall be pleased to hear I have another little darling to divide my affection with my precious Frances—in August or September [three or four months hence] I expect to inform you of such an event if no accident intervenes—I often think what I shall do with more, when one engrosses me so much.'"[9]

Similarly, Ellen Coolidge, Jefferson's granddaughter, also anticipating the birth of a second child, told her sister that "my present poppet is such a source of hope and comfort to me that I do not allow myself to repine at the thought of another, although I should certainly have preferred to defer the arrival of the little sister another year."[10]

In short, the eighteenth century was an era of primitive medical knowledge. Another sixty years would pass before people came to understand the importance of the simple act of washing hands before any type of medical procedure, including the delivery of babies. Although there is no definitive answer to the question of why Martha Jefferson had persistent problems with pregnancy and childbirth, it is certain that bearing children put her life in jeopardy. The fear that she might die must have surfaced with each pregnancy. That was certainly the case in 1782, when Jefferson wrote to James Monroe announcing the birth of his daughter and describing Martha's condition as "dangerous."

In fact, the events surrounding Martha's childbearing were largely the province of women, not men, at Monticello. Although none of the Hemings servants was a professional midwife, they were certainly involved in caring for Martha during her pregnancy and assisted at her births, according to slave historian Annette Gordon-Reed. "Taking care of a seriously ill and bedridden person is an emotionally and physically difficult task," observed Gordon-Reed, "and it must have been for the Hemings family. On the emotional side, the Hemings servants must have remained steady while attending to the needs of Martha, no doubt melancholy and depressed at her physical state. And when the sick person was a relative or friend, the caretaker feels frightened at the prospect of losing a loved one, like Martha Jefferson. Martha's sisters and her sisters-in-law no doubt experienced these aspects of caretaking to the fullest degree. They worked, and they surely grieved. But it is unlikely that they were primarily responsible for carrying out the more physical aspects of tending to 'Miss Martha.'"[11]

None of this would have been new to Betty Hemings, Martha's beloved "house servant" and mother to Sally Hemings. Betty had been caring for Martha from the time when she was a small girl, acting as something of a surrogate mother after Martha's mother and two stepmothers died by the time Martha reached twelve. "[Betty] Hemings was the one adult female fixture in Martha's life from the day she was born until the day she died," argues Gordon-Reed. "Even after Martha's death, the connection continued, as Hemings's daughter, Sally, was sent along with Martha's two youngest daughters to live with Martha and Sally's sister Elizabeth Eppes, while Jefferson took charge of his eldest daughter."[12]

Writing about Martha's physical and emotional ordeal with child-bearing, historian Jack McLaughlin concluded that "it is a tribute to her strength of will and dedication to what she perceived as her mission in life 'that she persevered in the face of all her difficulties.' But it also must be seen as a tribute to the enslaved women—Elizabeth Hemings, her daughters, and Ursula—whose labor sustained Martha through all her trials and allowed her to make a home for her family. Without their support she would not have made it as far as she did."[13]

How Martha entertained her children, Patsy and Polly, during the eighteenth-century holidays has always been somewhat of a mystery. As it is for many people today, Christmas was for Martha Jefferson a time for family, friends, and for celebrations, or in Jefferson's word, "merriment." In 1762, he described Christmas as "the day of greatest mirth and jollity." Although no documents exist to tell us how, or if, Martha decorated Monticello for the holidays, Jefferson noted the festive scene created by his grandchildren. On Christmas Day 1809, he said of eight-year-old grandson Francis Wayles Eppes: "He is at this moment running about with his cousins bawling out 'a merry Christmas' 'a Christmas gift' Etc."[14]

During Martha's time at Monticello, holiday celebrations were much more modest than those we know today. Socializing and special food would have been the emphasis of the holiday celebrations, rather than decorations or lavish gifts. The traditional ways of celebrating Christmas, particularly the decorating of evergreen trees and the hanging of stockings, derived from a variety of national traditions and evolved throughout the course of the nineteenth century, only becoming widespread in the 1890s.[15]

Yet references indicate that at Monticello, as throughout Virginia, mince pie was Martha's traditional holiday dinner favorite. Filled with apples, raisins, beef suet, and spices, Jefferson wrote of the delicious pie to Mary Walker Lewis on December 25, 1813: "I will take the liberty of sending for some barrels of apples, and if a basket of them can now be sent by the bearer they will be acceptable as accommodated to the season of mince pies." Of course, music also filled the scene in Martha's home. The Monticello music library included the Christmas favorite "Adeste Fideles."[16]

For slaves at Monticello, the Christmas season meant a few days of rest from the winter work. The winter celebration came to represent a time when enslaved families came together. In 1808, slave Davy Hern traveled all the way to Washington where his wife, Fanny, worked at the President's House (the White House) to be with her for Christmas. Two days before the Christmas of 1813, Bedford Davy, Bartlet, Nace, and Eve set out for Poplar Forest to visit relatives and friends.[17]

During the holidays, Martha would have provided the slave tables with wild game. Freshly slaughtered meats would have supplemented the usual rations of pork and cornmeal and "gills of molasses sweetened holiday fare. Music lifted spirits not fatigued by a harvest but by another full cycle of work in the fields, shops, and living quarters of Monticello. Enslaved people frequently recalled that Christmas was the only holiday they knew, filled with memories of gathering apples and nuts, burning Yule logs, and receiving special tokens of food and clothing."[18]

Years after Martha's death, Jefferson and his eldest daughter, Patsy, headed for Congress in Philadelphia, where Jefferson hired teachers and tutors to provide a first-rate and highly unusual education for a female child. He sent Patsy a detailed schedule for her day, one that Martha most probably had written or contributed to before her death at Monticello:

> From 8 to 10 o'clock practice music
> From 10 to 1 dance one day and draw another
> From 1 to 2, draw on the day you dance, and write a letter the next day
> From 3 to 4 read French
> From 4 to 5 exercise yourself in music
> From 5 to bedtime read English, write, etc.[19]

In 1801, the year Jefferson was sworn in as president, Patsy and Polly each produced a baby—it was Patsy's sixth (one of her children had died in infancy) and Polly's second (her first having died after only a few weeks). The demands of the nursery did not dissuade their father from encouraging his daughters to join him in Washington. By the fall of 1802, as the Sally Hemings scandal swirled,[20] the president needed his family by his side, and the young women agreed. Leaving the babies behind, Patsy and Polly and two of Patsy's older children moved into the White House, in an emotional display of filial devotion. But, as one historian has written, "years of living on Virginia plantations meant neither woman was quite city ready, and the flurry of preparations included a request from Martha to her father that 'Mrs. Madison [Dolley Madison] who very obligingly offered to execute any little commission for us, to send to Philadelphia for 2 wigs the color of the hair enclosed and of the most fashionable shapes, that they may be at Washington when we arrive.' That way the women would not have to do their own hair, "a business in which neither of us are adepts."[21]

The visit finally gave official Washington a good look at the president's daughters. After they had been in the capital for about a month, Margaret Bayard Smith reliably dispatched a report on the pair to her sister-in-law: "Mrs. Eppes [Polly] is beautiful, simplicity and timidity personified when in company, but when alone with you of communicative and winning manners. Mrs. R. [Patsy] is rather homely, a delicate likeness of her father, but still more interesting than Mrs. E. She is really one of the most lovely women I have ever met with, her countenance beaming with intelligence, benevolence and sensibility, and her conversation fulfills all her countenance promises."[22]

Patsy truly was her father's daughter and eventually produced twelve children and numerous grandchildren. However, her husband, Thomas Mann Randolph, was a miserable failure in life. Judged by tangible accomplishments, Randolph ignored his family, went bankrupt, alienated nearly all his friends and relatives with his terrible temper, acted irresponsibly as a military officer, served uselessly in Congress, and was one of Virginia's worst governors. Yet, he had come from an influential family, had a superb education, and inherited substantial property. Moreover, he was the son-in-law of Thomas Jefferson. But as historian William Gaines points out in his biography of Randolph, his "curious eccentricities, his irascibility, his fits of depression, his inability to finish anything, and his intense feeling of inadequacy compared to Thomas Jefferson were personal faults serious enough to have disgraced himself and Jefferson's daughter, Martha. At the same time Randolph failed to make a living as a farmer and he virtually abandoned his large family leaving their education up to Martha and Thomas Jefferson."[23] Most probably, this is why Patsy often retreated to Monticello and the tender succor of her father.

Years later, on a sunny November afternoon in 1824, fifty-two-year old Patsy Jefferson Randolph stood beside her father, Thomas Jefferson, and welcomed the Marquis de Lafayette to Monticello. The aging French hero, who was touring the United States to commemorate the fiftieth anniversary of American independence, kissed Patsy's hands and offered kind words, while his hostess "received him with a grace peculiarly her own." Historian Cynthia Kierner has noted in her biography of Martha (Patsy), that Patsy was "widely regarded as an exemplary woman and an accomplished plantation mistress. Martha Randolph presided over a celebration that showcased the Virginia gentry's gracious style of living and traditional rites of southern hospitality. After receiving Lafayette on Monticello's columned portico, twenty 'ladies & gentlemen,' including several of her own 'white robed' daughters and nieces, enjoyed a pleasant dinner in doors. By all accounts, the food was good and the company was congenial. As the sun set behind the distant Blue Ridge mountains, Martha Jefferson Randolph and her guests basked in the nostalgic glow of the reunion of the old revolutionaries."[24]

Jane Blair Cary Smith, Patsy's niece and a frequent visitor to Monticello, would later describe Patsy as an exemplar of genteel womanhood and domesticity. When Patsy received Lafayette at Monticello, Smith wrote, she exuded "the charm of a perfect temper—the grace of a nature which . . . possessed the truest dignity." Her unselfish cheerfulness was "the result of an unambitious spirit, and a contentment that lived in a sunshine all its own." Patsy, Smith wrote affectionately, was "highly cultivated and accomplished . . . [but] nevertheless happy in the domestic life of Monticello." According to historian Cynthia Kierner, "this Paris-educated daughter of a president and wife of a governor was universally popular in large part because she downplayed her own notable experiences and accomplishments and projected to every one she encountered an utmost simplicity of character and the most unaffected humility."[25]

Polly Jefferson, on the other hand, married well and seemed happy. On October 13, 1797, she married her cousin, John Wayles Eppes, and returned to live at their plantation, Eppington. John Wayles Eppes had been born near Petersburg, Virginia, and educated at the College of

William and Mary. Eppes studied the sciences and law under the direction of his uncle Thomas Jefferson and ultimately became a successful attorney and planter. He represented Virginia in the United States House of Representatives (1803–1811 and 1813–1815) and in the Senate (1817–1819).

Polly had two children, Francis Wayles Eppes and Maria Jefferson Eppes (b. February 15, 1804–d. February 1806). Their only surviving child, Francis Wayles Eppes, was born in 1801 at Monticello.[26] Yet, like her mother, Polly suffered from complications of childbirth, and she died on April 17, 1804, two months after giving birth to Maria. Jefferson wrote stoically, "This morning between 8 & 9. aclock my dear daughter Maria Eppes died."[27]

Sadly, Martha Jefferson had never known Patsy and Polly as adults, nor her numerous grandchildren. A third grandchild of Jefferson was born in 1796, while he was vice president. With this girl child, another apple had fallen close to the tree—six-year-old Ellen Randolph, Jefferson's granddaughter, was destined to also conquer the capital with her charm.

On a certain July morning in 1802, Ellen received a letter from her grandfather, the president of the United States:

Washington, Tuesday, July 20, 1802.
My very dear Ellen
I will catch you in bed on Sunday or Monday morning.
Yours affectionately,
TH. JEFFERSON.
Miss Eleanor Randolph.[28]

Historian Marie Kimball observed that "although the news of her grandfather's coming doubtless caused Miss Ellen no small degree of excitement, his threat was nothing new. Surprising his little granddaughter in the early morning hours was an established custom with Jefferson which he often jestingly alludes to elsewhere."[29]

"She was the favorite among his many granddaughters," Kimball concluded, "with whom he corresponded more frequently than with any other and of whom he spoke in terms of unique devotion . . . He [Jefferson] alludes to her as 'my peculiarly valued grand-daughter for whom I have a special affection'; and on another occasion, many years later, he writes: 'She merits anything I could have said of a good temper, a sound head and great range of information.'"[30]

Ellen received letters from her distinguished grandfather from her fifth year until his death some twenty-five years later. The letters have lost none of their quaintness and charm. They reveal a facet of his nature that Jefferson was usually careful to conceal. It was only his young correspondent who could lead the staid president to write as a birthday greeting: "On Sunday next, the 30th . . . receive the kisses I imprint for you on this paper." Ellen rewarded his devotion, as she herself wrote, with "all the affection of a child and something of the loyalty of a subject."[31]

The first letter from Ellen to Jefferson was written when she was only eight years old. A thoughtful mother had ruled the paper for her guidance with delicate double lines in pencil and had helped with the spelling. Ellen wrote in a large, round, regular hand, and, in her eagerness, she forgot to dot her "i's":

> My dear GrandPapa
>
> I received your letter and am very much obliged to you for it, as it is very seldom that I get one you cannot think how glad I was at it. I am very much obliged to you for the bantams you promised me and will take great care of them. I go on very slowly with my French for I have got through but one book of Telemachus but I hope that I shall now go on better since Mamma's health is so much better that she is able to hear us our lessons regularly.
>
> Give my love to Papa and Mrs. H. Smith [whose acquaintance she had made in Washington during the winter of 1802]. Adieu my Dear GrandPapa believe me to be your affectionate GrandDaught&er
>
> Ellen Wayles Randolph Feb 22, 1805.[32]

With his next letter, Jefferson inaugurated a custom, notes historian Marie Kimball, that he adopted with all his grandchildren, of sending them poems cut from the papers of the day. They were to keep these and learn them by heart:

Washington, Mar. 4, '05.

My dearest Ellen,

I owe a letter to you and one to your sister Anne. But the pressure of the day on which this is written and your Papa's departure permits me to write only to you, to inclose you a poem about another namesake of yours, and some other pieces worth preserving. As I expect Anne's volume is now large enough, I will begin to furnish you with materials for one. I know you have been collecting some yourself; but as I expect there is some tag, rag & bobtail verse among it you must begin a new volume for my materials. I am called off by company therefore God bless you, my child, kiss your Mamma and sisters for me & tell them I shall be with them in about a week from this time. Once more adieu. Th. Jefferson.[33]

Ellen's marriage on May 25, 1825, and her move to Boston did not deprive Jefferson of her solicitude and love during the last year of his life. Frequent gifts and a constant interchange of letters bear witness to Ellen's loyal devotion. None of these better expresses the spiritual connection of the venerable statesman and his granddaughter than the first letter from Ellen's new home. "One of my first cares," she writes, "is . . . to thank you for all the kindness I have received from you, & for all the affection you have shewn me, from my infancy & childhood, throughout the course of my maturer years: the only return I can make is by gratitude the deepest and most enduring and love the most devoted; and although removed by fortune to a distance from you, yet my heart is always with you."[34]

ELEVEN

DEATH

....

We are not immortal ourselves, my friend; how can we
expect our enjoyments to be so? We have no rose without
its thorn; no pleasure without alloy.[1]

— THOMAS JEFFERSON

MARTHA JEFFERSON attended to the family business
when Jefferson was away. But in the fall of 1773, John Wayles
became deathly ill. Martha now had a young child, a dying
father, and a plantation to run. Martha stayed at or near The Forest at
least through the spring, perhaps through the early fall. Consequently,
the Jeffersons were absent when another new cousin arrived at Shadwell
as Thomas's sister, Martha Carr, married to Jefferson's best friend and
groomsman at his wedding, Dabney Carr, gave birth.

And then tragedy struck again. Dabney Carr died suddenly. His
death, burial, and subsequent reburial as the first person interred in the
Monticello cemetery was the start of a sacred legend attached to that
small plot of hallowed earth. With Dabney Carr's passing, the mytholo-
gizing of the mountaintop as a place of destiny had begun.

Martha Jefferson was not present at her brother-in-law's death, being
in attendance on her ill father at The Forest. She was not yet twenty-five
years old when Wayles eventually died. Her world would never be the
same: her father had been the source of security during her entire life—as
a motherless child, a bereaved widow, and the heartbroken mother of a
dead son. Wayles was still looking out for her when he amended his will
in February 1773. His health failing, he worried about the debt he owed
his London agency, Farrell & Jones, a debt that was growing larger on

account of his last, immense foray into the slave trade. Wayles stipulated that all the tobacco he was growing on his various lands be shipped to pay that debt, "unless my children should find it to their interest to pay and satisfied the same in a manner that may be agreeable to the said Farrel and Jones."[2]

As the peach trees bloomed and the shoots of early peas poked up through the soil at Monticello in 1773 came the final grim news: John Wayles was dead at the age of fifty-eight. Jefferson had become fond of this genial man, and he knew how much he meant to Martha. Wayles had returned his son-in-law's friendly feelings, making Jefferson the executor of his will. The Jeffersons soon realized that, with Wayles's passing, they were, in fact, truly wealthy, but the knowledge did little to soothe Martha's emotional wound. She had inherited 11,000 additional acres of land and 142 slaves, most notably the Hemingses. Yet, there were also heavy debts to British merchants, and Martha sold almost half the land to settle them.

Martha Jefferson now had charge over three branches of her or her husband's family. There was her own husband and their infant daughter, Patsy. There was Thomas Jefferson's sister, Martha Carr and children, the Jeffersons' nieces and nephews, who came to live with them after Dabney Carr's untimely death. And there was Elizabeth Hemings and her slave family, including Sally Hemings. After her father's death, Martha surely took solace in married life and the building of her home and hearth at Monticello. During the first year of Martha's marriage, she and Jefferson no doubt entertained members of Jefferson's family a great deal. The extended family lived close by and would have been anxious "to meet the former widow Skelton, now Mrs. Jefferson." There is no historical record of the relationship between Jefferson's mother, Jane, and his young bride. The only mention of her by Martha is an item in her household account book: "borrowed 10 lb sugar of my mother." (She repaid it four weeks later.) Since Martha's own mother and stepmothers were dead, this obviously referred to Jane Jefferson. Although calling her mother-in-law "my mother" suggests a warmer relationship than most previous historians have thought, at the time this usage was common. Maria (Polly) Jefferson

Eppes was later to refer to her own mother-in-law as "mother." Still, it is likely that Jefferson's sisters and mother found Martha an extremely agreeable addition to the family. Her family connections were impeccable, even for a Randolph like Jane Jefferson, and her social skills, according to reminiscences by her grandchildren, were considerable. Martha not only impressed a French aristocrat like Chastellux, but, during the Revolution, she also became warm friends with the family of a Hessian baron who was a prisoner of war at Charlottesville.[3]

Much as he treasured the small pleasures of home, the torrent of public life was sweeping Jefferson away from Martha. In Williamsburg, when Jefferson and his allies proposed, in March 1773, a day of fasting and prayer in solidarity with their "sister colony" of Massachusetts, the governor, Lord Dunmore, responded by dissolving the assembly. Jefferson, by now a leader of the radicals in the legislature, joined the unofficial meetings at the Raleigh Tavern. As he looked back later, he would describe his younger self as "bold in the pursuit of knowledge, never fearing."[4]

During this recess of several months, Jefferson devoted himself entirely to his young family and to Monticello. Martha was enduring another difficult pregnancy, and the house was reaching the first stage of its perfection. No one, including Jefferson, imagined that in a few years he would tear it down and build another even a more remarkable version.

Across the hillsides where Monticello stood, Jefferson cut winding trails that he called roundabouts through the little mountain's forested slopes. Ultimately, he created four of these paths for woodland wandering, connecting them by oblique roads, while Martha planted more fruit trees and a vegetable garden on the southeastern slope. They were a couple attempting to create their own Garden of Eden for each other.

Martha gave birth on April 3, 1774. Everyone, above all the worried father, was hoping for a boy. But it was another girl, whom Jefferson named Jane Randolph in honor of his mother. One suspects that the name was really a tribute to his dead sister, with the "Randolph" a gesture of respect to his mother, still very much alive only a few miles away in his rebuilt boyhood home of Shadwell.

Once more, the pregnancy and postpartum took a toll on Martha's petite body. She recovered slowly from the ordeal. Jefferson fussed over her, repeatedly assuring her that he was the happiest man on the planet, with a loving wife and two thriving daughters. He played with little Martha, toddling at eighteen months, and began schooling Peter Carr, Dabney's oldest son. In the evenings, he and Martha read to each other from their favorite books, among them *The Poems of Ossian* translated by James Macpherson, a vivid example of the romantic movement in literature. Here is one their favorite passages from "The Songs of Selma":[5]

> Star of descending night
> Pair is thy light in the West
> Thou liftest my unshorn head From thy cloud
> Thy steps are stately on thy hill
> What does thou behold in the plains?
> The stormy winds are laid
> The murmur of the torrent comes from afar
> Roaring waves climb the distant rock.
> The flies of evening are on their foeble wings
> The hum of their course on the field
> What dost thou behold, for light?
> But thou dost smile and depart.
> The waves come with joy around thee:
> They bathe thy lovely hair
> Farewell thou silent beam!
> Let the light o' Ossian's soul arise!

The goal of such poetry was the emotion that Jefferson called "the sublime," a word that reveals the mystic side of Martha and Thomas Jefferson's shared soul. On Monticello's summit, their conjoined spirits soared in every direction.

Yet, there was little tranquility for Martha in her first few years at Monticello. A few weeks after Jefferson returned from Williamsburg, he watched his daughter, little Jane Randolph Jefferson, die in her weeping mother's arms. Unable to bear the thought of leaving Martha alone, Jefferson persuaded her to pay a visit to her half-sister, Elizabeth Eppes, and her husband, Francis, while he headed back to Philadelphia in his phaeton. Martha found the separation unbearable. She sank into a depression and was too ill to write a single letter. Jefferson devoted one day a week to writing letters home to Martha. When a month passed without a response from Martha, he grew frantic. Only a few weeks after his triumph as the author of the Declaration of Independence, Jefferson begged a Virginia colleague to replace him in Philadelphia: "For God's sake, for your country's sake and for my sake, come. I receive by every post such accounts of the state of Mrs. Jefferson's health, that it will be impossible for me to disappoint her expectation of seeing me at the time I have promised." He wrote to Francis Eppes, imploring him for news. Eppes assured him that Martha was not seriously ill, but the distraught and perhaps guilt-ridden Jefferson wrote that he wanted to hear that news from Martha herself.[6]

In the last week of December 1775, Jefferson abruptly left Philadelphia and returned to Monticello for the next four months. Together, Martha and Jefferson supervised the continued work on the house. Jefferson did his utmost to restore Martha's health and happiness. But on March 31, 1776, Jefferson's mother, Jane Randolph Jefferson, died suddenly at the age of fifty-seven.

Two years earlier, some scholars believe, the death of young Dabney Carr may have precipitated Jane Randolph Jefferson's own fears about her mortality. Sometime in 1773, Jane wrote her will, making bequests to her unmarried children: slaves for Anna and Randolph, and for Elizabeth a bed and some of Jane's own clothes. "By this time Jane had come to rely almost completely on Jefferson's direction of her affairs," historian Virginia Scharff observed. "For example, Dr. George Gilmer, the son of the Williamsburg doctor of the same name, paid many visits to Shadwell, and Jefferson paid Dr. Gilmer's fees and settled Jane's accounts." Local storekeepers appealed to Jefferson when his mother charged things. Jefferson kept careful track of Jane's expenses on her behalf, and, as the years passed, it became increasingly clear that she had no way to repay him. So, in September 1773, presumably "for his assumption of all her debts, she handed over to him her only property of value, the deeds to her remaining slaves."[7]

"Jane Jefferson lived out her last months amid the building fear and carnage of war," observed one historian, "though she would not survive to see the creation of a new nation." She may have been in failing health for some time before her death, since Jefferson made several payments to doctors on her behalf. He and Martha, in all likelihood, brought her to Monticello for nursing. Still, the end came more suddenly than anyone expected. As Jefferson wrote to his mother's brother, William Randolph, Jane had died "after an illness of not more than an hour," after what Jefferson called an apoplexy—a stroke. On March 31, he noted in his account book: "My Mother died about 8 o'clock this morning—in the 57th year of her age."[8]

According to funeral customs of the time, Jane's funeral was probably held two days later at Monticello. Her grave was located near Dabney Carr's recently erected memorial stone. The Reverend Charles Clay was most likely in attendance to preach a funeral service for the Jefferson family, the third in three years. Jane was survived by four daughters and two sons, numerous grandchildren, and a wide community of family, friends, and acquaintances in Albemarle County and across Virginia.[9]

Within a few hours of Jane's death, Martha nursed her distressed husband through a violent headache. Jefferson's headaches were reported to always come on his left side and not the right. Martha would comfort him by dimming the candles and offering him a bit of sherry. It was the only tonic that seemed to ease his discomfort. And although Jefferson did not seem to suffer any life-threatening illnesses, he continued to suffer from relentless migraine ("periodical") headaches during his life, which confined him to darkened rooms for weeks at a time.[10]

The emotional strain of Jane's death, coupled with Wayles's and Dabney Carr's deaths, caused his severe headache to incapacitate him for almost two months. In fact, he was so sick both physically and emotionally that he did not return to Philadelphia and the Continental Congress for six weeks.

Some historians have speculated that Jefferson never revealed a trace of sorrow about his mother's death in any letters, and this adds weight to the notion that Jane did not approve of Jefferson's revolutionary acts. Yet, as historian Virginia Scharff observed, "some historians have made a leap of logic from the absence of documents to insist that the most famous of Jane Jefferson's children did not write to her, or chose to destroy his letters, out of a desire to obliterate her influence on his life. They have concluded that the ever-scribbling Thomas Jefferson disliked his mother . . . these scholars presume that the lack of surviving letters implies a want of affection between Jane and her celebrated son. If that were true, we ought to have dozens and dozens of letters between Jefferson and his adored wife, Martha Wayles Skelton Jefferson. But we don't. Neither, for that matter, do we have letters between Thomas Jefferson and his closest male friend, Dabney Carr."[11]

Scharff argues that historians have ignored the absence of letters between Jefferson and Carr and have assumed that Jefferson burned his correspondence with his mother, as well as his wife's, reducing those precious documents "to ash as cold and silent as the remains of his childhood home. But why identify the lack of letters to or from Jane as proof that she and Jefferson were estranged? Perhaps some of Jefferson's biographers have let their own sentiments bias their readings of Jefferson's feelings about his mother," Scharff concluded.[12]

As historian Susan Kern pointed out, "Jane suffered greatly during the twentieth century at the hands of the Momists, psychohistorians, psychosexual historians, and worshipers of the patriarchy . . . [she] stands as the often-maligned mother with whom her son Thomas could just not relate. . . . Yet the family remembrances of Jane and the nineteenth-century biographers of Thomas Jefferson who relied on those remembrances present Jane in glowing terms, suggesting that in her own time, she was revered."[13]

Historian David McCullough observed that "possibly it was a deeply private love for his mother and the shock of her death coming so suddenly that explained his collapse. Or possibly it was worry over his wife's illness, or the stress of revolutionary politics. But there was no mistaking the intensity of his suffering. To his friend John Page, Jefferson wrote that it was only with 'great pain' that he remained in Philadelphia."[14] As Jefferson biographer Thomas Fleming remarked, "every man carries on a lifelong dialogue with his mother, sometimes in his conscious mind, more often in his unconscious. Mothers have an especially strong influence in the shadowy realm of emotions. George Washington and Thomas Jefferson seem to have inherited their mothers' temperaments. Some historians think John Adams's mother, Susanna Boylston Adams, was a manic depressive, who passed on the illness to her favorite son."[15]

Thus, gradually, a clearer historical image of Jane Jefferson emerges, one that shows her to be a woman who carefully ensured knowledge and a good education as part of her legacy to her children. No matter what their relationship might have been, it is a fact that Jefferson followed as a steward of her prayer book, having lovingly seen to it that it was rebound and maintained at Monticello. He not only preserved Jane's family records, but also fulfilled the duty of recording the family history in that same prayer book, which was in Jefferson's library on his death. After his death, his daughter Patsy claimed it and continued Jane's enduring legacy.

$$\mathcal{C}\sim$$

After a period of mourning had passed, Jefferson's neighbors urged him to participate in the Virginia Convention, which was rewriting the new state's laws. Jefferson agreed, and Martha eventually joined him in Williamsburg. They lived in the comfortable house of his friend and mentor George Wythe, who was serving in Congress. Martha was soon pregnant again. Jefferson consulted the best doctor in Williamsburg on Martha's behalf, but the physician could only tell the anxious husband that Martha was a fragile woman whose health would always be uncertain.

A few weeks later, the president of Congress, John Hancock, asked Jefferson to join Benjamin Franklin in the Paris embassy to seek French aid in the coming war. It was flattering evidence of how much Jefferson had impressed his fellow congressmen. It also confronted him with an agonizing decision. Finally, here was his chance to see Europe, something he had yearned to do since he was a student at the College of William and Mary. Hancock told him that his "great abilities and unshaken virtue" made him Congress's choice for this task, which was crucial to the future survival of America.

For three days, Jefferson remained conflicted. Could he take Martha and his children with him? The way she leaned on his arm like an invalid when they walked in George Wythe's garden dismissed that notion. Only someone in peak physical condition could endure six weeks on the rough Atlantic waters. Should he go alone? Martha would certainly acquiesce to his wishes, but they had both been unable, physically and emotionally, to tolerate a separation of a few months while he was in Philadelphia. This ambassadorship meant an absence of at least a year, possibly two. Jefferson could not even bring himself to discuss it with her. Again and again, love trumped ambition.

Instead, Jefferson wrote one of the most painful letters of his life, rejecting the appointment. He tried to defend himself against the imputation of cowardice or self-interest. "No cares of my own person or yet for my private affairs would have induced one moment's hesitation" to accept the appointment, he avowed. "But circumstances very peculiar to my family, such as neither permit me to leave nor to carry it" compelled him to refuse the offer.[16]

Ironically, those heartfelt words won him a scathing rebuke from Richard Henry Lee, who echoed other Virginia congressmen. "No man feels more deeply than I do, the love of and the loss of private enjoyment," Lee penned. "But if everyone followed Jefferson's example, America was beyond redemption, lost in the deep perdition of slavery."[17]

Meanwhile, Martha's pregnancy advanced, and her anxiety mounted with it. Once more there was dread as the day of delivery approached. On May 28, 1777, an all but distracted Jefferson waited on the first floor of his still unfinished mansion while Martha gasped and sobbed in labor. At last, down the stairs came his friend, Dr. George Gilmer, with a broad smile on his face. In his arms was a tiny red body swathed in blankets. It was a boy. Thomas Jefferson had a son.

However, seventeen days later, Jefferson, with a tight rein on his emotions, scrawled succinctly in his pocket diary: "Our son died 10 H. 20 M P.M." Regardless of the Jeffersons' deep sorrow, letters came to Monticello from John Adams and Richard Henry Lee, telling him how much he was needed in Congress. Lee's missive bordered on insulting, and Jefferson did not bother to answer either letter. He retreated from national politics, paying only sporadic attention to the ongoing war, with its perilous mixture of victories and defeats. Jefferson continued to accept election as a delegate to the Virginia Convention, but his attendance was erratic, depending largely on Martha's health.

As the Revolutionary War raged on for two years, on August 1, 1778, Martha gave birth to another child, a girl whom Jefferson named Mary, nicknamed Polly. She survived the first months, when so many babies died, and Martha also made a rapid recovery. With war, both husband and wife plunged into a near frenzy of planting and building. They were determined to finish Monticello for their growing family before the bloody war might destroy it.

TWELVE

THE GOVERNOR'S PALACE

....

Williamsburg could really be called a village rather than
a town.[1]

— PHILIP MAZZEI, neighbor of THOMAS JEFFERSON

BEFORE THE Revolutionary War formally started, Thomas Jefferson returned alone to Williamsburg shortly after his daughter Jane was born. The assembly met again, in the wake of the Boston Tea Party and closure of the port of Boston. To protect his family, Jefferson insisted that Martha stay behind at Monticello. Busy running the house and plantation while raising her daughters, Martha still took the time to record those things Jefferson would want to know when he returned. She duly noted eating the most ripe cherries from the trees he had planted and first peas of the season. When Jefferson returned, he would proudly look over her journal and record her observations in his own garden book.

Much as he treasured the small pleasures of home, the torrent of public life was sweeping Jefferson away. As he looked back years later, he would describe his younger self as "'bold in the pursuit of knowledge, never fearing' to follow truth and reason to whatever results they led, and bearding every authority which stood in the way."[2] The stalking of truth and reason was about to become a very dangerous hunt, and one may wonder how Martha, a mother of three little girls, felt about her young husband's willingness to take such bold risks for the Revolution. Jefferson was embroiled in controversy and formulating his first great statement of political philosophy, an incendiary pamphlet that would be printed, without his knowledge or consent—although not without pride—as *A Summary View of the Rights of British America.*

While Martha attended to family and the running of Monticello, in this season Thomas Jefferson, planter, lawyer, and provincial aristocrat, became a true revolutionary. In *A Summary View*, he rejected the authority of Parliament in America, arguing that although the colonies owed allegiance to the king, they elected their own representatives to local legislatures. The Continental Congress, then meeting in Philadelphia, would not tread that far. As one historian noted, "Jefferson must have known that his Summary View invited hanging."[3]

He was on perilous political ground, but Jefferson situated his argument deeply and firmly in the terrain of his real life as an Albemarle County planter and lawyer, clearing his lands, traversing the breadth of Virginia, leaving his family for weeks on end. Should such a man's fate be tied to a distant, negligent, sometimes abusive government? As he saw it, the original British colonists, like their Saxon ancestors, had left "the country in which they had been born."[4]

On June 3, 1779, and in the midst of war, Jefferson was elected governor of Virginia by his colleagues in the state assembly. Martha and their daughters—Patsy, Polly, and Lucy—now took up residence at the magnificent Governor's Palace in Williamsburg, although Jefferson could not have entertained notions of a lengthy stay. In fact, two days after his election, the Virginia Assembly passed a bill moving the government from Williamsburg to Richmond.

In those days, Williamsburg was really a small, busy village rather than a bustling city, even though the Governor's Palace, the Assembly Hall, the College of William and Mary, and the Bar were located there. It would have been crowded when the assembly was in session because all the representatives lived there while they were in session.

Nonetheless, Jefferson displayed a keen interest in the Governor's Palace and, with Martha's direction, soon embarked on a series of planning exercises aimed at remaking it on paper, if not in fact. These architectural designs were first identified by historian Fiske Kimball and reproduced, with commentary, in his 1916 study, *Thomas Jefferson, Architect: Original Designs* in the Coolidge Collection of the Massachusetts Historical Society. Since the appearance of Kimball's book, scarcely a decade has passed without some revision or reinterpretation of the facts surrounding these plans, yet there has been little discussion of what Jefferson had hoped to achieve.

The Virginia Assembly first authorized construction of a house for the governor in 1706. Work could scarcely have begun, however, before Governor Edward Nott died in August of that year. By 1709, only the walls and roof had been completed. With the arrival of Lieutenant Governor Alexander Spotswood in 1710 construction resumed. Although Spotswood was in residence by 1714, work continued into the early 1720s. Thereafter, the Governor's Palace witnessed little in the way of significant alterations until the arrival of Lieutenant Governor Robert Dinwiddie in 1752, when a rear wing for public entertainment was added.[5]

No stranger to this dwelling, Jefferson introduced Martha and his children to the grand house. As a student in Williamsburg, Jefferson had enjoyed the cultured atmosphere of Royal Governor Francis Fauquier's home as he joined the intimate palace group in the role of amateur musician. The young would-be lawyer and potential revolutionist found many opportunities to satisfy his appetite for music. He liked to hear Pelham play the Bruton organ, he enjoyed hearing the young ladies sing and play the spinet, and he entertained himself with the violin he had acquired. He admired Carter's organ so much that he even tried to buy the instrument.

As a protégé of Governor Fauquier, Jefferson had frequently dined at the palace during his student days in the early 1760s, accompanied by his mentor, prominent lawyer George Wythe. As a member of the House of Burgesses during the administrations of Lord Botetourt (1768–1770) and Lord Dunmore (1771–1775), Jefferson had surely attended assemblies there as well. Fauquier could not have been a more suitable mentor for Jefferson. Born in March 1703 into a wealthy French immigrant family from which he inherited 25,000 pounds, Fauquier was director of the South Sea Company, a fellow of the Royal Society, a member of the Society of Arts, and a former manager and governor of the Foundling Hospital of London. He was a friend of George Frederick Handel and was described in his proposal for membership in the Royal Society as "a gentleman of great merit, well versed in philosophical and mathematical inquiries and a great promoter of useful learning." He was also a fine musician, something of a religious skeptic and a gambler who made gambling fashionable in Virginia in a gentlemanly sort of way. He died of testicular cancer in March 1768.[6]

On these occasions, Jefferson, still in his mid-twenties, came to understand the building's role as a private residence and its function as a setting for imperial administration. As governor, his tenure in the house extended over a period between June 1779 and March 1780, broken only by brief visits to Monticello or Elk Hill.

Situated at the end of an imposing, tree-lined avenue, the governor's house was a cubic structure of brick, surmounted by a hipped roof with a flat deck and balustrade. A distinctive, two-stage cupola provided access to this rooftop platform and, with a pair of massive brick chimneys, served to elaborate the building's silhouette. To either side of the main dwelling were service yards and outbuildings associated with the stables (east) and the kitchen (west). In the rear, an elongated wing, embracing a ballroom and supper room, extended northward into a large formal garden. In front of the palace, two symmetrically arranged service buildings flanked a forecourt where approaching visitors alighted from their horses or vehicles.

Mounting the front steps of the main building, guests entered by way of the hall where ornamental displays of weapons—swords, muskets, and pistols—symbolized the status and authority of the chief executive. During Governor Botetourt's administration, the ceremonial importance of this entry was evident in its impressive furnishings—a royal coat of arms, a suite of globe lamps, and a fashionable set of backstools elegantly upholstered in red damask.

The hall was also important as a "room of access" where liveried footmen assigned priority to those persons seeking to bring business before the king's representative. From a pantry adjoining the west side of the hall, the governor's butler supervised this process and performed many other duties: dispatching servants to their tasks, handling disbursements, keeping household accounts, managing daily activities in the kitchen yard, and watching over "precious stores of the table" entrusted to his care.[7]

Seeking to materially redesign the Governor's Palace would be no easy task. Yet, Jefferson's architectural skills had already been praised by others, as in a design for his friend George Wythe and for an enlargement of a building of the College of William and Mary prepared at Governor Dunmore's request. Jefferson's plan for the Governor's Palace featured a great arcaded court reminiscent of the town palaces of Italy as shown by Palladio. "When he became Governor in 1779," historian Fiske Kimball observed, "he projected a transformation of the Palace at Williamsburg—by pedimented porticoes of eight columns, the 'full width of roof'—into the form of a temple, prophetic of extremes of the classic revival not yet even proposed abroad."[8]

Strategically located in proximity to the "little middle room" and the kitchen yard, the Governor's Palace pantry was ideally suited to its role as the center of the household. Across the hall was the parlor, a reception space that served by morning as a waiting room for persons seeking an audience with the governor and in the afternoon as a place where Martha could take tea with guests before dinner. After meals, the room may have functioned as a withdrawing room where Martha and the ladies socialized until their male companions rejoined the party. Those invited to share a meal with Martha and the governor moved deeper into the house, passing through a rear stair hall to reach the dining room. At an elegantly decorated table, Martha Jefferson entertained her guests, and afterward Thomas Jefferson would join his male companions for a glass of wine. If some item of business required attention, Martha made sure a desk and writing table with all the necessary supplies stood nearby.

In this same room, years earlier, Jefferson had often joined Governor Fauquier, George Wythe, and friends in food, drink, music, and conversation as a student at the College of William and Mary. Opposite this dining room was the imposing walnut staircase ascending to the governor's inner sanctum. To preserve decorum, just south of the great stair was the little middle room, a staging area where Martha supervised the servants preparing food and linen for delivery to the governor's table. On the other side of the stair was the so-called powder room. Furnished with a pair of dressers and a wig block, it was a private place in which to adjust apparel or renew the coating of white powder to a guest's coiffure. At the north end of the rear passage were the two largest rooms of entertainment, a ballroom and, beyond it, a supper room. Added during the early 1750s, these fashionable new spaces allowed Martha to entertain on a scale and at a level of sophistication befitting the dignity of her husband's office.

Led by Martha and Jefferson, select company of Williamsburg danced in the ballroom or enjoyed elegant refreshments in the supper room at evening's end.

On the second floor of the main house was Martha and Jefferson's own apartment. Beginning with the outermost room, this suite included the middle room, where the governor met with persons on official business; a chamber, where they slept; and the library, an inner sanctum where Jefferson read or conferred with intimate associates. Opposite Martha's apartment were two additional chambers for their children, Patsy, Polly, and Lucy, or certain guests. The larger of these, situated at the head of the stair, may have functioned like the state bedchamber in a great English house, reserved for important visitors and, on public occasions, open to company as a chamber of parade.[9]

As described here, the Governor's Palace that Martha lived in embodied two related yet distinct functions: to highlight the pomp of public business and to serve the private needs of the Jefferson household. This dual purpose supplied the underlying rationale for Jefferson's architectural exercise.

Historian Fiske Kimball observed "that Jefferson never occupied a house that he did not attempt to remodel. The palace drawings seem to uphold that statement. It is clear that Jefferson intended the measured plan as a record of existing conditions." As Kimball points out, the dimensions on the plan correspond closely with those set forth in the building act of 1705, and the occasional odd measurements surely reflect dimensions taken from a standing structure. Indeed, the excavated remains of the Governor's Palace corresponded with Jefferson's drawing in nearly every respect, save for the absence of a foundation for the hall/parlor partition.

Like the great mansion at Tuckahoe, the Governor's Palace as delineated by Jefferson's sketches would have drawn a line between family and business, allowing private existence and official endeavor to cohabit. He appreciated the similarity of these two schemes. The elaborate measures envisioned for Martha's personal privacy at the palace and those later undertaken at Monticello suggest a unique need for seclusion by the Jeffersons. "Actually, the couple's desire for privacy was remarkable only in degree," concluded historian Fiske Kimball. "By the time he sat down to consider possibilities for remodeling the palace, the trend toward greater domestic privacy was already widespread and ongoing among the colony's upper caste. Jefferson was only the most conspicuous of many Virginians who rebuilt their houses with this end in mind."[10]

Some historians have suggested that Jefferson acquired his taste for domestic privacy during his trips in Europe. As Kimball's detailed research concludes, the palace drawings demonstrate that he was thinking about the issue well before his foreign sojourns. Privacy was a growing part of the culture in which Martha and Thomas Jefferson moved, a trend with which his own deepest needs were in accord. "In the palace designs," Kimball observed, "in the remodeling of successive town houses, in the rebuilding of Monticello, and in the making of Poplar Forest, we see an earnest and continuous effort to create a tranquil world of solitude for the couple. The palace drawings constitute some of the earliest and most revealing evidence of that enterprise."[11]

In the Governor's Palace, Martha and Thomas Jefferson were able to indulge in their passion in music, with Jefferson, a serious master of the violin, often accompanied by Martha's harpsichord. In Jefferson's earliest surviving pocket account books, which begin in 1767, we find frequent items for fiddlestrings. With Governor Fauquier himself a musician, Jefferson formed a little group of amateurs who played often at the palace prior to Fauquier's death in 1768. Jefferson continued to study the violin with Alberti, a gifted virtuoso who had come to Williamsburg with some players, and to whom Jefferson's payments begin in 1769. Later, Jefferson persuaded Alberti to come and live at Monticello, where he took lessons for several years and introduced Alberti to Martha and his children for probable instruction as well.

"I suppose," Jefferson wrote, "that during at least a dozen years of my life, I played no less than three hours a day." He lost no opportunity of acquiring fine instruments: one violin purchased in May 1768 was probably the Cremona he still had when he died; another was one that "together with all his music composed for the violin" he pledged a large sum to John Randolph in 1771 and that he acquired when Randolph went to England in 1775. These two, he said, "would fetch in London any price." Nicholas Trist, who married Jefferson's granddaughter, quotes him as saying that he had to lay aside his violin on the eve of the Revolution, but we still find payments for fiddlestrings, as well as for a music stand, on his arrival in Paris, where in 1786, he bought a small violin, his third. Even after he broke his right wrist—indeed, even when he was secretary of state—he had his violin. In 1800, at the age of fifty-seven, he was still buying music.[12]

Jefferson's musical interests were not limited to the violin. In 1771, during his courtship of Martha, herself musically gifted, he ordered a clavichord from Hamburg, then wrote: "I have since seen a Forte-piano and am charmed with it. Send me this instrument instead of the Clavichord." In Philadelphia in 1783, he bought a clavichord; in Paris he first hired a piano, then bought a harpsichord; in Philadelphia in 1792, he had a spinet; in 1800, he purchased a piano for $264. Writing from Williamsburg to Paris in 1778, during a lull in the Revolution, he speaks of music as "the favorite passion of my soul" and makes his celebrated proposal to create a "domestic band of musicians" by importing workmen in various trades he ordinarily employed who could also "perform on the French horn, clarinet, or hautboy, and bassoon."[13]

During Jefferson's governorship, Williamsburg also had its professional musicians to entertain Martha and her children: Cuthbert Ogle before 1755 and Peter Pelham after 1750. The latter played the Bruton Church organ for almost fifty years, gave lessons on the harpsichord and organ, supplied copies of music to his friends, and played for the theater—but he also had to serve as the keeper of the public jail in order to make a living. When the church doors were open, Williamsburg was entertained with the strains of Felton's, Handel's, and Vivaldi's works.

Most of the homes in Williamsburg had one or more musical instruments, and, in some cases, there were enough to form small family orchestras. Even in the seventeenth century the violin, hautboy, virginal, and hand lyre were frequently mentioned in the inventories of personal estates. But none was more notable than that of an estate on a hill above the Potomac. There stood the impressive Georgian structure that was home to Councillor Robert Carter. With its 2,500 acres, avenue of towering poplars, and thirty outbuildings, the great house of white-limed brick with its five stacks of chimneys and three great pillars marked Nomini, the estate of a country gentleman, a Virginia tobacco planter. In 1732, when Carter was four years old, his grandfather, the "King," had died and left the estate of 300,000 acres, 1,000 slaves, and 10,000 pounds that had been accumulated over the years to make "King" Carter the wealthiest and most powerful of Virginia aristocrats. The young Robert Carter, heir to a portion of this vast estate, built up his own fortune until he held almost 80,000 acres of land by the dawn of the Revolution. Family wealth and prestige enabled Robert Carter to join Thomas Jefferson and the small group of planters who played important roles in the government of the colony and directed the political, economic, and social life of the Old Dominion.[14]

The Carters were the perfect example of the aristocratic families that dominated every field of activity, every aspect of the life of Colonial Virginia. And one of the larger collections of musical instruments belonged to Carter, including a harpsichord, fortepiano, "armonica" guitar, German flutes, and a violin at Nomini Hall, and a good organ in the house at Williamsburg.[15]

Martha's children probably had their music lessons whenever a "Mr. Stadley" stopped for a few days as he made his rounds of the Tidewater estates.[16] Jefferson also directly supervised the musical education of his family, pointing out the tunes to be learned and designating certain days and hours for practice. Jefferson's oldest daughter, Patsy, would have taken after her musical parents and played on keyboard instruments, probably spending two days a week practicing the piano and harpsichord. The children enjoyed the family concerts as listeners and players, and Patsy may have joined her father in evening performances. When snow and rain forced Martha and the children to stay indoors, the entire day might be spent playing music.[17]

The case of Jefferson and other plantation owners such as Robert Carter is by no means unique in the history of eighteenth-century Virginia. According to historian Maurer Maurer in his article "A Musical Family in Colonial Virginia," "the colony lacked the more spectacular evidences of a musical culture but nonetheless had an active musical life, and its capital was a musical little city. Carter also joined Washington, Jefferson, and the other Virginians who made up the audience at the Williamsburg theater for performances of the ever-popular *Beggar's Opera*, *The Virgin Unmask'd*, *Damon and Phillida*, or one of the Harlequin pantomimes. Since Virginia, unlike some of the other colonies, had no music publishing business, most of the printed music was imported from

England, although William Rind did make one venture into the business and brought out a collection of the 'newest' songs in 1773. In the 1760s, every week Governor Francis Fauquier and his friends, including Thomas Jefferson, staged their informal concerts."[18]

It is evident that music was not absent from the heart of Martha Jefferson. But it is significant that it was largely the music of amateurs who loved the art they practiced within the intimate circle of family and friends. No great artists, no great composers came out of the Old Dominion, but the musical life, fostered by men like Robert Carter, is worthy of the attention of any historian. As a result, music was kept alive as an important part of the cultural life of colonial Virginia when Martha Jefferson lived there.[19]

Skill with music was considered a social ornament by Williamsburg's young ladies of fashion, second only to dancing. Although young ladies were usually taught to perform on the spinet or the harpsichord, gentlemen preferred the violin, the horn, or the flute. As nationalism grew, so did the colonists' efforts to lessen their dependence on England. Life in Virginia became austere. Thriftiness was necessary, and the colonists were willing to pinch pennies in some areas—but not when it came to entertainment. Williamsburg was the center of hospitality in the colony. At "publick times" the taverns, inns, town houses, and theaters bulged with visitors. Few things were more important in the entertainment of these guests than music; fine musical instruments were commonly found in taverns, in churches, and in private dwellings.

Of course, it would be a mistake to imagine that every Virginian was a music-loving amateur who spent evenings with his harpsichord or flute. The unmusical ear, like that of Colonel Landon Carter of Sabine Hall, was disturbed by the "constant tuting" that came from every house along Duke of Gloucester Street in Williamsburg.[20] Carter wrote in his diary on August 21, 1771:

> Lord Dunmore's dogs had raised the price of beef in the market of Williamsburgh, and I do suppose they must make a goodly addition to the present modes of concepts, for I hear from every house a constant tuting may be listened to, from one instrument or another, whilst the vocal dogs will no doubt compleat the howl.[21]

Stringed instruments of all kinds were popular in Colonial Williamsburg, as well as in the Jefferson home, but the most popular were violins, violas, cellos, and basses. One of the earliest stringed instruments mentioned in historical records is that belonging to John Utie, a seventeenth-century colonist who brought a viol to play at sea. Another popular stringed instrument was the English guitar, a pear-shaped version of the cittern. A variety of wind instruments were played: among them were flutes (recorders) of all sizes, which were sold at the post office. A new instrument—the German or transverse flute—was also played in Williamsburg's music circles. Other woodwinds included oboes (usually identified by the French word "hautbois" or as "hautboys") and bassoons. Horns were popular brass instruments, and fifes and trumpets were important parts of military activities. Singing was also a popular diversion in Williamsburg. The ballads sung in London's taverns soon echoed in the public houses of the town of Williamsburg. English songbooks like *Pills to Purge Melancholy* were treasured by the colonists. Songs were also an important part of the culture brought to the colonies by African slaves.[22]

Although Pelham is the best-known "Musick Master" of colonial Virginia, several others are worthy of mention. Cuthbert Ogle came "to instruct those gentlemen that play other instruments (than the harpsichord or spinet) so as to enable them to play in concert." Unfortunately, Ogle died soon after reaching Williamsburg. Francis Russworm, "who played such a sweet fiddle," and William Attwood, a teacher of oboe, horn, and flute, both advertised for students in the *Virginia Gazette* in 1771. Francis Alberti taught the violin to young Jefferson and probably to Martha as well. For a while, Martha practiced three hours a day. Years later, Jefferson wrote, "subsequently I got him [Alberti] to come up here and took lessons from him for several years."

Jefferson procured a fine Italian violin from John Randolph, a Tory sympathizer who returned to England rather than break with the mother country. Jefferson's library contained many fine music books, some of which still survive. An interesting incident occurred when a group of Hessian prisoners of war, interned near Monticello, were invited to the house. When he learned that his guests were musical, Jefferson took out his violin and provided instruments for the Hessians. They all played chamber music, and afterward the prisoners wrote home about the delightful evening, asserting that their host was an extremely good violinist.[23]

The days and nights in Williamsburg must have been almost continuous enjoyment of beauty and family for Martha, in the company of the man she loved and the children he had given her, in the bountiful blooming world of nature that fascinated both the eyes and mind. It is easy to imagine how this sensitive woman must have treasured almost every hour she lived in Williamsburg and Monticello, and would willingly have spent the rest of her life there, yielding with reluctance the few days a year her husband was required to be away from her.

But events beyond Martha Jefferson's world were about to force her to surrender that dream.

THIRTEEN

WAR

Such terror and confusion you have no idea of, Governor,
Council, everybody scampering.

— BETSEY AMBLER, daughter of REBECCA BURWELL[1]

THE REVOLUTION that exploded in Boston in 1773 soon
swept into Martha Jefferson's Virginia. This was the season in
which Martha and Thomas Jefferson, wife and husband, father
and mother, both became revolutionaries.

In fact, Martha was informed by Martha Washington of a "Letter
from an Officer at Camp" in late June that was printed in newspapers up
and down the eastern seaboard. The "officer" reported that the soldiers
who had felt "neglected" were pleased by the "mark of respect" shown by
Philadelphia women, who supported their revolutionary cause. Esther
Reed, the wife of Pennsylvania Governor Joseph Reed, penned a letter
of support for the soldiers. Her "Sentiments" letter had become known
throughout the land through the newspapers. Esther sent form letters
to ladies of note in all of the states, including Martha Jefferson, and as a
governor's wife, especially tried to engage other "first ladies" on behalf of
the soldiers.

The *Virginia Gazette* published Martha Jefferson's announcement of
a collection for the soldiers in churches, since it would be impractical
to go house to house in rural Virginia. Martha sent the plan to a friend
explaining, "Mrs. Washington has done me the honor of communicating
the enclosed proposition of our sisters in Pennsylvania and of inform-
ing me that the same grateful sentiments are displaying themselves in
Maryland. . . . I undertake with cheerfulness the duty of furnishing to my

country women an opportunity of proving that they also participate of those virtuous feelings."[2]

It is the only letter of Martha Jefferson's that survives.

Other women were literally draping themselves in the cause of liberty. "At a fancy ball in Williamsburg, Virginia, in December 1769 held for the governor and ladies and gentlemen of the town," noted historian and author Cokie Roberts, "women arrived at the gala affair in simple homespun gowns, leaving their imported silks and brocades at home. The Daughters of Liberty organized up and down the colonies, with hundreds of women spinning their wheels and sipping 'Liberty Tea,' a mixture of herbs and flowers rather than the real thing." The *Boston Evening Post* published a boycott agreement on February 12, 1770: women from three hundred families, including "ladies of the highest rank and influence," publicly promised "totally to abstain from the use of tea." They continued: "This agreement we cheerfully come into, as we believe the very distressed situation of our country requires it."[3]

And it was not just Boston that made a stand. In 1774, the *Virginia Gazette* published "A Lady's Adieu to Her Tea Table" because "Its use will fashion slavish chains upon my country." And in Edenton, North Carolina, fifty-one members of the Ladies' Patriotic Guild met in October 1774 at the home of Mistress Elizabeth King to sign an agreement to boycott tea and British cloth "for the public good." The agreement was published in the *Morning Chronicle and London Advertiser*. One North Carolinian living in London, Arthur Iredell, saw the mean-spirited drawing depicting incredibly ugly women and wrote with dripping sarcasm to his brother in America: "Is there a female Congress at Edenton too? I hope not, for we Englishmen are afraid of the male Congress, but if the ladies, who have ever, since the Amazonian Era, been esteemed the most formidable enemies, if they, I say, should attack us, the most fatal consequence is to be dreaded."[4]

The English criticism of these ladies was not well founded. "Almost all of the women who mothered and married the Founders," noted one historian, "were of the wealthier classes, and even if they had no formal education, they did know how to read and write, and many of them, like Abigail Adams, read extensively, though they never went to school. Abigail never got over the injustice of excluding girls from proper schools, and she advocated vociferously for women's education." John Adams wrote heavy-handedly from Paris to Abigail, who was busy running his business and raising his children in Braintree, Massachusetts. "I admire the ladies here," he said. "Don't be jealous. They are handsome and very well educated. Their accomplishments are exceedingly brilliant." Abigail had a ready reply: "I regret the trifling narrow contracted education of females in my own country. . . . You need not be told how much female education is neglected, nor how fashionable it has been to ridicule female learning."[5]

Although many of the marriages of the Founders, like that of Martha and Thomas Jefferson, were true partnerships, yet in the context of the marriage itself, the women literally owned nothing, not even their own jewelry. "Some colonies allowed for divorce," observed one historian, "but since it was not legal in England, the subject became another bone of contention between the Mother Country and her colonies. In fact, Catharine Littlefield Greene, the widow of Revolutionary War hero Nathanael Greene, caused a scandal by living with a man not her husband. Her old friend President Washington advised her to marry when she and her gentleman came to visit. Kitty was to petition Congress for repayment of her husband's payouts to clothe his soldiers, but Washington thought her sinful state of cohabitation caused resistance to her cause. But Kitty Greene, rambunctious, flirtatious, and highly competent, had legal reasons to resist marriage: she wanted to control her own property."[6]

During his first year and a half as governor, Thomas Jefferson had presided over a state that had not yet felt the lash of war. But the British were coming. Jefferson struggled to secure money, supplies, and soldiers, and he kept an eye on reports from the northern front while coping with urgent requests for help from the Continental Army. For a short time at least, Martha was with him in Williamsburg, sharing something of his public life. For the first time, instead of trading bacon for eggs and chickens and cabbages, she dealt extensively in cash. She started out asking for small sums for her household expenses, but soon found she needed much more of the fast-inflating Virginia currency.

The legislature, with Jefferson's consent, decided to transfer their operations to Charlottesville, which they thought was deep enough in

Virginia's interior to be immune from British attack. Since he and Martha were not safe in Williamsburg, Jefferson took Martha and the children to nearby Richmond and joined the lawmakers in the city. Some of this energy was inspired by good news about the war. France had signed a treaty of alliance, and the British army had abandoned its grip on the American capital, Philadelphia. General Washington pursued the retreating redcoats and claimed a victory in a brutal clash at Monmouth, New Jersey. Jefferson and many other Americans hoped peace was imminent. In May 1779, Jefferson informed his friend Edmund Pendleton—prematurely it would turn out—that he was planning to retire from both state and national politics with a war quickly settled.

The crime of "treason" against the British Crown was punishable by not one death, but three. When rebels were convicted of treason they were taken to a public place and there they were hanged by the neck. Hanging, however, was too clean a death, so after they had suffered but before they were unconscious, they were cut down and disemboweled. To make this second death complete, their entrails were burned before their eyes. Once gutted, their bodies were cut into four large pieces and then, at last, beheaded.[7]

In fact, during this time, one of the most horrific acts of British savagery took place. No doubt Jefferson was aware of this and may have related the incident to Martha. Two soldiers in the Queen's Rangers had robbed a local home when they came upon a nine-year-old girl. According to contemporaneous journals and letters, the soldiers "ravished" the girl. The commander of the Queen's Rangers, John Graves Simcoe, investigated the incident and informed General Cornwallis on June 2 that "I have not the least doubt but that Jonathan Webster & Lewis Terrpan . . . of the Queen's Rangers, were guilty of a rape on Jane Dickinson yesterday." After a brief trial, the two men were given an hour "to prepare for their death." By order of Cornwallis, the men were then hanged "in the presence of the whole army." Word of the crime spread quickly, further terrifying Virginians, and perhaps Martha Jefferson, who had young daughters of her own.[8]

With fear and trepidation, Martha took her two daughters with her to the safety of Richmond, to which the legislature again had decided to move because it was less vulnerable to seaborne assaults from the British.

But the British landed troops from their fleet with ease, and Governor Jefferson could do little to stop them.

In the fall of 1779, Martha and the children again fled Richmond to their nearby plantation, Elk Hill, until British raiders withdrew. In the midst of all this chaos, Martha became pregnant again, adding yet another worry to Governor Jefferson's lengthening list of woes. In November of that year, in a small Richmond house Jefferson had rented from Martha's uncle, she gave birth to another daughter, whom Martha named Lucy Elizabeth. Both the baby and Martha recovered quickly, the first good fortune to come the Jeffersons' way in months.

Little more than a month later, another British raid, led by the traitor Benedict Arnold, now a British brigadier general, sailed boldly up the James River. Martha and her children again were forced to flee, this time in foul winter weather, while Jefferson frantically tried to rally the state's militia. Barely two hundred men turned out, and "Jefferson had to sit helplessly on his horse on the south side of the James River and watch Arnold burn millions of dollars worth of cotton, tobacco, and other property in Richmond."[9]

Desperate to be together as a family, Martha and the children came back to the ravaged capital, and she struggled with her husband to keep a semblance of government alive. As spring approached, their spirits seemed to be reviving. But on April 15, a raw, rainy day, came a devastating personal blow to Martha. "Our daughter Lucy Elizabeth died about 10 o'clock a.m. this day," Jefferson wrote in his account book. Martha was inconsolable at the death of a third child within a few years, and with a bloody war raging in the background. Jefferson did not dare leave her. He sent his colleagues a note, telling them that Mrs. Jefferson's "situation" made it impossible for him to attend their daily session. Three days later, Jefferson wrote to a friend, "I mean shortly to retire."[10]

Even with more than 50,000 militiamen on its rolls, Virginia was unable to stop 180 British dragoons from riding into the heart of the state. No one had fired a shot at them. Martha's distress grew when a letter from a friend arrived to inform Jefferson that the Virginia legislature had approved a resolution calling for an investigation of his governorship. Behind this nasty move was Jefferson's former friend, Patrick Henry. He may well have been sincerely disgusted with Jefferson's performance, but it was also a chance to taunt a potential political rival.

Henry and others basically accused Jefferson of cowardice—yet, to be historically fair, no person has ever accused Samuel Adams or John Hancock of similar cowardliness in fleeing from Lexington when warned by Paul Revere that the British were coming. Some historians have overlooked the fact that Jefferson was a county lieutenant before he was governor and head of the local militia. He was entitled to be addressed as "Colonel," as his father had been, and occasionally he was, but the title did not hold. Jefferson did not take up arms in the struggle for American independence, but he went to war as truly as any civilian could. To him, this was a momentous, ideological conflict. The war cost him much, but in his mind this cause never lost its nobility, and Jefferson continued to invoke the "spirit of 1776" during his entire life.

The assembly adjourned until the fall, leaving Jefferson dangling between guilt and innocence. Adding to Martha's emotional distress, at dawn on June 4, 1778, her worse fears came true. Her beloved home, Monticello, and family were directly threatened by the war. It was not unlike her close escape from Richmond and the British months earlier, when a British column set up several cannons to the horror of Richmond's inhabitants. The cannons boomed, and, as Isaac Granger, Martha's servant, recalled, "everybody knew it was the British." As cannonballs knocked the top off a butcher's house, "the butcher's wife screamed out and holler'd and her children too and all." According to historian Henry Wiencek's description of the scene, "the ensuing panic was instant and total. In ten minutes not a white man was to be seen in Richmond." Jefferson called for his fastest horse, Caractacus, and galloped off. The arrival of the invaders, to the grim beating of drums, terrified young Isaac: "it was an awful sight—seemed like the Day of Judgment was come."[11]

Isaac remembered that his mother "was so skeered, she didn't know whether to stay indoors or out." But his father, George, kept calm and turned his attention to the task of saving Jefferson's most valuable possessions. He went through the house gathering all the silver, which he laid in a bed tick "and hid it under a bed in the kitchen." When the British marched up, Granger was prepared.[12] "Whar is the Governor?" demanded a mounted officer. "He's gone to the mountains," Granger replied. "Whar is the silver?" "It was all sent up to the mountains."[13]

The British searched the house, smashed Martha's wine bottles, emptied the corncrib for their horses, but they did not find Martha's silver. The day after sacking the governor's house, the British returned and grabbed little Isaac. "When Isaac's mother found they was gwine to car him away, she thought they was gwine to leave her. She was cryin' and hollerin'. The British took her as well."[14]

"The British hunted Governor Jefferson fruitlessly," Wiencek observed, "raiding the plantation west of Richmond where he had hidden his family, only to find the quarry gone. After Jefferson placed Martha and the children at a farm deeper in the interior, the British withdrew to the east, carrying off many slaves, leaving Richmond a shambles, and permanently scarring Jefferson's reputation as a wartime leader. The tumultuous winter ended with a personal tragedy: the Jeffersons' infant daughter Lucy died in April."[15]

George Granger's heroism may have led Jefferson to set him free, but the record is ambiguous, according to Wiencek. In his memoir, Granger's son Isaac said that his father "got his freedom by it. But he continued to serve Mr. Jefferson and had forty pounds from Old Master and his wife." There is no direct evidence for this manumission in the records, but Jefferson's list of taxable servants includes two free people, one of whom might have been George Granger.[16]

Now, riding fast, British dragoons were again pursuing Jefferson and his family, passing the Cuckoo Tavern in Louisa on Sunday, June 3. It was late—somewhere between nine and ten p.m.—when the British rode by. A giant of a Virginia militiaman named Jack Jouett, six foot four and 220 pounds, was in Louisa at the same time. Realizing that the enemy was en route to capture Jefferson and his family, Jouett thundered off in a now famous, daring nighttime ride of forty miles. Mounted on a horse said to be "the best and fleetest of foot of any nag in seven counties," Jouett crashed through the wilderness. Careering through thick and tangled woods, Jouett avoided well-traveled roads, staying clear of the British. According to one account, his face was "cruelly lashed by tree-branches as he rode forward, and scars which are said to have remained the rest of his life were the result of lacerations sustained from these low-hanging limbs."[17]

Jouett arrived at Monticello just before dawn. Martha greeted him with a glass of Madeira, but it was not hard to imagine the growing terror registering on her face. Not even at Monticello could she and her children be safe. If they captured her husband, the British might hang him on the spot or transport him to England for a degrading show trial as a traitor, followed by an even more grisly execution. At the very least, these rampaging dragoons were likely to loot Monticello and burn it to the ground. In fact, a strike force of 180 British dragoons commanded by Lieutenant Colonel Banastre Tarleton, the most feared cavalry leader of the war, was heading for Charlottesville to capture the retiring governor and the legislature.

Martha had good reason to fear Tarleton, the twenty-two-year-old officer later known for his bloodthirsty tactics in the South. In fact, he had captured General Charles Lee, who had been hiding at an inn. When Lee spied Tarleton's horsemen outside his window, he gasped, "For God's sake, what shall I do?" The widow who owned the inn tried to conceal Lee above a fireplace as bullets ripped through the windows. After [Tarleton] threatened to burn down the inn," wrote historian Ron Chernow, "Lee surrendered in slippers and a filthy shirt to the derisory cheers of his captors and a mocking trumpet blast. To make his degradation complete, the British didn't allow him to don a coat or a hat in the wintry weather. After all of his abrasive lectures to Washington, Charles Lee hadn't known how to protect himself, and his embarrassing capture proved the punch line of a grim joke. He would spend sixteen months in British captivity."[18]

With growing trepidation, Martha ordered breakfast served to the household, summoned a carriage for her children, and bade farewell to the legislators, who descended the mountain back to Charlottesville. Jefferson shook Jouett's hand and held it for a fraction longer than was necessary. He told Jouett to head for Charlottesville to warn the legislators. No one, including Jouett, knew when Tarleton and his horsemen might arrive. But it seemed probable that Jouett had made far better time than the dragoons, who were riding in slow military formation. In Charlottesville, Jouett had barely sounded the alarm when another Virginian reported Tarleton was only minutes away. The lawmakers scattered in all directions, many barely dressed.

On Monticello's crest, Jefferson remained calm. He studied the empty road through a telescope. He had asked Martha to collect important personal papers and hide them in the woods. It was at this time that a twenty-three-year-old Virginia lieutenant named Christopher Hudson happened to be traveling on the road about four miles east of Monticello, on his way to join Lafayette's army. Hudson knew Jefferson, having been in Richmond during Arnold's invasion, and he observed how Jefferson was "constantly on duty." As Hudson continued along the road, he met a man named Long, who discussed the movements of British soldiers near Monticello. Long mentioned that Jack Jouett had gone to Charlottesville to warn the legislators about Tarleton's advance toward the village. Hudson asked whether Jouett had gone to Monticello to inform Jefferson of the impending danger. Long said he did not know.[19]

Hudson tugged at his horse's reins and switched direction, determined to warn Jefferson of the approaching troops. He arrived at Monticello and "found Mr. Jefferson, perfectly tranquil, and undisturbed." Hudson also noticed that Monticello, normally busy with laborers, was dead silent and empty. "I was convinced his Situation was truly critical since there was only one man (his gardener) upon the Spot." Hudson told Jefferson that Tartleton's men were ascending the hill. Hudson begged Jefferson to depart. Finally, "at my earnest request he left his house," Hudson recalled.[20]

Jefferson mounted his favorite horse, Caractacus, his six-year-old stallion and one of the fastest horses in Virginia. Jefferson kicked with his heels and whipped Caractacus through a dense forest dominated by chestnut trees. He "knew that he would be pursued if he took the high road," so he "plunged into the woods of the adjoining mountain"[21] to get a better look at the advancing British troops.

At Monticello, Martha began to give orders to her house servants. A wild scramble ensued. Martha hurried their daughters into a carriage as Jefferson returned and guided Martha, their two children, and two slaves to an escape path. They set off to nearby Blenheim Plantation. She did not know if she would ever see her husband alive again. Back at Monticello, Jefferson was largely alone. But at least two slaves were still present, one of them Martin Hemings, hiding silver in anticipation of the raid.

Jefferson tried to rescue his documents: "In preparing for flight, I shoved in papers where I could," he later wrote. The searing memory of his boyhood home, Shadwell, burning to the ground with nearly all of his books and papers, was probably in the back of his mind.[22]

As Martha and the children vanished down the road, Jefferson gave orders to the house servants to hide as much of the silver and other valuables as they could. The mortified ex-governor (his term had legally expired two days earlier) told other servants to walk his horse from the blacksmith's to a point in the road between Monticello and adjoining Carter's Mountain. Jefferson rushed into the woods, cutting across his own property to rendezvous with his horse.

On Carter's Mountain, Jefferson resorted to his telescope again and saw no trace of Tarleton's green-coated horsemen. Underscoring his desire to capture Jefferson, and his contempt for Virginia's ability to stop him, Tarleton had divided his small force and ordered Captain Kenneth McLeod to take a detachment of dragoons to Monticello. Jefferson was about to return to Monticello when Charlottesville's main street swarmed with sabre-waving horsemen in hasty pursuit of scurrying legislators. Jefferson rode hastily down the other side of Carter's Mountain and soon joined Martha and his family at Blenheim Plantation, their temporary refuge. "Martha's anxiety remained acute," observed historian Thomas Fleming, "and so did Jefferson's mortification. Tarleton's incursion was a savage final commentary on his failed governorship."[23] Jefferson would later make a cryptic notation about the day's extraordinary events for his memorandum book: "June 4, British horse came to Monticello."[24]

Merely five minutes after Jefferson had left, Captain McLeod and his men arrived at Monticello. As Great George Granger, faithful servant and slave, had been the man to save the family silver in Richmond as Tarleton's men approached, that fabled task now fell to twenty-six-year-old servant Martin Hemings. According to one of the most famous stories in Monticello lore, Tarleton's troops pounded up the mountain while Martin and another slave hid the silver beneath the planks of the steps of one of the front porticos. The British arrived just as they finished, with Martin slamming the planks down on the other man, who was trapped below. That man would be stuck in the tight, dark hole until the next day. Meanwhile, Martin faced down soldiers armed with loaded guns and bayonets. They threatened to shoot him if he did not reveal the whereabouts of

Jefferson. One of the dragoons jammed a pistol into Martin Hemings's chests. "Fire away, then," Hemings replied, and refused to say anything else. As the Jefferson grandchildren recounted the story, Hemings stood his ground, "fiercely answering glance for glance, and not receding a hair's breadth from the muzzle of the cocked pistol." Unbeknownst to the British, the other servant, named Caesar, lay in silence beneath their feet under the floor of the portico with silver he and Martin had just finished hiding when the raiding party rushed in.[25]

Martin escaped unharmed, and Tarleton's cavalry left Monticello intact, for reasons unknown. Perhaps he found it as magnificent an estate as did others. But British General Lord Cornwallis was not as kind and inflicted a cruel blow at Edge Hill. In Jefferson's words, Cornwallis was "the most active, enterprising and vindictive Officer who has ever appeared in Arms against us." He aimed at Jefferson but struck the lives of Martha and many enslaved people the hardest. Cornwallis took his army to Elk Hill and occupied the place for ten days. There he wrought his vengeance on the fugitive governor "in a spirit of total extermination." Writing seven years later, the memory of Cornwallis's destructions at Elk Hill still burned bitterly for Jefferson. He recalled that the British general destroyed all his growing crops of corn and tobacco, and burned all of Jefferson's barns "having first taken what he wanted; he used, as was to be expected, all my stocks of cattle, sheep and hogs for the sustenance of his army, and carried off all the horses capable of service: of those too young for service he cut the throats, and he buried all the fences on the plantation, so as to leave it an absolute waste."[26]

There was also a heavy human cost at Elk Hill. Some thirty slaves left with Cornwallis, either as captives or, as Jefferson put it in his farm book in 1781, "fled to the enemy," "joined enemy," or simply "ran away." Jefferson blamed Cornwallis for "carrying off" those enslaved people: "Had this been to give them freedom he would have done right, but it was to consign them to inevitable death from the small pox and putrid fever then raging in his camp." Most of Jefferson's slaves died in enemy hands. Some made it back to Elk Hill and Monticello, bringing smallpox with them.[27]

One historian described Cornwallis's later surrender at Yorktown and noted the slain black slaves dotting the battlefield. "The next day soldiers waded across a hellish battlefield paved with cadavers, one recalling that 'all over the place and wherever you look [there were] corpses lying about that had not been buried.'" The majority of the bodies, historian Ron Chernow noted, were black, "reflecting their importance on both sides of the conflict. Some of these black corpses likely belonged to runaway slaves who had sought asylum with Cornwallis, only to be stricken during the siege with smallpox or 'camp fever'—likely typhus, a disease spread by lice and fleas in overcrowded camps."[28]

Historian Dumas Malone acknowledged the devastation at the Jeffersons' estate, Elk Hill, but concluded that Jefferson's "supply of slaves was not seriously depleted, for he still had more than two hundred," including "his very special 'people,'" Jupiter and Suck, George and Ursula, "and the superior Heming [sic] of 'bright' mulattoes." Life at Monticello, said Malone, soon "resumed its normal character and tempo." The "normal character and tempo" of Martha Wayles Skelton Jefferson's life for the past two years had throbbed with death and loss, but nothing had ever come close to this: her family physically threatened and her husband in disgrace and despair.

Martha, meanwhile, arrived at the Enniscorthy estate, owned by a friend, John Coles. Set upon the Green Mountains, the two-story mansion was one of the largest in Albemarle County. Still, with British troops patrolling the area, Jefferson decided it was too dangerous either to stay overnight or to return to Monticello. Instead, he guided the family toward the home of another friend, Hugh Rose, who lived forty miles farther to the southwest. It would be a difficult trip for Martha and her young daughters along treacherous mountain roads that might be patrolled by British troops. "Jefferson normally preferred to travel by longer routes if it meant he could avoid raking his carriage on bumpy mountain roads, especially when traveling with his wife and daughters, but there was no time for such a luxury," historian Michael Kranish observed. "The fastest route would take the Jeffersons along mountainous byways, over fast-moving streams, and through dense forests."[29]

The carriage ride was slow and tortuous. From the nearby Blue Ridge Mountains, silhouetted by the almost constant flashes of lightning, came the distant rumbles of an approaching thunderstorm. As the horses slipped and strained on the ascending and mud-rutted road, the carriage pulled to a halt. Finally, Jefferson made a decision to take Martha and the children to the most remote of his three plantations, Poplar Forest, their plantation in Bedford County, an arduous journey of seventy miles.

Poplar Forest was a large estate of several thousand acres, which came to Jefferson from Martha shortly after their marriage. Martha had inherited the property upon the death of her father, John Wayles, in 1773. It was encumbered to the extent of nearly four thousand pounds sterling. "In order to pay the debt," historian Norma B. Cuthbert explained, "Jefferson was compelled to make great sacrifices in land, because of the depressed condition of land values, the tobacco market, and the necessity for taking bonds which were redeemed in paper money so depreciated by the war that he lost virtually half of the property. This staggering blow was the first of a succession of financial catastrophes that pursued Jefferson to the end of his life. Curiously enough, upon his death the only bequest of land which actually passed to a member of the family was a fragment of Poplar Forest. Everything else was swept away."[30]

Poplar Forest was an estate Jefferson and Martha had not visited in eight years. However, the British were unlikely to go there, and he did not have to face angry legislators when they returned from their hiding places in the woods. Poplar Forest was bordered by the Bear and Tomahawk Creeks and dominated by a stand of enormous tulip poplars. Years later, Jefferson would build a retreat there, "creating an elegant octagonal structure with triple-sash windows and Palladian porticoes. The property at this point, however, had only barns, slave cabins, and a two-room dwelling occupied by an overseer, Thomas Bennett. An unused overseer's cabin may have also been standing. In one of these cabins, Martha and her family apparently lived for the next five weeks." It was as far as Martha could have gotten from the comforts of Monticello, but it was also as far as she could get her family from the British, so it suited her.[31]

Arriving after the brutal journey over rough terrain with Martha and their children, Jefferson cantered out one morning for a ride on his favorite horse, Caractacus. Unfortunately, the horse reared and threw his master from the saddle, breaking Jefferson's left wrist. It took a full six weeks for Martha to nurse a badly shaken Jefferson back to health.

Rumor that Jefferson had been taken captive by the British spread rapidly and as far as Europe, "where it had so distressed John Adams." In fact, Jefferson and his family were in safe seclusion at Poplar Forest. They remained there for six weeks, during which time Jefferson, to occupy himself during what had become as depressing a time as he had ever known, began making notes in answer to a series of questions sent by a French aristocrat, the Barté-Martois, on the state of Virginia. These now famous notes would one day be published as Jefferson's first and only book.

Thus, *Notes on the State of Virginia* was largely written between November 1780 and the winter of 1782–1783, under conditions of public and private trauma for Jefferson. "Not only had Jefferson been driven from his home by British troops," concluded one historian, he had been "nearly censured by the Virginia legislature for failing, as the state's governor, to prepare adequately for Cornwallis's invasion of 1781, two days after his thirty-eighth birthday . . . beginning a seventeen-month period of depression and grief in his household, complicated by Martha Jefferson's seventh pregnancy."[32]

Jefferson's *Notes* include the now famous description of Williamsburg and its public buildings. He wrote extensively about the Governor's Palace, and he believed the governor's house "capable of being made an elegant seat."[33] The time of seclusion following Tarleton's raid was also Jefferson's first opportunity to become intimately acquainted with his property at Poplar Forest. Accommodations were minimal when the family arrived. Architectural historian Allen Chambers suggests that the family lodged with overseer Thomas Bennett, as Jefferson himself is later known to have done. Was it the rude sufficiency of these accommodations that prompted him to consider architectural improvements? At Poplar Forest, Jefferson had sufficient time to sketch a survey and plan a dwelling, even while working on his *Notes*, for with one exception he completely suspended his correspondence during this period. Jefferson made his drawings on a large sheet, cobbled together from several oddly shaped pieces of paper. The two paper types used in assembling this sheet are most commonly associated with drawings Jefferson made during the late 1770s and early 1780s, dates that coincide with his Poplar Forest seclusion.[34]

The following description of Poplar Forest was given by one of Jefferson's granddaughters in 1856:

> The house at Poplar Forest was very pretty and pleasant. It was of brick, one story in front, and, owing to the falling of the ground, [artificially contrived] two in the rear. It was an exact octagon, with a centre-hall

twenty feet square, lighted from above. This was a beautiful room, and served as a dining-room. Round it were grouped a bright drawing-room looking south, my grandfather's own chamber, three other bedrooms, and a pantry. A terrace extended from one side of the house; there was a portico in front connected by a vestibule with the centre room, and in the rear a verandah, on which the drawing-room opened, with its windows to the floor.[35]

The very similarity of the Governor's Palace and Poplar Forest plans provides a further argument for dating the latter to 1781. It stands to reason that Jefferson used his knowledge of the palace sooner rather than later—that within months of completing the palace drawings, he applied the lessons of that exercise to the design of their house at Poplar Forest.

At summer's and war's end, Jefferson was asked to become one of the peace commissioners in Europe. He declined, telling friend and kinsman Edmund Randolph in a letter, "[I] have retired to my farm, my family and books from which I think nothing will ever more separate me." A month later, Cornwallis surrendered at Yorktown to the combined American and French forces under Washington and Rochambeau.

Doubtlessly, Martha longed to return to her true home and inner sanctum, Monticello.

Months later, Jefferson took a group of French officers, Comte de Rochambeau and his aide-de-camp, Baron Ludwig von Closen, who had defeated Cornwallis at Yorktown on a tour of Monticello. They arrived at midafternoon at Monticello, on February 21, 1782. Jefferson showed them the mountains and where he had escaped Tarleton's troops. They discussed Jefferson's role in the Revolution and the war, including Tarleton's raid on Monticello, which had "much alarmed his family." The Frenchmen settled in for the night, having found Jefferson "very interesting and [his] family very agreeable."[36]

Years later, Jefferson's friend and former neighbor, Philip Mazzei, attributed Martha's eventual death partly to the horrific events of the invasion of Virginia, during which she endured repeated flights from Richmond, the death of the first Lucy Elizabeth, the harrowing escape from Monticello, and the further flight to the home of Hugh Rose and onward to Poplar Forest. Mazzei concluded:

In Jefferson's house I had been greatly saddened by the memory of his angelic late wife, a sadness that solitude made even more deeply felt. While he was Governor of the State, during the second year of independence, he had gone home for a few days when a sudden enemy raid forced him to flee. He fell from his horse, broke an arm, and his angelic wife's death was the aftermath of her fright. His irreparable loss induced him to accept the appointment as minister plenipotentiary to France.[37]

According to Mazzei, the innumerable rough rides on short notice and the narrow escapes from the British, combined with her frail health, had eventually taken their emotional and physical toll on Martha Jefferson.[38]

FOURTEEN

MISTRESS OF
MONTICELLO

Monticello is like no other home in America, so well does
it express the character of its designer and builder.[1]

— Author, ROBERT L. POLLEY

AS THE WAR came to an end, life at Monticello resumed
some state of normalcy for Martha Jefferson and her children,
and she was strongly and undoubtedly influenced by the aes-
thetic considerations of Monticello. Her husband was often asked why
he chose to live on a mountain, and he replied that he had "never wearied of gazing on the sublime and beautiful scenery . . . and that the
indescribable delight he here enjoyed so attached him to this spot, that
he determined when arrived at manhood he would here build his family mansion." According to historian Gene Waddell, "Jefferson was also
convinced that climate had a direct influence on one's intelligence. In his
Notes on the State of Virginia, he responded to a question about everything
that might "increase the progress of human knowledge" with an answer
devoted almost wholly to how preferable the climate of Monticello was
to Williamsburg. Jefferson's architectural mentor, Andrea Palladio, had
also stated that living in the shadow of a mountain would make people
"stupid" (stupide) and that living in a valley with stagnant vapors would
seriously injure health. He recommended "building on an 'eminence'
(monte) for these reasons and to take advantage of the views that such a
situation would afford, both of and from the site."[2]

As life resumed on the sparkling mountain, Martha's household
accounts are one of the few surviving documents in her own handwriting.

The records reveal that Martha accumulated tallow in March, oversaw the manufacture of soap and candles, and took an inventory of beds, bolsters, mattresses, pillows, and blankets. In April, she took stock of her husband's shirts, listed a variety of other clothing for herself and their four-year-old daughter Patsy, and made more candles and soap. In May, she planted vegetables—French beans and "garden peas"—then made forty more candles.

As she slowly recovered from the trauma of the British raid on Monticello, Martha oversaw the carpentry work at Monticello that reflected her husband's views of classical norms. Here, Martha reigned, as Jefferson's Venus would have done in his gallery of statues—among aristocrats of talent, beauty, and virtue. Much later, Jefferson would lovingly reflect that the dozen years of their marriage and courtship before Martha's death were unmatched in bounty and fulfillment. They entertained guests such as French diplomat Chastellux, who found the "Sage" of Monticello wholly "retired from the world and public business." Several days in Martha and Thomas Jefferson's company disappeared like minutes, Chastellux later wrote. They talked of art, literature, and natural history as work on the house continued about them. The racket of construction was hardly the tranquil setting one would imagine for a sage, but Chastellux thought the house unlike anything he had seen in his American travels. Of Martha, then in the ninth month of pregnancy, he wrote only that she was "mild and amiable," words that would be used to describe her by many others. (With the death of Martha less than five months later, everything changed. In a letter to Chastellux then, Jefferson described himself as emerging from a "stupor of mind which had rendered me as dead to the world as she." He had lost all interest in Monticello, believing he could never be happy there again.)[3]

The aura of Monticello impressed Chastellux, as it did every guest who visited. Martha's love for antiques and Renaissance and late Baroque architectural models contributed to the heart of her Monticello in its evolving form. The same feminine, encompassing dome at Monticello was also central to Jefferson's last, absorbing designs for the University of Virginia's pantheon rotunda-library, the principal building in another ideal, cerebral community. Perhaps they both were lasting tributes to his beloved Martha.[4]

Martha adorned Monticello with paintings and statutes, including a portrait of George Washington and a plaster bust of Washington by Jean

Antoine Houdon. Jefferson had always revered Washington's patriotism and determination. "He was, indeed, in every sense of the word, a wise, a good, and a great man," he stated in later years. Jefferson claimed that his dealings with President Washington were always amicable and productive. "In the four years of my continuance in the office of secretary of state," he was to say, "our intercourse was daily, confidential, and cordial."[5]

Jefferson's source books also mentioned many ancient versions of the architecture and statutes he and Martha preferred as they planned to acquire modern copies for the growing Monticello. His lists included three large statue groups that Jefferson eventually intended to be ceramic figurines. Contemporary journals, correspondence, advertisements, and export declarations, all show that, by Martha's time, many of those objects were being manufactured full size, as marble copies and casts. A thriving industry centered in Florence and Rome catered to palatial houses with such objects of virtue.[6]

Unfortunately, the plan for the Jefferson's statue gallery was never realized. As with many of Jefferson's enlightened and progressive schemes, his imagination ran ahead of immediate opportunity. None of the sculptures on his list was ever obtained for Monticello. Jefferson did, however, eventually acquire a marble copy of at least one famous ancient work—the Sleeping Ariadne in the Vatican Museum, then popularly called the Dying Cleopatra or Nymph. In 1771, Jefferson had contemplated using such a reclining nymph by a picturesque brook in his garden. It was a project comparable to his plans for the gallery. Earlier in the century, these same elements had been assembled at Twickenham, for the country house of Alexander Pope. Jefferson intended to use Pope's translation of the inscriptions in his own erudite celebration of his and Martha's domestic privacy.

Martha had been bred to be a plantation mistress, and, during ten years of married bliss with her illustrious husband at Monticello, she worked hard at being a successful one. Indeed, the mistress of a Virginia plantation was also expected to assume the management of the domestic life of the plantation house. This included the normal household duties of preserving meat, dairy, and fresh foods and supervising their preparation;

knitting or sewing bedding materials, linen, and slave clothing; and man-
ufacturing soap, candles, dyes, and, during the Revolutionary War, cloth.
Martha, as well as her scientific husband, would have been the plantation
physician, too. She most probably tended to the illnesses of her own family and of the families of the household slaves. We know for a fact that
the Jeffersons inoculated their slaves against smallpox. Martha also managed the feeding and clothing of the house servants and was the ultimate
arbiter of their disputes.

Yet Martha possessed advantages that set her apart from the vast
majority of colonial women. She had money, education, and the confidence of first her father and then her husband. But even though the cities
on the eastern seaboard, with their shops and conveniences, were growing, most women, like Martha, still lived on farms and produced everything they used. "As towns sprouted up," observed author Cokie Roberts,
"women started specializing—one doing the soap making, another the
cheese and butter churning, another the weaving. They bartered with each
other for goods and services, creating an off-the-books economy entirely
run by women."[7]

In fact, despite their lack of legal rights, many women still ruled their
households. There was an elaborate view of "spheres." The men were "in
the world," whereas a woman's place was in the house, the "domestic
sphere." "The men handled relations with England—deciding whether to
declare independence and what kind of government should be formed;
the women handled pretty much everything else," concluded one historian. "That's not to say that these women were unaware of the sphere outside of their homes, quite the contrary. Their letters and diaries are filled
with political observations and, in the case of Abigail Adams, instructions. Newspapers and magazines of the day kept women as well as men
up to date on the news, as well as the fashions, both at home and in
England. Visitors from Europe were amazed to see how stylishly their
colonial counterparts were."[8]

In addition to these domestic and childrearing duties, Martha also played
an important role in Jefferson's political life, as hostess and social companion. Her formal education included music because an ability to sing

and play at the keyboard was considered a valuable social skill. She invariably studied dance with a dancing master, and she was encouraged to draw and paint. Martha also read verse and novels suitable for ladies. Indeed, reading was often one of her main amusements. Robert Carter, a neighbor at Nomini Hall, boasted of his own wife that he "would bet a Guinea that Mrs. Carter reads more than the Parson of the parish!"[9]

How Martha dressed herself was a reflection of her relative prosperity with Jefferson, so her clothing was expected to be suitably stylish and tasteful. Although there were professional milliners, dressmakers, and tailors in the larger towns such as Richmond and Williamsburg, and clothing was purchased regularly from England, no plantation mistress could afford not to be able to sew.

In all, the life of a plantation mistress was a challenge to the hardiest of women, and even the most robust were oppressed at times by the burden of the multiple duties demanded of them. They may not have expressed their dissatisfaction as strongly as did one colonial woman who felt that the domestic duties to which she was chained "Stagnate the Blood and Stupifie the Senses," but many plantation mistresses believed they were overworked and their labors undervalued.[10]

How much of this discontent with their plight was shared by Martha can only be guessed at because Jefferson destroyed virtually all written traces of her existence. Only one letter by her survives, this an impersonal one. There is, however, a household journal in her hand, and, for several of the early years of their marriage Jefferson copied Martha's yearly household accounts into his own memorandum books. From these two sources, as well as reminiscences by family members, slaves, and Jefferson's own daily record of his financial transactions during their marriage, it is possible to piece together an imperfect portrait of Martha as mistress of Monticello.

As mistress of Monticello, an indication of how Martha's domestic interests dictated the eventual design of the her beloved house is best illustrated by her particular pride in brewing beer. When she first arrived at Monticello to set up housekeeping with her new husband, one of her first domestic acts was to brew a fifteen-gallon batch of "small beer."

This was a low-alcohol beer probably brewed from wheat and bottled and consumed without aging as soon as fermentation was completed, usually about a week after it was brewed. Martha brewed ten fifteen-gallon casks and one twenty-gallon cask of beer in one year, enough for 1,700 twelve-ounce cups or tankards of beer. Thus, an average of close to thirty-five servings a week were being consumed at Monticello. Martha's beer was obviously one of her specialties and was probably tasty, for, unlike some small beers, it was hopped; we know this because she purchased hops frequently. One bargain was recorded: "bought 7 lb hops with an old shirt."[11]

Although Thomas Jefferson was known throughout his life to prefer cider and wine, as a devoted husband to Martha, who was proud of her beer making, he undoubtedly consumed a lot of small beer. In fact, much later in his life, he established a commercial beer-making operation at Monticello. Significantly, Jefferson's architectural drawing for the house's dependencies shows that the kitchen under the south pavilion was to be converted to a brewing room with a circular masonry firebox to hold a large brewing kettle, an homage no doubt to Martha. There is little doubt that Martha Jefferson, beer maker, had a voice in its design and location.

Martha continued to work toward regaining a sense of normalcy upon her return to Monticello, and she started by emulating Jefferson's business habits. She borrowed from him a 1768 leather-bound notebook in which he had taken notes on General Court cases. Starting at the empty pages at the back of the book, in rather cramped handwriting—the letters separated, tight, and vertical—she made her entries. For example: "1772 Feb 10 opened a barrel of col: harrison's flower." It is quite likely that Jefferson reviewed her entries, for the next time she wrote the word "flour," it was spelled correctly. This was followed by daily notations of what was killed for the table: pullets, turkeys, and mutton. On February 28, an industrious Martha took an inventory of the house linen, tablecloths, napkins, towels, and sheets. These were nearly all Jefferson's, purchased the year before his marriage, probably in preparation for his life with Martha, for they bore his initials. In subsequent years, Martha also inventoried her clothing, her husband's clothes, and those of their first daughter, Patsy.

Because dairy products were not produced at the mountaintop during the first few years of Martha's residence, she recorded in her household account book regular purchases of butter from Thomas Garth, the Monticello overseer. It was not until January that she noted: "made at mottcello 3 pots of butter." Her spelling of Monticello indicates how she may have pronounced it. Jefferson established an Italian pronunciation for their mountain home because there are contemporary references to its being spelled "Montichello." One workman, however, spelled it "monnttesello" and "mounteyselley," suggesting that there were variations in the pronunciation then, as there are now.[12]

The butter that Martha made was not enough for the table at Monticello, however, because it continued to be purchased. By the fall, large quantities of butter were being hauled to the mountaintop from Jefferson's Bedford plantation, Poplar Forest. In Martha's household, dinner was a communion of all of her family, including children and whatever visitors were present. All shared the fruits of Monticello's labor and gardens. Daniel Webster, who visited Monticello, recalled that "in conversation Mr. Jefferson is easy and natural." Martha's table was set to nurture the presence of both the muses and the meal, offering the abundance of her husband's library as well as her kitchen, both of which were renowned for their European sophistication. Martha made sure that guests were set at ease in convivial, free-ranging conversation with a choice of dinner table topics that avoided business or belief. Neither too heated nor too cool, table talk was leavened with wit and philosophy and was most likely lightened with her anecdotes.[13]

Like any good hostess, Martha probably also ensured that the dinner party was physically insulated from the rest of the household, which at Monticello often included more than thirty house servants. Even though Jefferson had a chronic concern for privacy, he had a respect for the intellect and power of the enslaved people in his own household. Thomas Jefferson later attributed "much of the domestic and even public discord to the mutilated and misconstrued repetition of free conversation at dinner tables by those mute but not inattentive listeners."[14]

Jefferson, as well as Martha, knew that good food and wine loosened the tongue to a more playful language of wit distinct from other forms of daily chatter. Jefferson's friend the Marquis de Chastellux wrote of an evening spent overlooking the lawns, sharing a bowl of punch, and recalling the poetry of Ossian. The talk was like "a spark of electricity that passed rapidly from one to another as we recalled the passages in those sublime poems which particularly struck us. . . . In our enthusiasm the book was brought forth and placed by the bowl. And before we realized it, book and bowl carried us far into the night."[15]

The orchestration of Martha's Virginia dinners was in contrast to the pace and formality of a European banquet. Taking a meal and talking at dinner was a social ritual described in ancient texts, several of which Jefferson held in his library. Dinner is portrayed there as a gathering set aside from daily business, an occasion when family and guests came together, suspended their quarrels, and enjoyed one another's conversation. The Jeffersons, as social hosts, assumed Cicero's "convivium" (from the Latin *convivere*, meaning to live together) at their feasts. Both Plutarch and Plato invited philosophy to the table because "it is an art of living and therefore must be admitted into all our gay humors and our pleasures."[16]

Martha's Monticello kitchen and dining room matched one another stroke for stroke in the bounds of necessity. Jefferson would later install two devices to traverse the space between these two realms, each lending its own drama—bordering on magic—to the setting for dinner guests. The first, a hoisting machine modeled on those he had seen in France, carried spirits from the wine cellar up through shafts on either side of the dining room chimney. Fitted within a box, bottles were lifted out of the darkness with a pulley and crank, to emerge into view carrying with them a scent of the cellar underworld. The second device, a door mounted on a central pivot, turned at a touch to reveal on its other face a set of semicircular shelves laden with dishes. Jefferson may have operated the dumbwaiter himself, but it is likely that his butler, Burrell, and perhaps others served "in the French manner" when the party was larger.

On these grander occasions, Martha had small wheeled carts that could be drawn up beside each guest so each could serve himself subsequent courses without interruption. Martha clearly wished the performance of dinner to be an accompaniment to conversation, not to take center stage. A typical Monticello meal would probably have consisted of fried apples and bacon. A favorite dish was squab pie, always served when Benjamin Franklin was a visitor at Monticello. And of course, "spoon bread," that southern favorite; the story goes that on one very special occasion at Ashlawn-Highland (James Monroe's estate), in the cook's effort to make good cornmeal mush she put it into the oven where it baked into a soft "pudding" with a crisp crust—and thus "spoon bread" was invented.

Guests at Monticello noted that the first dinner bell customarily rang at three o'clock, and the second called them to the table at four. In the eighteenth century, as the meal ended, the ladies would retire to leave the gentlemen to their conversation. The women would then return at about seven o'clock, when tea was served in the adjoining tea room and talk continued into the night as long as the company pleased. This habit does suggest a scene where Martha and her husband enjoyed their wine as the setting sun lit the piedmont and shone onto the loving couple through the western windows of both the dining room and the tea room.

When Monticello was finally completed after her death, Martha's formal rooms overlooked the magnificent landscape from her piano mobile that was set above extensive service areas in the basement. The formal entry presented a villa in the Palladian manner, as a body with colonnaded façade or face, domed vault, and two arms that reached into the landscape to embrace lawns and Martha's flower gardens, which were maintained for the view. Below, the rooms in the "rustic" reflected the advice of Jefferson's neighbor, Leon Battista Alberti, to segregate servants and gentry, dining room and kitchen. In contrast to the rooms above, the service level had no façade, no symmetry about its kitchen entry, and a view more into the fireplace than out to the land.

Martha's kitchen would have received raw produce and meats from Monticello's fields, vineyards, gardens, and orchards and transformed these into food for the family, guests, and slaves. Whatever could not be produced on site would have been purchased from merchants and workshops along Mulberry Row, the adjacent slave quarters situated on the side of Monticello, and from the markets in nearby Charlottesville. Butcher shops, local and foreign wineries, bakeries, dairies, and importers of fine teas and spices all answered the inquiries of Martha Jefferson's cook.

Martha planned the immediate landscape of the plantation of Monticello to provide as much of the table's fare as possible. Her approach to planting was as experimental as was Jefferson's approach to architecture. His garden book lists orchard plantings of pomegranates, cherries, apples, peaches, apricots, almonds, figs (which Jefferson particularly liked), and nectarines. The couple made several attempts as vintners, but the grapes suffered in Virginia's heavy soils and humid air and produced a disappointing wine. Martha's vegetable garden was sown with imported seeds, which Jefferson kept cataloged in his bed chamber, and it provided many of the delicacies he later enjoyed in Europe. Martha also oversaw a grove of forest trees with sweet underbrush planted to attract game, hare, pheasant, and quail. As a gourmet and gardener, Martha shaped the creative processes of the landscape of Monticello as much as Jefferson through the habit of the kitchen and with the skill of the craftsmen of Mulberry Row.

Martha was also adept at the messy task of making soap. Her first soap was made two months after her arrival: "Mar. 26 made 46 lb. of soft soap."[17] Thereafter she made hard and soft soap regularly and in large batches, as this inventory of the cellar indicates: "put in the sellar a jar that had 32 gallons of leaf fat, two firkins & two iron pots of gut fat, two store pots of sauce fat and half a barrel of craknels [cooked pork fat], made 229 Ib of hard soap, 200 Ib ditto soft." Soap was produced by adding assorted fats to lye that had been made by leaching water through ashes gathered from the plantation fireplaces. The lye was strong enough and ready for use if an egg floated in it. The lye and fat were boiled, usually in a large kettle over an open fire outdoors. Making soap was normally a cold weather chore, when ashes were plentiful and pork was butchered. Hard soap, made by adding salt to the lye, was used for general-purpose cleaning as it is today. Martha's soft soap had the color and consistency of butterscotch pudding and was used for the plantation laundry. Tallow for candles was derived from beef suet. It was not until more than two years after her arrival at Monticello that Martha made her first batch of candles. She recorded on March 13, 1774: "made 12 doz: candles" and two months later, she made three dozen more.[18]

Records show that during the years of her marriage, extraordinarily large amounts of food were eaten for a household of two adults and an infant. Much of the killing of farm animals was to provide meat for workmen, but on August 13, 1773, she recorded the staples consumed at her own table: "Eat 6 hams, 4 shoulders, 2 middlings [of bacon] in 3 weeks and 2 days. used 3 lo[a]ves of sugar in preserves, one d[itt]o in punch." This was only the pork and sugar, however. She regularly purchased poultry, fruit, and vegetables from the plantation slaves and from the construction workers and their wives.

Martha's six granddaughters were thoroughly schooled in the domestic arts, and each of them carefully copied their favorite "rules" and "recipes" of the household, compiling their own manuscript collection from Martha. "The book of Monticello recipes here reproduced," as one author explained in the first chapter, "is the one made by Virginia Randolph, Martha Jefferson Randolph's fifth daughter, who was born in 1801 and who, in 1821, married Nicholas P. Trist, later diplomat to Mexico." On her death, it passed to her only daughter, Martha Jefferson Trist, and subsequently to the latter's daughter, Fanny M. Burke of Alexandria.[19]

The versatile Martha Jefferson was also interested in culinary art and collected and copied recipes for macaroons and blanc mange as carefully as she recorded making candles. Here, from notebooks and letters, one historian has revealed both Jeffersons as epicureans, seeking new and unusual culinary delights. How much Thomas was influenced by Martha in his epicurean endeavors we will never know. Yet during his travels in Europe after her tragic death, he readily sampled the foods and fruits of each locality he visited. In France, he acquired a fondness for intricate and elaborate dishes, a habit that made Patrick Henry denounce him in a political speech as a "man who abjured his native victuals." Daniel Webster later remarked that dinner at Monticello, served at 3:30 in the afternoon, was "in half Virginian, half French style in good taste and abundance." From Holland, Jefferson brought a waffle iron; from Amsterdam, half a pound of tea; and his secretary, William Short, made a special trip to Naples to secure a "maccaroni mould." Jefferson is credited here with introducing both macaroni and vanilla to the United States. From Philadelphia, he wrote to Short, then American charge d'affaires at Paris, "Petit informs me that he has been all over the town in quest of vanilla, & it is unknown here. I must pray you to send me a packet of 50 pods."[20]

Later, during the years of his presidency, Jefferson kept a record of the earliest and latest appearance of each vegetable in the Washington market, listing thirty-seven kinds. At Monticello, his garden book recorded the progress of Martha's own vegetables, and their library contained various books on cookery. Represented in these books are people and their recipes such as Lemaire, his maitre d'hotel during his presidency; Petit, his Paris valet de chambre who was promoted to maitre d'hotel; Julien, the French chef in Washington; and Annette and James, cooks at Monticello. The name of Soyer, the famous French chef, appears more than twenty times. There is even a Mexican bean soup recipe "furnished by the grocer who sold the beans," and beef olives attributed to "Septimia Randolph Meikelham's cook Nancy."[21]

The recipes, such as "beef a la daube," "minced collops," "forcemeat," and "syllabub," are names common to the eighteenth century. A larger proportion than is customary shows a decided French influence due, of course, to Jefferson's years abroad. A "Capitolade of the remains of roast fowl" is explained in a footnote as a "ragout of cold meat." Many of the recipes transcribed by Jefferson were partly, if not entirely, in French. There is individuality in a recipe for meringues as given in the biographical chapter:

> 12 blanc d'oeuf, les fouettes bien fermes, 12 cueillerres de sucre en poudre,
> put them by little and little into the whites of eggs, fouetter le tout ensemble,
> dresser les sur un papier aver un cueiller de bouche, metter les
> dans un four bien doux, that is to say an oven after the bread is drawn
> out. You may leave them there as long as you please.[22]

The Monticello servant cooks, however, would have been grateful for the translated recipe in the chapter of "Paris recipes" that begins: "Beat the whites of 6 eggs to a stiff froth." If they were adapted for modern use and proportioned to the current practice of serving six persons, substitutions would have been made: gelatin for calves' hoofs, junket for chicken gizzard, and the food chopper for the mortar and pestle.[23]

Monticello is where Martha spent most of her married life with Jefferson, although she took frequent sojourns to Elk Hill when Jefferson was away in Richmond or Williamsburg. The short interval between the births of the six Jefferson children, coupled with her perpetually frail physical condition, would have prevented her from extensive travel. Arguably, the defining event of her life at Monticello was motherhood. However, another role for Martha would have been that of a social hostess.

Martha hosted a steady stream of guests and visitors at Monticello. Lavish affairs for fifty guests, who were fed fine French foods and expensive wines, are documented. This meant planning large dinners and other accommodations for guests, who extended their thanks to the lady of the home: "I embrace this opportunity of assuring you that I retain a particular remembrance of the Civilities I received when in Virginia from you, Sir, and Mrs. Jefferson to whom I request my Compliments."[24]

When Martha was pregnant or ill, she appears to have excused herself on occasion from hosting duties during such times. Nor did Martha officially serve as first lady of Virginia or as a presiding lady during the war, as did the wives of other prominent revolutionaries. There were, however, many visitors to Monticello during the early years of the republic, and Martha would not have been without adult or female company. After the death of Jefferson's dear friend and brother-in-law, Dabney Carr, Carr's widow and six children came to live at Monticello. Other members of the large Jefferson family—Jefferson's sister Mary and her husband, John Bolling, had eight children, and his sister Lucy and her husband, Charles Lewis, had six children—were guests at Monticello. Martha also had a large and close family of her own. Her half-sister Elizabeth "Betsy" Eppes and her husband, Francis Eppes, had eight children, and Martha's half-sister, Anne "Nancy" Skipwith and her husband, Henry Skipwith, had six children.

Of course, life at Monticello was not entirely filled with work. Martha's home was stocked with fine wines, featured one of the country's premier collections of books, and was the site of parties and frequent guests. The stables boasted many fine horses, and the woods nearby were stocked with domesticated deer. The couple worked together in the gardens, delighted in reading poetry and fiction to one another, and frequently performed musical duets. Monticello was, after all, noted for its serenity, architecture, elegance, and prosperity.

Martha not only impressed a French aristocrat like Chastellux, but, during the Revolution, she also became warm friends with the family of a Hessian baron who was a prisoner of war at Charlottesville. Major General Baron de Riedesel, commander of the Hessian troops, was one of the officers of Burgoyne's troops who had been captured at Saratoga in 1777 and subsequently marched to Virginia for holding. Although technically a prisoner, the German baron was permitted to live far more comfortably than most Virginians, and, in the peculiar manner of eighteenth-century warfare, was soon socializing with his distinguished American neighbor. His wife, a large, exuberant woman, apparently sang very well and enjoyed Martha's musical talents. With the Riedesel's three young daughters close in age to seven-year-old Patsy, she and Martha undoubtedly found much in common. The Riedesels spent many social evenings with the Jeffersons, joined from time to time by other Hessian officers from Riedesel's staff. These civil and sophisticated social gatherings gave Martha not only a respite from her busy life as Monticello's domestic manager, but an opportunity to demonstrate the social graces her position called for.

In fact, some 4,000 British and German prisoners were brought to Albemarle County. Many of the "captured" officers rented homes in the neighborhood, and many became friends of the Jeffersons. Establishing close friendships with captured enemy troops may seem strange in an age of modern warfare, but in the eighteenth century, warfare was a game practiced by civilized men. A loss on the battlefield did not deprive one of rank. Losers and winners were still gentlemen.[25]

General Riedesel, therefore, was not an ordinary prisoner of war. He and his wife rented a house close to Monticello and proceeded to live in the style they were accustomed to. These aristocrats fell in with rebels Martha and Thomas Jefferson as easily as if they had met at one of the courts of Europe. The Riedesel girls became particularly attached to Martha. The baron and his wife, who shocked local Virginians by appearing in public wearing riding boots, entertained frequently. In a letter to Jefferson, Riedesel writes, "Madame de Riedesel, who never can forget the esteem and friendship she has so justly consecrated to Mrs. Jefferson, desires me to insert her sincerest compliments both to her and your Excellency." Nights with the Riedesels often included other German officers and were filled with food and music. Another German, Baron de Geismer, joined Jefferson on the violin. In fact, Martha appears to have befriended the wives of a number of her husband's friends, whose letters to Jefferson often include such pleasantries for his wife as "Lucy unites in most sublime Compliments to Lady & famely."[26]

Music helped bring the Jeffersons, the Riedesels, and other German officers together. One of the officers wrote of his impressions of Martha:

"As all Virginians are fond of music, he is particularly so. You will find in the House an elegant Harpsichord, Pianoforte & some violins. The latter he performs well upon himself, the former his Lady touches very skillfully & who is in all respects a very agreeable, sensible & accomplished Lady." Indeed, a music book belonging to Martha survives, and this book may well have been open at the harpsichord when Martha and her husband performed for the German officers.

In the fall of 1773, an Italian gentleman, Philip Mazzei, who was planning to start a vineyard in Virginia, stopped at Monticello for the night, and, by the next day, Martha and her wine-loving husband had persuaded him that the land in the immediate vicinity was the place to do it. Mazzei brought in a corps of Italian workmen for his vineyard and to build him a suitable house. Before long, he was established, together with his wife and daughter, as a nearby residents. The Jeffersons entertained them frequently, and Martha began to pick up whiffs of a way of life different from what she was accustomed to. When Mazzei departed for Europe in 1779, it was his house that was rented by Major General Friedrich Riedesel.

"The war which was to break the yoke of a British aristocracy, and establish a republican form of government in America," noted historian Jack McLaughlin, "brought to Martha, a woman who had most likely never been out of Virginia, a temporary opportunity to live the cultured life of European aristocrats. Monticello became almost an American Liechtenstein, a center of tasteful talk, good music, fine wine, and feminine charm."[27]

During the eight years spanning her marriage to her association with the Riedesels, Martha had blossomed from a well-born but provincial young mother to a woman who would have held her own in the salons of Paris. Martha was also capable of carrying on an exchange of gossip with the French vice consul in Virginia, Charles-François Chevalier d'Anmours. A letter to Jefferson, with a witty anecdote to be passed on to Martha, shows the comfortable relationship between the French aristocrat and his charming hostess:

On my way here I Call'd on Col. mercer, who now is Become a Compleat farmer. This piece of news is for Mrs. Jefferson, who will Scarce believe it. Yet Madam, nothing is truer. By his present appearance you Could never guess that he was once one of the first-Rate-Beaux. Red coats, Gold frogs, Gold and Silver embroider'd Jackets, Powder, Puffs, Smelling Bottles, &c. all is vanished. And if you, now and then, see some Remains of them, they appear like the Ruins of those ancient magnificent cities, which serve to show what they once were: indeed the Reformation is as Compleat as Can be imagined.[28]

Historian Jack McLaughlin concludes that "if Martha the hostess was all charm, wit, and music, Martha Jefferson the housewife tried to be all business. Although after a few years she stopped keeping records of how much she spent and for what, she continued to enter inventories of food and clothing in her borrowed account book until her death. During the years she kept accounts of cash payments, she noted them on separate sheets of paper and turned them over to Jefferson, who copied them into his pocket memorandum book at the end of the year."[29] On January 30, 1772, Martha noted: "sent to buy cyder 10/," and Jefferson, in copying it into his pocket Memorandum Book, noted for posterity "(which was 6/3 too much)."[30]

Martha also established herself as manager of the household servants. In fact, the Jeffersons were slave rich, and there were many servants to care for, house, feed, and clothe. Running a plantation household was labor intensive for Martha. She personally oversaw the household servants, since their skills were often highly specific—seamstress, nurse maid, gardener. Those who were house servants, including the Hemings family, were divided between Monticello and the Elk Hill plantation, which was included in the 11,000 acres of land also inherited by Martha.[31]

Before coming to Monticello, Betty Hemings stayed for some time at Elk Hill with her younger children. Her older children, Mary, Bett, Martin, Bob, and James, were then brought to Monticello. Martin, who was to stand up to the British a few years later when they charged up the mountaintop in a vain attempt to capture Jefferson, became the house butler. Bett, also known as Betty Brown, was a seamstress and trusted servant to Martha from a young age. Bett most probably sewed the clothing

Martha gave to the other slaves. Jupiter's wife, Sukey, cooked, and Mary Hemings was a pastry cook, as was Ursula, Great George's wife. Jefferson purchased Ursula and her two children, George and Bagwell, a year after his marriage, before John Wayles's death brought the talented Hemings family of cooks and household servants to Monticello.

Ursula was undoubtedly purchased for Martha because of her skills as a pastry chef, but there was also a bit of serendipity in her acquisition. She became a wet nurse for Martha's sickly infant daughter, Patsy, shortly after Ursula arrived at Monticello. In later years, Jefferson recalled that his eldest daughter's health was recovered "almost instantaneously by a good breast of milk from Ursula." In his memoir, Ursula's son, Isaac, recalled the working relationship between Ursula and Martha Jefferson: "Mrs. Jefferson would come out there with a cookery book in her hand." This account indicates that Martha directly supervised food preparation and was in the kitchen giving instructions when meals were cooked. Managing so many servants and supervising their duties while nursing and caring for children, all in the middle of a Monticello construction site, no doubt taxed her energies, both physically and emotionally.[32]

Although there is no known documented portrait of Martha, in all probability one or more existed at some point. Jefferson himself had no less than ten portraits made of himself by the following artists: Mather Brown, 1786; John Trumbull, 1786 and 1787; Jean Antoine Houdon, 1789; Giuseppe Ceracchi, 1790 or 1791; Charles Willson Peale, 1791; William Joseph Williams, 1792; Gilbert Stuart, 1800 and 1805; Saint-Memin, 1804; Rembrandt Peale, 1805; Bass Otis, 1816; William J. Coffee, 1818; Sully, 1821; and, for a life mask, John Henri Isaac Browere, 1825—thirteen painters and sculptors in all. It would be remiss not to add the pencil sketch by architect Benjamin Henry Latrobe who, although he scarcely had a formal sitting, appears to have drawn Jefferson from life, as their close collaboration over a considerable period of years readily permitted.[33]

Family tradition describes Martha as "slightly but exquisitely formed," with a "brilliant" complexion, "expressive eyes of the richest shade of hazel," and "luxuriant hair of the finest tinge of auburn."[34] How Martha's beauty held up under the strain of frequent childbearing and poor health is questionable. There is some hint that she may have had some difficulty with her teeth, and it is quite possible she lost some of them. Shortly after his marriage, Jefferson paid John Baker, a prominent Williamsburg dentist, for two visits, on April 14, and May 2, 1772, a time when his wife was with him in Williamsburg. It is quite possible that Martha, four months pregnant, suffered from calcium deficiency, with dental problems as a result. If so, a pregnancy every two years could not have improved her smile. Jefferson, in his later life, claimed that his own teeth were good. In 1819, at the age of seventy-six, he wrote, "I have not yet lost a tooth by age."

Martha transferred her own physical qualities to only one of her two surviving daughters, Polly, who is said to have most resembled her mother. The eldest, Martha (Patsy), was her father's daughter. Like Jefferson, she was tall, and her features resembled his, but she was regarded as plain by those who described her. Anna Maria Thornton made the laconic comment in her diary, "she is not handsome." On the other hand, she found Polly, who favored Martha, "very beautiful but much more reserved than Mrs. Randolph." According to historian Jon Kukla, Martha Randolph (Patsy) inherited Jefferson's immune system, as well as his features, and passed it on to her children. In spite of the inevitable illnesses accompanying twelve pregnancies, she was physically robust and lived to be sixty-four. Eleven of her twelve children lived to maturity. Polly, on the other hand, died at twenty-six, after complications of childbirth.[35]

The phrase "unchequered happiness" that Jefferson uses to describe his marriage to Martha tells much about the character of his relationship with her. His words tell us that, regardless of external turmoil, nothing had been allowed to intrude upon their deep love affair. By the scant evidence we can accumulate, it becomes apparent that, at Monticello's summit, Martha's spirit must have soared, her days and nights filled with books, music, gardens, the man she loved, her unique house, and her children. Monticello was her home in every sense of the word, and it is easy to understand how this sensitive woman must have treasured almost every hour she lived on the mountain.

FIFTEEN

A Promise

> In every scheme of happiness she is placed in the
> foreground of the picture, as the principal figure. Take that
> away and it is no picture for me.[1]
>
> — THOMAS JEFFERSON to ROBERT SKIPWITH,
> August 3, 1777

> My dear wife died this day at 11:45 a.m.[2]
>
> — THOMAS JEFFERSON, in his diary,
> on September 6, 1782

B Y SEPTEMBER 1782, Martha Jefferson had grown so weak over the course of the summer that she was spitting up blood and could scarcely walk. By early August, Martha had been confined to her bedroom at Monticello, and Jefferson did not expect her to survive much longer.

Soon, physical love would literally kill Martha Jefferson at the tender age of thirty-three.

Two days after Thomas Jefferson's thirty-eighth birthday, on April 15, 1781, his four-and-a-half-month-old daughter, Lucy Elizabeth, died. This tragic event triggered a seventeen-month period of depression and grief for Martha, complicated by her seventh pregnancy. Martha's profound desire to nurture a big family was ruining her fragile body. Her health had worsened with each pregnancy and childbirth. The loss of so many children at such a young age also took a toll on her mental and physical health. Already weak and emotionally drained, this seventh pregnancy was even more precarious than the others. Martha gained far too much weight and was too ill to receive guests, perform any household duties, or even sit comfortably. She remained bedridden and turned over the management of Monticello to her servants, the Hemingses. Jefferson declined all public duties offered him in an effort to remain at Martha's side, concerned for her life.

The child of Martha's last and fateful pregnancy—named after baby Lucy Elizabeth who had died a year earlier—was born on May 8, 1782. In spite of Martha's grave condition, the baby was healthy and weighed an astonishing sixteen pounds at birth. But Martha's condition declined further, causing Jefferson to pen an ominous letter to his friend and colleague James Monroe twelve days after the delivery, writing, "Mrs. Jefferson has added another daughter to our family. She has ever since and still continues very dangerously ill."[3]

On or about September 6, 1782, a few weeks short of her thirty-fourth birthday, Martha's health began to seriously wane. Perhaps it was fate or written in her genes, since her own mother had died when she was born. Martha never regained her health following the birth of Lucy Elizabeth, who in turn died of whooping cough only two years later. Of the six children born to Martha, only two daughters survived to adulthood, Patsy and Polly.

At Monticello, Martha could always breathe the fresh mountain air, delight in the blazing autumn foliage, and gaze at the majesty of the Blue Ridge Mountains. She would revel in the cool night air that was alive with crickets. In those days, she could dream about her husband and her children. From the beginning, Martha and Thomas Jefferson had sketched their plans for their big house together, for it was surely a home for Martha and their children that Jefferson had envisaged.

Outside, the late afternoon August sun slanted down in the yard, throwing gleaming brightness into the dogwood trees that were solid masses of white blossoms against the new green. Jefferson's horses would have been hitched in the driveway, big animals, red as their master's hair.

Around their legs quarreled a pack of possum hounds that accompanied Jefferson wherever he went.

Day after day for three months, Jefferson had gazed into Martha's eyes, bright and unspoiled despite the disappointments life had shown her. Now, her light, loving eyes had sunken into drowsy sickness. Her tender mouth fought pain for breath. In the middle of the night, Martha awoke with a burning sensation in her chest and a suffocating lapse of breath. It had been nearly four months since she had given birth to little Lucy, but Martha had failed to gain her strength.

Before retiring that night Martha had refused the doctor's usual dose of laudanum with such vigor that it was omitted. As she slept, a terrible constriction consumed her with a great force. Martha broke out in a fevered sweat, nausea overcoming her. Her whole body revolted against this attack. She gasped, choking, lost in a swirling black darkness. She flung out her arm, but was unable to raise herself to stop the dizziness. The pain continued, searing, engulfing her. She cried Jefferson's name in a strangled voice before she began to retch.

Hours later, her sister, Lisbet, tiptoed into the bedroom, which was furnished in black walnut. She took Martha's cold hand as the flaring light of the fire threw tall dim shadows on the carved furniture and rose strewn carpet. Martha managed to sit up. Two auburn braids fell on either side of her face. Her eyes sunk into twin purple circles. Her face drained of life's blood, with a pinched look about her nose. Jefferson had stayed up all night with her and had finally fallen asleep in the dressing room next to their bed. It had been his habit in the afternoons to go riding at Martha's insistence, then sit up with his cherished wife all night, not allowing Martha's sisters to wear themselves out.

On the morning of September 6, 1782, it had started to rain, with the wind hastening decayed leaves from the magnolia trees. Martha did not have the strength to lie back down. She had spent her days drifting in and out, sleeping a good deal. The doctor had given her laudanum, which increased her fuzziness, but at least the pain in her chest had subsided.

Betty Hemings, her faithful and loving servant since childhood, removed the warm cloth on her head, replacing it with a cool one. Betty, Nance, and Critta Hemings had taken care of Martha these last months. Betty spoke to Martha in a quiet voice, gentle, solicitous as always. She had nursed Martha since she was two years old, and had become more of a mother to her than anyone. Betty was nurturing in her care, not only of her, but the other Jefferson children as well.

She came over with baby Lucy. Betty held her low by the bed as she knelt by Martha. Lucy's dark hair was gone. Martha reached out to her little head and found fine blonde fuzz. Dark hazel eyes gazed back at her. How sweet it was to Martha to feel the vibrancy of her little baby against her and to breathe in her warm baby smell.

Martha's four-year-old daughter, Polly, quietly entered the candle-lit room. Martha took several breaths with great difficulty and took Polly's soft hand. She was nearly smothered by Polly's firm embrace. Her beautiful Poll. She was so gentle hearted and kind. She would be a lovely woman. Martha drifted awhile and came back again to the hand of her older daughter, Patsy, on her arm. "Miss Patt." Her ten-year-old big girl. Her young lady, who would forever capture this death bed scene in correspondence and remembrances for many years to come.

Jefferson stroked Martha's soft hands as she drifted in and out of consciousness. His face paled at her sight. There was so much they had yet to do. They had talked of traveling to Paris and building two new wings at Monticello. They talked of having another baby, a son. Of Martha playing her spinet, the couple digging and humming in the garden. Now, all Martha could do was stare into the depths of Thomas Jefferson's hazel blue eyes, where all boundaries between flesh and spirit were dissolved. Martha wept, but she had no tears left in her wasted body. She fell asleep in Jefferson's arms as she had done so often before, safe and warm.[4]

Once before—in the summer of 1776—Martha had been so seriously ill that her life was feared for. Jefferson, in Philadelphia for the Second Continental Congress, had become frantic about her health. He wrote to Richard Henry Lee, who was to relieve him as a Virginia delegate. "For god's sake, for your country's sake, and for my sake, come. I receive by every post such accounts of the state of Mrs. Jefferson's health, that it will be impossible for me to disappoint her expectations of seeing me."[5]

During her final illness, Jefferson was again under pressure to be separated from her, but he steadfastly refused to leave her bedside.

During the week of Lucy's birth, he had been, against his wishes, elected Albemarle delegate to the Virginia legislature. In spite of his refusal to serve, he was threatened with being forcibly taken to Richmond by the sergeant-at-arms because a delegate could not legally be excused from serving unless he first appeared at Richmond and formally requested leave. In a letter to Monroe, Jefferson raged against the idea that one could be forced into public service as a lawmaker for an indefinite period. "Nothing could so completely divest us of . . . liberty as the establishment of the opinion that the state has a perpetual right to the services of all its members," he wrote. Finally, after reflecting on the fact that "public service and private misery [seemed] inseparably linked together," Jefferson closed his letter with this cryptic and ominous statement, the real reason for his refusal: "Mrs. Jefferson . . . still continues very dangerously ill."[6]

In spite of the pressures from Richmond, for the final four months of Martha's life, Jefferson stayed with her at Monticello. As his daughter Patsy was to recall, "when not at her bed side he was writing in a small room which opened immediately at the head of her bed." This would be the "anti-chamber," the small room between the entrance hall and the Jefferson bedchamber. The chamber could be closed off from the bedroom to provide Jefferson with a sanctuary, where he could be close to his wife and work at his writing desk at the same time.[7]

Jefferson spent the rest of that summer watching Martha slip away from him. He fed her food and medicine and sat up with her during her final months, when finally he had to summon his sister, Martha Carr, and Martha's sister, Elizabeth Eppes, to help him. But he did most of the nursing himself. He sat beside Martha's bed for hours, reading to her from her favorite books when she was awake. When she slept, he retreated to his study adjoining the bedroom, where he tried to work on a book he was writing, *Notes on the State of Virginia*, a response to a set of queries sent to him by an inquisitive French writer.

Years later, his daughter Martha, who was ten at the time, remembered that her father "was never out of [her mother's] calling" during these four depressing months. Husband and wife could not conceal from each other, no matter how hard each tried, that both knew what was happening. "He nursed my poor mother . . . sitting up with her and administering medicines and drink to the last," and, after she died, "he kept his room for three weeks and I was never a moment from his side. He walked almost incessantly every night and day only lying down occasionally. . . . When at last he left his room he rode out and from that time he was incessantly on horseback rambling about the mountain . . . in those melancholy rambles I was his constant companion, a solitary witness to many a violent burst of grief."[8]

Either at her bed or in a small room nearby that opened onto hers, Jefferson kept the sacred vigil. Patty too, craved Jefferson's presence. "Her eyes ever rested on him, ever followed him," historian Henry Randall recorded. "When he spoke, no other sound could reach her ear or attract her attention."[9]

Most of their conversations are lost to history, but throughout the summer no doubt Jefferson read to Martha from *Tristram Shandy*, a novel they both admired. Martha doubtless found in Sterne a confirmation of life's fragility and uncertainty that echoed her own poignant experience. "It was with this consciousness of death's imminence," concludes historian Andrew Burstein, that the Jeffersons turned to their literary commonplace book, "a scrapbook of significant quotations that he had been keeping since his college days, and made an entry from one of the final chapters of *Tristram Shandy*."[10]

Shortly before her death, Martha copied some lines from Sterne's book:

> Time wastes too fast: every letter I trace tells me with what rapidity life follows my pen. The days and hours of it are flying over our heads like clouds of a windy day never to return.

Martha was too weak to complete the passage, so Jefferson finished it for her in his own hand:

> and every time I kiss thy hand to bid adieu, every absence which follows it, are preludes to the eternal separation which we are shortly to make!

Whether prompted by hope or despair, he ended the text just short of Sterne's next line: "Heaven have mercy on us both."

Jefferson saved the paper for the rest of his life, adding to it a lock of Martha's hair.

By Friday, September 6, 1782, the family and household servants sensed that Martha's death was mere hours away. The following account of the death scene is taken directly from Jefferson's daughter Martha:

> As a nurse no female ever had more tenderness nor anxiety. He [Jefferson] nursed my poor mother in turn with aunt Carr and her own sister—sitting up with her and administering her medicines and drink to the last. For four months that she lingered he was never out of calling; when not at her bedside, he was writing in a small room which opened immediately at the head of her bed. A moment before the closing scene, he was led from the room in a state of insensibility by his sister, Mrs. Carr, who, with great difficulty, got him into the library, where he fainted, and remained so long insensible that they feared he never would revive. The scene that followed I did not witness, but the violence of his emotion, when, almost by stealth, I entered his room by night, to this day I dare not describe to myself.
>
> He kept his room three weeks, and I was never a moment from his side. He walked almost incessantly night and day, only lying down occasionally, when nature was completely exhausted, on a pallet that had been brought in during his long fainting-fit. My aunts remained constantly with him for some weeks. I do not remember how many. When at last he left his room, he rode out, and from that time he was incessantly on horseback, rambling about the mountain, in the least frequented roads, and just as often through the woods. In those melancholy rambles I was his constant companion—a solitary witness to many a violent burst of grief, the remembrance of which has consecrated particular scenes of that lost home beyond the power of time to obliterate.[11]

Edmund Bacon, who had been chief overseer at Monticello for many years, gave this account of the death scene in 1862:

The house servants were Betty Brown, Sally, Critta, and Betty Hemings, Nance, and Ursula. . . . They were in the room when Mrs. Jefferson died. . . . They have often told my wife, that when Mrs. Jefferson died, they stood around the bed. Mr. Jefferson sat by her, and she gave him directions about a good many things that she wanted done. When she came to the children, she wept, and could not speak for some time. Finally she held up her hand, and spreading out her four fingers, she told him she could not die happy if she thought her four children were ever to have a stepmother brought in over them. Holding her other hand in his, Mr. Jefferson promised her solemnly that he would never marry again. And he never did. He was then quite a young man, and very handsome, and I suppose he could have married well; but he always kept that promise.[12]

Bacon was wrong about the number of surviving children—there were only three, Patsy, Polly, and little Lucy, but in other respects his recollection is convincing. Martha herself had to endure more than one stepmother, and there were other obvious reasons why the thought of being replaced was painful. In return, it seems quite believable that to Jefferson, in those last mortal moments, the idea of another woman was abhorrent.

Martha's deathbed request is an extraordinary psychological puzzle. Why would she ask such a thing of Jefferson? One historian suggested that Martha "may have been as possessive of him in death as she seems to have been possessive of him in life, as jealous of any future wife as she had been jealous of his 'passion' for politics." Or was Martha "simply revealing her terrible sadness in relinquishing him altogether with life." Most probably, the "promise" suggests the root of Martha's concerns about Jefferson's remarrying. Her words were not motivated by a desire to die knowing that her husband would always belong just to her. This was not about Jefferson—it was about Martha's children. She was concerned that her daughters would grow up under the control of another woman, a cold stepmother like Martha had experienced.[13]

Yet, Martha's request was an extraordinary demand to make on a thirty-nine-year-old man, especially when we consider how frequently Virginia men remarried after losing a wife. But consider Martha's request against the backdrop of her own childhood: she had never known her own mother, who died after childbirth, and she endured a number of years with her first cruel stepmother, who gave birth to Martha's sisters. After her death, there came a second stepmother who lived for only one year of her marriage to John Wayles, dying when Martha was twelve. Her sisters were surely close to Martha and played very important parts in her life. They helped care for her, and one, Elizabeth (Lisbet), loved and looked after Martha's motherless children as if they were her own. If Martha's experiences with her stepmothers had been loving, she would not have required assurance that her own children would not suffer a cold or cruel stepmother. Martha probably felt it better that Jefferson raise the girls alone or with the help of the numerous women in both their families. These women were there at the end of Martha's life, just as they had been there throughout her short life.

According to the Hemings's oral history, during her final hours, Martha gave Sally Hemings, then nine years old, a handbell as a memento. The young girl, called by that very bell, had run errands for Martha. Oral histories of Monticello's servants note how stories passed down can be literal or symbolic. Some historians have argued that, on the surface, the story of the handbell is about Martha giving something concrete to her suspected half-sister, Sally, singling her out as someone to whom she had a special link, even though Martha had known Sally, the youngest of the female slaves, the shortest time.

However, it should also be noted that when the bell that the Hemings descendants loaned to official Monticello was examined, including metal identification by researchers at Colonial Williamsburg, it was dated to 1845. Therefore, the bell being shown at Monticello cannot be the bell that was given to Sally Hemings by Martha Jefferson when she died in 1782. In all likelihood, the story was apocryphal.[14]

Finally, Martha sank into a coma and her breath became the shallow gasps of the dying. There is some medical evidence that not only did she suffer from complications from childbirth and diabetes, but also from some form of tuberculosis at the time of her death. The spewing of bloody septum would indicate this as well.[15]

It was nearly noon on Friday, September 6, 1782, when the end finally came, and Jefferson literally blacked out. The account of Martha's death gives a vivid description of Jefferson's grief. He was so emotionally devastated that his sister, Martha Carr, called to his sister-in law, still bending over Martha's lifeless body, "to leave the dead and come and take care of the living."

A pallet to lie on was brought to give Jefferson some comfort in the little library, although it took the better part of an hour to revive the grieving husband. His grief was so terrifying their fear of his death was replaced by fear of madness. For three weeks, Jefferson did not come out of the library. Hour after hour he paced up and down, collapsing onto a couch only when, in the words of his daughter Patsy, "nature was completely exhausted." When Jefferson emerged from his library like a ghost from a tomb, he was still a haunted man. All he could do was ride around the countryside hour after hour, swaying in the saddle like a corpse. Ten-year-old Patsy rode beside him, reaching out to this reeling, incoherent man to hold him erect, offering herself as a mostly wordless companion on their aimless rambles along unfrequented roads.

Patsy knew from the household slaves or from her aunts that Jefferson had promised never to marry again, for her and her sisters' sake. Her mother's death was the beginning of a bond between father and daughter that became stronger and more meaningful to both of them with the passage of the years.

On October 3, after Martha's death, Jefferson wrote to Elizabeth Eppes, who had returned to her home, Elk Hill. He told of Patsy riding with him and her determination to accompany him to Elk Hill when he made a visit that he had apparently promised Mrs. Eppes. "When that may be . . . I cannot tell," he wrote, "finding myself absolutely unable to attend to business." His grief burst uncontrollably onto the page: "This miserable kind of existence is really too burdensome to be borne and were it not for the infidelity of deserting the sacred charge left to me, I could not wish its continuance for a moment. For what could it be wished?"[16] He did not write another letter for eight weeks.

After Martha's death, following eighteenth-century custom, Lisbet and Betty Hemings most probably washed and laid out her body, tying the jaw shut with a strip of cloth tied up under Martha's hair, hair that had

gone from pure auburn to streaked with gray as a result of her long illness. As Lisbet moved through the drawers and clothes press, she would
have found a gown Martha had planned to wear again after Lucy was
born. It would have been in the new fashion, with a round neckline and
long sleeves, in fine muslin, of a pale blue-grey, the color of moonstone. It
was an utterly plain gown save for muslin ruffles at the neck and wrists,
pure and beautiful in its simplicity.

Although no historic record has survived, in all probability the burial
was held the next morning, and, as Martha may have wished, it would
have been small and quiet with just the family and servants. Jefferson
would have walked down the long path to the graveyard in the fine rain,
with the Hemings boys carrying the coffin, and Patsy and Polly probably
walked beside Jefferson.

Martha Jefferson was buried in the eighty-square-foot graveyard
Jefferson had set aside on his mountaintop in 1773, the year after his
marriage. The graveyard had been cleared from the surrounding forest to
receive the body of his boyhood friend and brother-in-law, Dabney Carr,
who died suddenly at twenty-nine of "bilious fever." The spot selected for
the graveyard was a sentimental one. The two young men had read and
talked together under a great oak at this spot and had made a pact that
they would both lie there in death one day.

After Martha's interment, Jefferson placed on the grave a slab of
white marble with her birth date and the lines:

TO THE MEMORY OF MARTHA JEFFERSON, DAUGHTER
OF JOHN WAYLES: BORN OCTOBER 19TH 1748 INTER-
MARRIED WITH THOMAS JEFFERSON JANUARY 1ST,
1772: TORN FROM HIM BY DEATH SEPTEMBER 6, 1782
THIS MONUMENT OF HIS LOVE IS INSCRIBED IF IN THE
HOUSE OF HADES MEN FORGET THEIR DEAD YET WILL
I EVEN THERE REMEMBER YOU, DEAR COMPANION

The last words were a quotation from the *Iliad*, in Greek. Jefferson used
these same words for other reasons than a display of classical learning,
noted famed biographer Dumas Malone. "He thereby revealed his devotion to the initiated while veiling it from the vulgar gaze."[17]

⌁

The ironic fact that Martha's death was connected to childbirth and thereby to their physical passion could not have been lost on Jefferson. He had, in effect, loved her to death. If a sense of guilt aggravated his grief, it was compounded by the knowledge that the completion of their dream mansion had been woefully delayed. As one historian wrote, "It was by his own admission a house only half finished, and this was the only Monticello she knew."[18]

Modern psychology would say that Jefferson had experienced a trauma, a psychic wound so intense that it may have affected his relationship with women for the rest of his life. Martha's death was the climax of a series of personal losses, compounded by his failure as a political leader during his governorship. The two streams of anguish blended into a terrible regret for the time he had given to his public career. He could not avoid thinking that the separations and the frantic flights from British raiders were the reasons for Martha's death. Perhaps Jefferson could not help but face this conclusion and hold himself responsible for his wife's death. Throughout his life, he had practiced a stoic control over his passions, but the liberties of the marriage bed were a temptation he was unwilling or unable to check—even though he knew the inevitable pregnancies placed her at risk. During Martha's long illness, he probably had ample time to brood over his own complicity in her condition. Had he sacrificed her to the Revolution—and for what? All he had received in return was a blotted name and sneers from political foes, that he was a man who preferred "domestic pleasures" to serving his country.

From a psychological perspective, the two most common dynamic emotions in cases of violent bereavement are guilt and anger. Jefferson may well have felt anger at his wife's being taken from him. In her tombstone epitaph he used the expression "torn from him," and Martha's death literally shredded his future. But if, indeed, his thoughts had run in that direction, they had inevitably to also confront a terrible fact: her death was ultimately caused, not by Martha's weakness of will or lack of determination to survive, but by the pregnancies resulting from the sexual predilections of her husband.

At some point after the death of Martha Wayles Skelton Jefferson, her husband destroyed all of their correspondence, but for the slip of paper on which Martha, slowly dying after a difficult childbirth, wrote: "Time wastes too fast . . . everything presses on." Among the family relics found after Patsy's death in 1836 was a folded sheet of paper with a lock of hair and this notation in her handwriting: "A Lock of my Dear Mama's Hair inclosed in a verse which she wrote." The paper on which these lines were written was found after Jefferson's own death forty-four years later, "in the most secret drawer of a private cabinet which he constantly resorted to." The condition of the note indicated that it had been folded and unfolded many times over the years.[19]

Later, Jefferson wrote stoically into his account book: "On September 6, 1782, My dear wife died this day at 11:45 a.m."[20] He did not gratify the curiosity of history with a description of the death scene. The most deeply felt dream of Thomas Jefferson's life was over. The figure who stood "always in the forefront" of his vision of happiness was gone. In all the twists and turns of a renewed public career that would transform America, Martha remained a profound presence in her husband's mind and heart. His final act of destroying his departed lover's correspondence was a cathartic ritual, a final communion that forever sealed their private relationship against intrusion. By destroying their love letters, Jefferson placed Martha eternally beyond desecration. Posterity must simply accept that its best glimpses of their genuine intimacy are like fleeting shadows. The rest is lost to history.

SIXTEEN

SUICIDE

....

Mrs. Jefferson has at last shaken off her tormenting pains,
by yielding to them, and has left our friend inconsolable.[1]

—JEFFERSON friend EDMUND RANDOLPH
to JAMES MADISON

JEFFERSON'S SISTER, Martha, and his sister-in-law, Elizabeth, "remained constantly with him for some weeks" until "at last
he left his room." Then Jefferson spent most of October riding aim-
lessly about the plantation, accompanied only by his daughter Patsy. "He
was incessantly on horseback rambling about the mountain in the least
frequented roads, and just as often through the woods," Patsy wrote. "In
those melancholy rambles I was his constant companion—a solitary witness to many a violent burst of grief, the remembrance of which has consecrated particular scenes of that lost home beyond the power of time to
obliterate."[2]

The intensity of Jefferson's grief bore testimony to his deep love for
Martha. His friends were surprised, his family alarmed, by the utter failure of his famed self-control, but no more alarmed than Jefferson himself. His towering intellect and will had succumbed to emotion. Head had
been conquered by heart. The man who had "folded himself in the arms of
retirement, and rested all prospects of future happiness on domestic and
literary objects" had discovered instead that "a single event wiped away all
my plans and left me a blank which I had not the spirits to fill up."[3]

After weeks of virtual solitude, Jefferson began "emerging from that
stupor of mind which had rendered me as dead to the world as was she

whose loss occasioned it." He did not sleep but paced the rooms of Monticello endlessly in spasms of grief. He cleared out the room of everything that was Martha's, every article of clothing, every trinket, every scrap, looking them over carefully one by one, touching, feeling, remembering. He came upon her copied lines from the poet Laurence Sterne and was undone.

For weeks after Martha's death, Thomas Jefferson was prisoner to his unquenchable grief. His friends feared for his sanity. Rumor had Jefferson nearing madness. Edmund Randolph, then serving in the Continental Congress, wrote to James Madison that "Mrs. Jefferson has at last shaken off her tormenting pains, by yielding to them, and has left our friend inconsolable. I ever thought him to rank domestic happiness in the first class of the chief good; but scarcely supposed that his grief would be so violent as to justify the circulating report of his swooning away whenever he sees his children."[4]

And what of his children? Like her own mother, Martha had left a motherless baby, little Lucy Elizabeth, too young to have any memory of her mother. Even in a private letter to Martha's sister, Jefferson could not bring himself to utter Martha's name. He assured Elizabeth Eppes that the children "are in perfect health," but his rationality seemed perplexed that the girls were "as happy as if they had no part in the unmeasurable loss we have sustained." Elizabeth urged Jefferson not to mourn forever, to seek happiness at the first opportunity. He was finding that task impossible:

> I forget that I began this correspondence on behalf of the children and am afflicting you at the distance of 70 or 80 miles with sorrows which you had a right to think yourself out of the reach of. I will endeavor to correct myself and keep what I feel to myself that I may not dispirit you from a communication with us . . . I say nothing of coming to Eppington because I promised you this should not be till I could support such a countenance as might not.[5]

"Thomas Jefferson loved his wife with all his heart," historian Virginia Scharff has written. "The only way he knew to grieve was to draw a shroud of silence over her, to obliterate all trace of her, to ruthlessly suppress memory of her presence."[6]

In the months after Martha's death, Jefferson poured himself into Monticello's redesign to take his mind off his deep loss. Building and rebuilding, one visitor later noted that she was unprepared for what she found at Monticello. "When she finally reached the entrance," wrote historian Jack McLaughlin, "she was admitted by a servant. Winded, tired, and feeling ill from a harrowing trip, she no doubt thought she would at last step into the furnished comfort, indeed the luxury and ease, of the house of the . . . man of courtly polish and acknowledged taste. She was, however, sorely disappointed. The stately columns and portico that would one day embellish the front of the house were not yet completed, and the large entrance hall was a cavern of raw brick, with boards covering window openings. It was lit by a single lantern, which dimly revealed a ceiling of rough beams and a floor of dangerously unnailed planks thrown loosely over floor joists. 'Tho' I had been prepared to see an unfinished house,' she later recorded in her diary,' still I could not help being much struck with the uncommon appearance . . . which the general gloom . . . contributed much to increase.'"[7]

Jefferson's friends launched a campaign to lure him away from Monticello, a place that could do nothing for the moment but deepen his despair. In the Continental Congress, James Madison persuaded Congress to reappoint Jefferson as a commissioner to negotiate a peace treaty. Madison immediately wrote to Edmund Randolph in Virginia: "The resolution passed a few minutes ago. . . . Let it be known to Mr. Jefferson as quickly as secrecy will permit. An official notification will follow. . . . This will prepare him for it." Knowing Jefferson's sensitivity about his controversial governorship, Madison added that the resolution passed unanimously, without a single negative remark.[8]

The news reached Jefferson a short time after Martha's death, when he was at Amphill in Chesterfield County, the residence of Colonel Archibald Cary. Cary had kindly offered his house to Jefferson so that he might have his three daughters inoculated against smallpox. In a letter to a French friend, Jefferson confessed he was "a little emerging from the stupor of mind which had rendered me as dead to the world as she was whose loss occasioned it."[9] That same day, he wrote to Madison and to the president of Congress, accepting the appointment. Leaving his daughters with their maternal aunt and uncle, Francis and Elizabeth Eppes, he journeyed to Philadelphia and then to Baltimore, where a

French ship was supposed to take him to France. Yet, before he could sail, word arrived in America that Benjamin Franklin and his fellow diplomats had signed a satisfactory peace treaty, and he dejectedly returned to Monticello.

However, a year later, Jefferson and Patsy would be off to Paris to soothe his psyche and to help him recover from the death of his beloved wife. In that year at Monticello without Martha, there is no doubt that he suffered from a deep depression and possible suicidal thoughts remarking on his "miserable kind of existence."[10]

Martha Jefferson never had the chance to be first lady, yet there is no doubt that she influenced Jefferson in every aspect of his life and, most probably, in his political thoughts as well. What would have been her role and possible influence on Jefferson had she lived to become first lady for eight years?

Historical scholarship on the first ladies has revealed that many White House wives had considerable influence on their husband's careers, decisions, and policies. Edith Mayo, director of the Smithsonian's First Ladies Exhibit, has written, "It is sad and telling that the press and public alike are unaware that Presidential wives since Abigail Adams have been wielding political influence."[11] Considering the social forces limiting a woman's involvement in politics and influence in society and the fact that women could not even vote until 1920, the political activism and influence of several pre-twentieth-century first ladies is remarkable. In fact, a new view of an "activist political partner" is emerging as possibly the rule rather than the exception for the female occupants of the White House.[12]

Historically, on one hand, the first lady is deserving of study simply because the institution has been a part of the presidency since the founding of the nation. Most presidents, after all, have been married, and most of them have had their partner with them while serving in the White House. Only two bachelors were elected to the presidency: James Buchanan and Grover Cleveland, the latter marrying while in the White House. Only a few presidents have occupied the White House without their spouses, Jefferson being one. Both Ellen Arthur and Rachel Jackson died shortly before their husbands' presidencies, Ellen Arthur just prior to Chester A. Arthur's vice presidency and Jackson in the interim between election and inauguration. Martin Van Buren and Jefferson lost their wives well before their White House days, and the wives of Benjamin Harrison, John Tyler, and Woodrow Wilson died during their presidencies. Wilson and Tyler remarried before leaving the White House. The fact remains that, from a historical point of view, the presidency can be viewed as a "team."[13]

It is wrong to assume that scholarly study of the first ladies should be limited to that of the post-1933 or "Eleanor Roosevelt era." Several first ladies prior to Eleanor Roosevelt were active and influential in their husbands' administrations. This includes Dolley Madison and Abigail Adams, both of whom probably knew and met Martha Jefferson. Some of the first ladies who were especially influential in the president's life as full partners also include Ida McKinley, Edith Roosevelt, Helen Taft, Florence Harding, Lou Hoover, Eleanor Roosevelt, Bess Truman, Rosalynn Carter, Nancy Reagan, Hillary Clinton, and Michelle Obama. To this list we can add the name of Martha Jefferson.[14]

"In the 18th century," writes historian Robert Watson "the first ladies had no blueprint to follow in defining a role and identity for themselves and for their office. Yet, they shaped the institution as a public ceremonial office that was responsible for social functions and hosting formal affairs of state. The institution emerged as a highly visible one. While the institution evolved in an apolitical and unofficial capacity with respect to political and public affairs, these first ladies did forge a role as confidante and informal adviser to the president on political matters. During Jefferson's time, this was especially true of Abigail Adams, an articulate, intelligent, and assertive life-long counsel to her husband, and Dolley Madison, who was quite politically astute and a close neighbor, in Orange county, to the Jeffersons. Others like Martha Washington were not only less active politically, but also avoided the public eye, whereas spouses such as Dolley Madison attracted and celebrated it."[15]

Although Martha Washington and Abigail Adams were intensely private individuals, as was Martha Jefferson, they were widely known and competent, respected hostesses. It could be argued that, with Martha's background, education, and cultural and musical talents, had she lived to become first lady, she would have been one of the most popular and successful. Martha was known as a charming, capable hostess at Monticello, and one whose presence in and around Washington could have been felt for many years. There is no doubt that Martha Jefferson would have played a vital social and political role as first lady to Jefferson.[16]

But there is a still more interesting historical question to be pondered: if Martha had lived a healthy life, would Jefferson have truly retired to Monticello, "to his books, his farm and his family," as he had always wished to do, and not sought the presidency? Think of the ramifications. If Martha Jefferson had lived, Jefferson could have retired in 1781. Perhaps he would have kept the abolition of slavery as one of his true causes and forged a political solution or compromise, one founded in light and reason, that might have avoided a bloody civil war eighty years later. On the other hand, perhaps the famed Louisiana Purchase would never have been consummated, and there would have emerged two or three countries where the one United States stands today. Perhaps no other president would have been bold enough to purchase territory that doubled the size of the United States. Jefferson fully expected America to spread across a continent, undergo economic and social change, and emerge as a global actor. Perhaps this dream would not have been fulfilled if he had not become president.

Some historians have opined that Martha had a "pillow" influence over Thomas Jefferson, the greatest political theorist and author in the history of the United States. A good case can be made for that very scenario. It is more than mere coincidence that Jefferson's most brilliant writings came during his marriage to Martha. After Martha's death, he may have reflected on the fact that the decade that he shared with Martha was far and away the most creative period of his long and remarkable political career. During his ten years of married life to Martha, his *Summary View of the Rights of British America* was published in Williamsburg in 1774, launching his reputation in Virginia. His Declaration of Independence, written in Philadelphia in 1776, established his subsequent fame throughout America and the world. In three years of labor revising Virginia's legal code between 1776 and 1779, Jefferson wrote the Virginia Statute for Religious Freedom (adopted a decade later in 1786) and drafted the legislation that was ultimately passed in 1819 to create the

University of Virginia. And, finally, in the last years of their life together, Jefferson began the compilation of his only book, *Notes on the State of Virginia*.

All of these writings were political masterpieces. And they all were penned in the years of his marriage to Martha (1772–1782), a fact that is certainly not a historical anomaly or mere coincidence. No doubt Martha had an apolitical and informal sphere of influence on Jefferson, including behind-the-scenes influence that simply came from being one's partner, lover, and confidante. Here, Martha's home and family life, social interests, and moral beliefs on slavery most probably highly influenced Jefferson. This type of influence probably cannot be measured but should not be ignored by scholars studying the presidential spouses or the presidency.

And when it came to influence on Jefferson, it should be historically noted that females dominated his world: wife, sisters, daughters, and granddaughters filled Monticello, yet somehow they have never been given credit in the Jefferson historical tableau. And what of Jefferson's daughters—Martha (Patsy) Jefferson Randolph, who dutifully served as mistress of his house (and later at the White House), and Mary (Polly) Jefferson Eppes, who refused to sacrifice her marriage on the altar of filial piety? What about Jefferson's educated sisters or his granddaughters who kept diaries that reveal educational lessons learned at Monticello? The voices of these women, who knew Jefferson's personal and political sentiments and who married men who figured prominently in local, state, and national government, have largely been neglected as a significant part of Thomas Jefferson's political history.

SEVENTEEN

PARIS

....

I do not say that his five years in France were the happiest
period in his private life . . . the French period was almost
certainly the part of his public service he enjoyed the
most.[1]

—Historian and biographer DUMAS MALONE

J EFFERSON WAS so distraught over Martha's death that he
sought sanctuary overseas, away from Monticello and his inconsolable grief. In the spring of 1784, delegates chose Jefferson to join
Benjamin Franklin and John Adams in Paris to negotiate commercial
treaties with other European states. Jefferson welcomed the change of
scenery for his own emotional health. He accepted the post, and, after
two false starts, he arrived in France to begin a five-year exploration of
the Old World, one that he had dreamed of making with his beloved
wife, Martha.

To lessen the pain of separation, he took his twelve-year-old daughter, Patsy, with him. He left the two younger girls, Polly and Lucy Elizabeth, whom he called "Lu," with their aunt, Elizabeth Eppes. Jefferson
also took one of Betty Hemings's sons, James, to Paris with him. A bright,
lively young man, James had welcomed his master's offer to apprentice
him to a French *traiteur* (caterer), where he could learn the art of French
cooking. Contrary to much popular speculation and myth, Jefferson did
not take Sally Hemings with him to Paris.

Outwardly, most people saw Jefferson as a serene, confident diplomat,
vastly enjoying the architecture, the paintings, the plays and operas of
Paris, a city that was the artistic center of the civilized world. But, for a

year, Jefferson found it difficult and frequently impossible to shake off his depression over Martha's death. In November 1784, he wrote to a friend that he had "relapsed into that state of ill health, in which you saw me in Annapolis [where Congress met in 1783] but more severe. I have had few hours wherein I could do anything."[2]

Franklin and Adams gave Jefferson the warmest of greetings and opened doors for him throughout Paris. Soon Jefferson was enjoying the French talent for charming visitors who were "so polite," he remarked in one letter, "that it seems as if one might glide through a whole life among them without a jostle." Pretty and charming Madame de Corny, wife of one of the Marquis de Lafayette's closest friends, liked Jefferson so much that they began walking together in the leafy Bois de Boulougne. Jefferson was delighted by her exquisite femininity, which she combined with a penetrating intelligence. In Paris, one of his favorite people was also the Comtesse de la Rochefoucauld d'Anville, dignified and sarcastic, but with an amazing love for America. Her son, Louis-Alexanre, the Duc de la Rochefoucauld d'Anville, lived in a magnificent mansion where Jefferson met intellectuals such as the Marquis de Condorcet, one of the philosophers who were hoping to transform French society.[3]

Young Patsy Jefferson, still very much a country girl, was more amused than dazzled by French femininity. With the help of Lafayette's wife, Jefferson soon found a school for Patsy, the Abbaye de Panthemont. The abbess, Patsy's father was assured, "was a woman of the world who understands young Protestant girls." Martha did not speak French, and none of her fellow pupils spoke English. But in the Abbaye lived fifty or more older women, "pensioners" from good families who quickly taught her the language. Soon everyone called her "Jeffy," and she was "charmed with my situation." Jefferson visited her often and found no fault with the education she was receiving.[4]

Patsy and her father were barely settled in their lodgings, she told a friend, when "we were obliged to send immediately for the stay maker, the mantua maker, the milliner and even a shoemaker before I could go out." She also submitted to a *friseur* (hairdresser) once, but "soon got rid of him and turned my hair down in spite of all they could say." Thereafter, she put off Monsieur Friseur as long as possible, "for I think it always too soon to suffer."[5]

But in January 1785 came a devastating letter to Jefferson: little "Lu" Jefferson was dead of "complicated evils of teething, worms and hooping cough." The letter had arrived from Jefferson's sister-in law, Elizabeth Eppes:

Eppington, October 13th, 1784

Dear Sir

It is impossible to paint the anguish of my heart on this melancholy occasion. A most unfortunate whooping-cough has deprived you and us of two sweet Lucys within a week. Ours was the first that fell a sacrifice. She was thrown into violent convulsions, lingered out a week, and then died. Your dear angel was confined a week to her bed, her sufferings were great, though nothing like a fit; she retained her senses perfectly, called me a few minutes before she died and asked distinctly for water. Dear Polly has had it most violently, though always kept about and is now quite recovered. . . . Life is scarcely supportable under such severe afflictions. Be so good as to remember me most affectionately to my dear Patsy, and beg she will excuse my not writing till the gloomy scene is a little forgotten. I sincerely hope you are both partaking of everything that can in the smallest degree entertain and make you happy. Our warmest affections attend you both.

Your sincere friend
E. EPPES.[6]

Jefferson lapsed into total gloom and arranged for his other daughter, Polly, to sail to France to be with him and Patsy. His beloved family was dwindling by the years, and Jefferson was sure his "sun of happiness had clouded over, never again to brighten." Throughout the winter, he was dogged by migraines, poor digestion, and sad thoughts of his departed wife and daughter. John Adams's wife, Abigail, who had become fond of him, reported he was "very weak and feeble" in March. Jefferson told his friend James Monroe he was "confined the greater part" of the winter. Spring sunshine and new responsibilities lifted his spirits when Polly arrived from Virginia. Benjamin Franklin returned to America, and

Jefferson was appointed ambassador to France in his place. John Adams went to London as the ambassador to Britain, and Jefferson soon realized his new role was a "lesson in humility."[7]

℮ ➲

Finally recovering from Martha's death after two years of grief and comfortably enjoying life with his two daughters, Jefferson arguably met another "Martha Jefferson": twenty-six-year-old Maria Cosway, a beautiful artist and skilled musician. It cannot be lost on history that Jefferson first met Martha when she about the same age as Maria—twenty-three—and that one of his own daughters was named Maria (Polly).

Maria Cosway was "a golden-haired, languishing Anglo-Italian, graceful . . . and highly accomplished, especially in music." According to physical descriptions, Maria had voluptuous lips, startling violet-blue eyes, and fashionably coifed golden hair. Born near Florence in 1759—she was sixteen years younger than Jefferson—Maria Louisa Catherine Cecilia Hadfield was the daughter of an expatriate English merchant who ran an inn popular in Italy. Maria enchanted Jefferson, then forty. "Jefferson's infatuation with her appears to have been instantaneous," historian Jon Meacham noted. "In a way, he disappeared into those eyes and did not emerge for air for nearly a month. Hungry for her company, he put the rest of the world at bay."[8]

Maria was artistic, musical, and intelligent, a woman physically and culturally much like his true love, Martha. Was Jefferson looking for another Martha? Jefferson became infatuated with Maria, the lovely wife of bisexual British portrait painter Richard Cosway, spending time with her exploring the environs of Paris. He eventually wrote her a nearly 5,000-word essay, a sensitive and revealing love letter. Maria became a part of Jefferson's intimate circle of friends during his time in France, and Jefferson described her as having qualities and accomplishments belonging to her sex that set her apart from other women, such as "music, modesty, beauty, and that softness of disposition which is the ornament of her sex and charm of ours." Her knowledge of art and her immense popularity in Paris and London no doubt contributed to Jefferson's fondness for Maria's companionship.[9]

Maria Hadfield was born of English parents in Italy, where she spent her youth and was schooled in drawing, music, and languages. She furthered her study of drawing in Florence and Rome and was elected to the Academy of Fine Arts in Florence at nineteen. Maria met her mentor, Angelica Kauffmann, when she returned to England after her father's death, and her circle of English friends included Francesco Bartolozzi, the engraver of her portrait.[10]

Kauffmann introduced Maria to her future husband, Richard Cosway, a member of the Royal Academy who was famous for his portrait miniatures of London's aristocracy, including the royal family. Cosway was also a collector and connoisseur of Old Master paintings and drawings, prints, sculpture, and decorative art, and his duties as principal painter to the Prince of Wales including overseeing the royal collection. The Cosways frequently hosted members of London's literary and artistic circles at fashionable salons or musical evenings at Schomberg House in Pall Mall, which was filled with their eclectic collection.[11]

Jefferson met the Cosways in August 1786 at the Halle aux Bleds in Paris through a connection with the American artist John Trumbull. According to Trumbull, the entourage "was occupied with the same industry in examining and reviewing whatever related to the arts . . . Mr. Jefferson joined our party almost daily." Their excursions included sites such as Versailles, the Louvre, Louis XIV's retreat at Marly, the Palais Royal, St. Germain, and the Column at the Désert de Retz.[12]

John Trumbull knew the Cosways from London, and their paths had crossed in Paris, too. Now he made the proper introductions, and suddenly everything changed. By midafternoon, Jefferson's heart was "dilating with [his] new acquaintances, and contriving how to prevent a separation from them," especially from Maria. The Cosways, Jefferson, and Trumbull all had evening commitments from which they excused themselves by dispatching "lying messengers . . . into every quarter of the city."[13]

As historian Jon Kukla described their first meeting, Jefferson put off his dinner engagement with the Duchesse de La Rochefoucauld d'Enville with a note feigning that a packet of urgent letters demanded his immediate attention. Off the foursome went for dinner in Saint-Cloud, a popular resort town midway between Paris and Versailles and the site of a chateau that Louis XVI had recently purchased for Marie

Antoinette. After dinner, they headed for the gardens near Montmartre, where the Ruggieri family of Italian pyrotechnists were drawing enthusiastic crowds to their "lyric pantomimes in fireworks."[14]

There is no doubt that Jefferson was smitten with Maria. On this point, his foremost biographer observed "a generally philosophical gentleman, hungrier for beauty and a woman than he realized." Dumas Malone wrote that Jefferson "was quite swept off his supposedly well-planted feet."[15] For the next week or so, Jefferson and Maria Cosway roamed Paris and its environs together, sometimes accompanied by Maria's husband, by Trumbull, or by Jefferson's secretary, William Short. One historian detailed their first romantic week together: "on Monday or Tuesday they visited the Royal Library (now the Bibliotheque Nationale), where the sculptor Jean-Antoine Houdon had one of his studios. On Tuesday they traveled west to the ancient Chiteau de Madrid in the Bois de Boulogne, the huge forest park in which Jefferson often walked. On Thursday they traveled to Saint-Germain, and had a picnic at the royal retreat overlooking the Seine at Marly-le-Roi near Versailles. On Friday evening Jefferson took Maria to a concert of Haydn symphonies at the Tuilleries. On Saturday, while Trumbull set out for Frankfurt and Brussels on his return trip to London, Jefferson and Maria viewed the crown jewels, tapestries, and objets d'art exhibited at the Hotel du Garde-Meuble near the place de la Concorde."[16]

Jefferson was enchanted by Maria. Her departure from Paris in October 1786 compelled him to write the only existing love letter in the vast collection of his correspondence, "The dialogue between my Head and my Heart," dated October 12–13, 1786. The letter is a mock dialogue between Jefferson's calculating intellect ("head") and his suppressed emotions ("heart"). There can be little doubt that Maria provided a soothing tonic to Jefferson's fractured psyche. Contrary to some historians' speculation, in all historical probability, it was not Sally Hemings who held Jefferson's romantic interest, but the worldly and beautiful Maria Cosway, who reminded Jefferson in every way of Martha, from her physical beauty to her accomplishments and musical ability.[17]

After the departure of Maria for London, Jefferson wrote that her attributes set her "a chapter apart." He referred to himself as "the most wretched of all earthly beings." Responding to his "head's" admonishment for allowing himself to become emotionally attached to Cosway, his heart defends itself by proclaiming that "assuredly nobody will care for him who cares for nobody." Jefferson's head tells him that "the art of life is the art of avoiding pain" and that to prevent such pain one must "retire within ourselves, and to suffice for our own happiness."[18]

Jefferson's romantic sojourns with Maria ended painfully just two weeks after they met. Walking with Maria, Jefferson impulsively attempted to jump a fence, and his forty-three-year-old right wrist broke. His pain was excruciating and it continued for months. Jefferson did not regain use of his right hand until early November, and the wrist plagued him for the rest of his life. "That began the denouement of their summer romance," historian Jon Kukla observed, "beginning with the remarkable letter that Jefferson wrote to Maria Cosway on October 12, 1786, shortly after her husband abruptly ended their sojourn in Paris."[19]

On Friday, October 6, ignoring his pain as best he could, Jefferson accompanied the Cosways north to the little town of Saint-Denis, on the Seine, where they boarded a carriage headed for Antwerp en route home to London. Returning despondently to Paris, Jefferson had the company of his daughter Patsy for the weekend. On Tuesday, in a brief letter, the second written with his left hand, he referred to the "dislocated wrist which for some time interrupted my attention to affairs."[20] Although the injury distracted him from mundane business, so did a week of pensive brooding after Maria's departure. Jefferson spent days sorting out his feelings for Maria Cosway in the first draft of a 4,600-word essay—and then neatly copying it onto three fresh sheets of paper, all with his left hand.

Julian Boyd, founding editor of the definitive edition of Jefferson's writings, opined that the October 12 dialogue between Jefferson's "Head and his Heart" letter to Maria "is one of the most revealing in the entire body of TJ's correspondence, and one of the notable love letters in the English language." Boyd claims that the twelve pages of eloquent indecision comprise a "notable love letter." Historian Andrew Burstein's perspective is somewhat different. "This stylish, evocative composition," Burstein writes, was created as "a testament to sentimental friendship" and serves posterity as "a window to the inner life of the man who fashioned it." Dumas Malone's description of the Head and Heart dialogue was "a feat of ambidexterity, and . . . one of the most unusual tributes ever paid a pretty woman by a distinguished man," referring to Jefferson's left-handed letter writing capability.[21]

What was the true nature of the relationship between Jefferson and Maria Cosway? Opinions vary from one historian to the next, depending on how each has interpreted the evidence available to them, but most agree that a laissez-faire morality prevailed in Parisian society. "Illicit love-making was generally condoned," Dumas Malone readily acknowledged, "and if [Jefferson] as a widower ever engaged in it, this was the time." If Jefferson and Cosway had spent months together, it would be easy to envision a passionate love affair. Yet, they only spent two weeks together. In all historical probability, although Jefferson may have wanted more, most scholars have concluded that "the overall relationship between Jefferson and Maria Cosway was a flirtatious friendship enhanced by shared cultural interests rather than a passionately erotic affair. And this interpretation gains further support as we consider both their subsequent correspondence."[22]

Jefferson returned to America in 1789, and Maria eventually moved to Lodi, Italy, and established a convent school for girls. Cosway and Jefferson corresponded sporadically over the years, with letters coming first from Cosway. At her home in Lodi, Cosway possessed a portrait of Jefferson by John Trumbull that is now at the White House, presented by the Italian government on the occasion of the 1976 Bicentennial.

The correspondence continued intermittently until a year before Jefferson's death. Her letters told of the birth and short life of her only child, Angelica, and her founding of a girl's convent school in Lodi, Italy, where she died in 1838.[23]

Could Maria Cosway have been the proverbial "second" Martha Jefferson for the Virginian? Given time and different circumstances, perhaps. In Maria, Jefferson saw all of the qualities that had attracted him to Martha: physical beauty, musical talent, intellect, and a sweet nature, a woman who could have easily been a loving mother to his two young daughters. Had they met in Virginia and not Paris, in a different time and circumstance, a romance could have blossomed. Maria no doubt would have thrived at Monticello with a renaissance man like Jefferson. Yet, in the end, circumstances and geography prevented what could have been a romantic relationship, and we will never know. One wonders how Jefferson would have psychologically reacted to a new "Mistress of Monticello" with that eternal reminder—Martha's grave—just down the hill. Perhaps the shadow and memory of Martha and Jefferson's deathbed promise never to marry again made the difficult decision for him.

Much has also been speculated about Jefferson's stay in Paris and a possible sexual liaison with his slave, Sally Hemings. Other than rank speculation by some, I have not found any historical, primary evidence of it. In fact, one could argue that Jefferson fell back into a recurring historical pattern in Paris—his taste for married women: Martha Jefferson had been a widow, Maria Cosway was married, and the only known instance of a youthful indiscretion before his marriage was his unsuccessful advances made to a married woman, Betsy Walker. Sally Hemings, in short, did not fit his penchant, nor Jefferson's apparent physical type: Rebecca Burwell; his wife, Martha; and Maria Cosway were all petite, blue-eyed, charming, artistic, educated women and with a proper social background.

Jefferson may have been "deeply in love" with Maria, as famed Jefferson historian Dumas Malone considered. And the historian went one step further: if the widower ever made love to another woman, "this was the time."[24] Yet, ultimately, Malone believed that their relationship was merely a flirtatious friendship, with the memory of Martha Jefferson overshadowing every other woman in his life, in Paris and always.[25]

EIGHTEEN

EPILOGUE

John Wayles and Betty Hemings

....

The loss of Mr. Jefferson is one over which the whole
world will mourn. He was one of those ornaments and
benefactors of the human race, whose death forms an
epoch, and creates a sensation throughout the whole circle
of civilized man.[1]

> —THOMAS JEFFERSON's nephew DABNEY CARR JR.

All should be laid open to you without reserve, for there is
not a truth existing which I fear, or would wish unknown
to the whole world.

> —THOMAS JEFFERSON to HENRY LEE, May 15, 1826
> (fifty days prior to Jefferson's death)

O N JULY 4, 1826, family members began to surround Thomas
Jefferson in his bedchamber as his strength ebbed. He said good-
bye to his family, addressing each in turn. To an eight-year-old
grandson, he smiled and said, "George does not understand what all this
means." To a great-granddaughter he quoted the Gospel of Luke: "Lord,
now lettest thou thy servant depart in peace." His grandson, Thomas Jefferson Randolph, suggested he was looking better, but Jefferson demurred.
"Do not imagine for a moment that I feel the result," he said. "I am like
an old watch, with a pinion worn out here, and a wheel there, until it can
go no longer." He was nearing what he referred to as "that eternal sleep
which, whether with or without dreams, awaits us hereafter."[2]

Prize-winning biographer Jon Meacham described the death scene: "At ten he stirred and stared at a grandson, trying but failing to signal what he wanted. It was Burwell Colbert, his trusted servant, who interpreted the glance correctly. Jefferson wanted his head elevated; the butler arranged him as he wished. An hour later he was moving his parched lips but saying nothing. Much to his evident relief, a grandson lifted a wet sponge to Jefferson's mouth. It was over. At ten minutes before one o'clock on Tuesday, July 4, 1826, Thomas Jefferson died in his bed, three miles from Shadwell, where he had been born a subject of the British Empire eight decades before."[3]

He died with his eyes open. Six hundred miles away, John Adams, ninety years old, had died on the same day as Jefferson, also at home in bed. Daniel Webster prepared a eulogy for both men in Boston. Webster penned his remarks one morning before breakfast, recalling that when he was done "my paper was wet with my tears." He wrote glowingly, "On our fiftieth anniversary, the great day of national jubilee, in the very hour of public rejoicing, in the midst of echoing and reechoing voices of thanksgiving, while their own names were on all tongues, they took their flight together to the world of spirits."[4]

Wormley Hughes, Monticello's gardener, dug Jefferson's grave on the western side of the mountain in the family cemetery, next to his beloved Martha. The weather had been wet when the funeral party gathered inside Monticello for Jefferson's final journey. The mourners were few. Jefferson had not wanted a large service. A small group of family, friends, and slaves escorted the wooden coffin down the hill. The Reverend Hatch read the burial prayer from the Episcopal Book of Common Prayer. "'I am the resurrection and the life,' saith the Lord," Hatch read, "'he that believeth in me, though he were dead, yet shall he live: and whosoever liveth and believeth in me, shall never die.'"[5]

Jefferson was buried next to his beloved Martha. Finally, after many detours, many wanderings, and many triumphs, Martha and Thomas Jefferson had come home to rest at Monticello for good.

Controversial and lingering questions remain about Martha Jefferson's true "family." Was Betty Hemings the slave mistress of Martha's father,

John Wayles, thus making Martha a half-sister to the infamous Sally Hemings, as several prominent historian have argued? Did Martha know or suspect that her father had an affair with his slave, Betty Hemings? Did Wayles father slave children? Or was this all distorted myth contrived by Wayles's political enemies?

Beyond these large controversial questions, as historian Thomas Fleming has observed, we should not allow differences about Hemings and Jefferson to obscure the most important woman in Thomas Jefferson's life: Martha. Hundreds of vivid letters tell us how much he loved Martha and his daughter Polly, those two beautiful tragedy-haunted "seraphs" who died too young and whom he hoped to greet beyond death's darkness.[6]

Martha's relationship with the slave Sally Hemings and her descendants has now entered the realm of mythical significance. Many people, for reasons that have little to do with historical accuracy, passionately want to believe that Wayles was the father of mixed-blood children by a slave mistress. The accusation has been aired mostly on the basis of innuendo and assertions made on insufficient historical evidence. Famed Jefferson biographer Dumas Malone argued that both Wayles and later Thomas Jefferson "suffered open personal attacks which, in severity and obscenity, have rarely if ever been matched."[7]

The historical evidence against John Wayles is lacking, and, in all probability, he was entirely innocent of the charge of having sexual relations with Betty Hemings. To understand this historical debate, one must delve into the genesis of the Hemings-Jefferson relationship. We start with the initial, basic historical question: Was John Wayles Sally Hemings's father? The answer, in all historical probability, is simply no.

John Wayles is at the center of this story, and the information on his life and activities has not been fully presented prior to this time. Wayles epitomized the rising middle class of the developing nation. Until now, Wayles's involvement in the "Sally Hemings" controversy was a footnote to the history of Thomas Jefferson. In fact, John Wayles had been simply a footnote to a footnote. Yet, most historians place Wayles prominently in the "Sally story." If Wayles were indeed the father of Sally Hemings, then Sally was the half-sister of Martha Jefferson. This notion has led some historians to speculate about the relationship of Jefferson and Sally Hemings based on a "half-sister" idea. However, the most verifiable, historical evidence has no hint of Wayles being involved in such a relationship, and strong, though not incontrovertible, evidence exists against it.

Slave historian Annette Gordon-Reed has written that John Wayles, thrice wifeless, did not live out his days alone and that he took "a concubine. He turned to a slave, Elizabeth 'Betty' Hemings, the daughter of an English sea captain and an enslaved African woman. She had come to the Forest at about the age of thirteen, as Martha Eppes's slave." According to Gordon-Reed, John Wayles was the father of six of Betty's children, three boys and three girls: Robert, James, Thenia, Critta, Peter, and Sally. "John Wayles," argues Gordon-Reed, "grew rich himself off of Africans. He used them as items of trade, held them in bondage, and mixed his blood with theirs."[8]

As indicated by this premise, Betty's other children, according to her grandson Madison Hemings, had other fathers who were not Wayles; Mary, Martin, Bett, Nance, John, and Lucy. Madison Hemings stated in his interview in 1873 that John was the son of a hired white worker at Monticello, Joseph Nielson. Yet, there is a fundamental historical flaw in this theory and rank speculation about Wayles being the father of either Sally or Critta, Betty Hemings's daughters. Critta was born in 1769. If Wayles had been her father, she would have been described as a mulatto or very light skinned. Yet, Critta's emancipation refers to her as "Negro," and the 1833 black census of Albemarle County specifically listed her name in the Negro column—not the "mulatto" column. Historian Cynthia Burton observes "that it is interesting to see how census takers and court clerks perceived persons of color and sometime that was apparent in inconsistencies. This may have been the mistake, but her husband's name was listed before her, and he was definitely designated 'mulatto.' The court clerk, Alexander Garrett, was familiar with Jefferson's slaves, and Jefferson was not known to differentiate the mulattos from Negros in his slave lists, but Critta's description is cause for skepticism about Wayles being her father."[9]

The most detailed research on John Wayles was conducted by historians Rebecca and James McMurray. In short, they concluded that the evidence is sparse and speculative at best for this alleged sexual relationship, and, in fact, the entire claim is historically dubious. John Wayles was a decrepit fifty-eight years old and dying at the time of the alleged sexual relationship with Betty Hemings that produced Sally Hemings.

The accusation that John "Wales" was the father of "SALLY" first surfaced in the form of a slanderous political letter in 1805 from a "Thomas Turner" of Virginia, although it also appeared in a letter between Federalists from one passing through Virginia in December 1802, following the summer announcement of the candidacy of John Wayles Eppes for Congress as a Jefferson supporter. These children of Betty Hemings, which are described in this passage, also appear on Jefferson's list of slaves in his farm book and are noted with the Hemings surname. Jefferson reported dates of birth for them that range from 1762 to 1773.[10]

Yet, Wayles's role in this controversy dates back more than forty years. Wayles briefly received a degree of attention in his community, although it was probably not the kind he wanted. For a few astounding weeks in 1766, Wayles's name appeared in Virginia's leading newspaper in connection with a sensational murder case. Wayles represented John Chiswell, who was accused in 1766 of killing Robert Routledge during a quarrel in a Williamsburg tavern. Chiswell was let out on bail, causing a firestorm of controversy among the citizenry who believed he had received special treatment because he was well connected. The case split people along class lines. As the lawyer for the accused, John Wayles, the former "servant boy" turned lawyer, merchant, and trader, was on the side of the grandees.[11]

This already sensational case gained further attention when the president of the Virginia council, John Blair, a man who had twice served as acting governor of Virginia, took to the pages of the newspaper, the *Virginia Gazette*, on Thursday, January 1, 1767, to accuse John Wayles of lying in his deposition recounting the facts of Chiswell's encounter with Routledge. Wayles denied the charge, but Blair and other correspondents who joined in the fray did not back down. Several more items appeared on the subject, with Wayles being parodied in two poems printed in the *Gazette*. Both attack his veracity, one beginning,

> When Judas lavish'd laud on honest Wayles
> Men, laughing, thought they heard Vermillio's tales;
> To him should grateful like praise return,
> Mankind would swear all language forsworn.

A stanza in the other poem is notable for its reference to Wayles's background:

> See Manners beam, from ill-bred Wayles; See Manners fraught with
> fairy-tales—The bastard of St. Judas!
> God send that Manners, praising Manners (And all who follow Folly's
> banners) Were banish'd to Bermudas.[12]

The sarcastic reference to him as "the ill-bred Wayles" suggests that people considered him of lowly birth and were willing to play that card when necessary. Indeed, the tone of some of the criticism was so contemptuous that one wonders if Wayles's background did not make his critics think they had extra license when attacking him. In one letter addressed "To Mr. Wayles" and printed in the *Virginia Gazette*, the correspondent ridiculed Wayles's claim that his reputation was defamed by Blair's allegation:

> You are pleased to intimate that your veracity has been called in question, and your reputation like to suffer, by the President's indiscretion. Pray sir, was your veracity never questioned before? And as to your reputation, would you not be obliged to those who would take away or annihilate it, provided they furnish you with another, as it is not at all probable that you could be a loser by the exchange. I think it will not be unreasonable to suppose that you will throw abundance of scurrility and abuse (of which you always have plenty at command) about on this occasion considering with what ill manners and disrespect you have treated a Gentleman who I believe deserves the regard and esteem of every honest man in the country, and that is beloved and respected by all that have the pleasure of knowing him, yourself excepted; but men do not expect to "gather grapes of thorns, nor figs of thistles."[13]

Wayles's response to the charge that he had lied in his deposition appears in the same edition: "Out of tender regard to the President, I have long both patiently and silently born the blame of his indiscretion; but for reasons obvious enough, I must beg to be excused from doing it longer, and put the saddle on the right horse."[14]

Thus, Wayles, as well as Jefferson later on in years, had political enemies out to defame him in any way that they could. Yet, on balance, it is less likely that John Wayles was the father of any of the children of Betty Hemings. For example, Wayles had been in ill health for most of the last two years of his life, and in February 1773 his health deteriorated rapidly. Wayles finally died in May 1773. Sally Hemings was born at Guinea Plantation several months after Wayles died. Thus, in all historical probability, Sally was conceived at Guinea Plantation and not at The Forest. Guinea Plantation was a hard two- to three-day trip from The Forest, a trip that Wayles was not healthy enough to endure.

Thus, in all likelihood, according to historians Rebecca and James McMurray, "Betty Hemings was the one-time mistress of William Hemings of Hobbs Hole and/or Robert Hemons, an overseer of Colonel Thomas Bray in Charles City County. According to the best evidence, men of one period gave way to others in Betty's life."[15]

William Hem(m)ing(s) of Essex was "imported" into Virginia by Colonel William Beverley about 1741, who claimed title to western land due him by right of paying passage for William Hemings and other persons to Virginia. The patent was presented October 1, 1747. Hemings was in Virginia for some time before Beverley finalized his land patents. Hemings had a tavern for a short time in the busy port town of Hobbs Hole (Tappahannock). The town was booming in that period, and it was frequented by mariners from around the world. According to the McMurrays' detailed genealogical research, Hemings must have been an educated man because he was readily available for witnessing legal work at the courthouse or in his tavern. His name appears among rolls of the wealthy families of Essex County in the court records. Hemings dealt in merchandise, and, at his death, the inventory listed many valuable items, such as prints of Hogarth's "Marriage ala Mode" and "Diana and Venus."

"Hemings's demise must have come suddenly," the McMurrays noted, "because he left no will, nor were a wife or children acknowledged. Among his 'inventory' were Edward Field and Mary Jones, servants; a Negro man named Harry; a Negro woman named Bess; and a Negro boy named Ben. His appointed executor was a well-known merchant, James Mills of Urbanna (in adjacent Middlesex County). Mills operated several stores in the Tidewater and the adjacent 'frontier.' He had married Colonel William Beverley's daughter, Elizabeth. Colonel Beverley's uncle, Colonel William Byrd II, was a close friend and neighbor of Colonel Francis Eppes among whose family Betty (Hemings) lived and labored. Slaves and bond-servants were often leased out and their lives were not stationary."[16]

Betty "Hemings" in all probability was sent to Hobbs Hole for a time. The Eppes family had connections there, and the "tripartite" agreement between Martha Eppes Eppes, John Wayles, and Martha's kin provided for this leasing of Betty, her family, and companions. It is possible that some of these servants were apprenticed and trained during periods of lease. In addition, relatives owned Bowler's Wharf a few miles south of Hobbs Hole/Tappahannock, and leasing arrangements may have been made in the Hemings tavern.[17]

Robert Hemons, another probable candidate for a sexual liaison with Betty Hemings, was an overseer in the neighborhood of the Eppes family. In 1741, he was accused of forcing Colonel Thomas Bray's slaves to work on the Sabbath and of using profanity. Lewellyn Eppes's mother was Angelica Bray, so there was commerce between these families. Little more is known about Robert Hemans, but his presence in Charles City County establishes him as a potential sexual partner for Betty Hemings.[18]

In contrast to these two likely sexual partners for Betty Hemings, on balance, "it is less probable that John Wayles was the father of any of the many children of Betty Hemings," concluded historians Rebecca and James McMurray. For instance, John Wayles had a houseful of young daughters and likely sons-in-law during the time that Betty Hemings was part of the Wayles household from 1760 to his death in 1773. Despite an active grapevine and much gossip in colonial Virginia, the editor of the *Virginia Gazette* who slandered Wayles in 1767 mentioned nothing to suggest that he had any children with a slave mistress. As one historian argued, "It would have been just too juicy to pass up, if rumored, much less if true. However frequently or infrequently men of Virginia used slave women as their 'mistresses,' it was not respectable behavior. Yet, the daughters of John Wayles named their own children for him, signifying their respect for him."[19]

Wayles fell ill in February 1773, and at that time he added a codicil to his will. He died in May 1773. His estate was divided between his three surviving daughters, known to him as "Patty" (Martha) Jefferson, "Betsey" Eppes, and "Nancy," who was engaged to Henry Skipwith. Their husbands, Thomas Jefferson, Francis Eppes, and Henry Skipwith, respectively, became the executors. One of the codicils to Wayles's will made a bequest of £200 to Robert Skipwith, husband of "Tibby," and there was no further mention of Tabitha, who apparently had died by February 1773.

It is interesting to note that Wayles left an estate of almost 5,000 acres of Virginia land to the future Martha Jefferson, not to Betty Hemings, his alleged slave mistress or to any of their alleged children.

As a side note, an interesting anecdote was related by historian Henry Wiencek. As he was leaving the Monticello graveyard with Frasier Nieman, an archaeologist who later participated in a 1998 DNA study matching a male Jefferson descendant to a male Hemings descendant, Wiencek turned and saw a bouquet of flowers lying on the ground. Wiencek asked Neiman if he thought Betty Hemings and her family might be buried here. Nieman replied that the Hemingses were more likely to have been buried closer to the summit. "A sign of this appeared in the 1950s in the most startling manner," Wiencek wrote. "Monticello's then director, James Bear, was walking in the area of the Ancient Field when, amazingly, he came upon a headstone from the 1830s wedged in the crook of a tree. How it got there nobody knows . . . A marked headstone for a slave is very rare. Slave cemeteries are also rarely found. Indeed, given the size of the population of enslaved people—in Jefferson's time 40 percent of Virginians were slaves—so few of their cemeteries have been found that one would think that slaves never died."[20]

The place of John Wayles in the Hemings paternity claims began on May 31, 1805, when a Boston newspaper, the *Reparatory*, printed a letter from a "Thomas Turner" who recounted the James Callender slander on Jefferson three years earlier in the *Richmond Recorder*. This time, however, Sally Hemings had now become, "the natural daughter of Mr. Wales, who was the father of the actual Mrs. Jefferson." This was the first suggestion that John Wayles was the father of Sally Hemings. The allegation was resurrected in 1873 in the so-called interview by abolitionist editor S. F. Wetmore of Sally's son, Madison Heming (with the same misspelling of "Wales's name). Some historians have speculated that if Wayles were indeed the father of Sally Hemings, then Sally was the half-sister of Martha Jefferson. Some historians have also speculated that Sally was more attractive to Jefferson because she resembled her "half-sister" (Martha Jefferson), whereas others historians have argued that Sally Hemings, her siblings, and her children were accorded special privileges because of the "half-sister" relationship, rather than because of some long-term affair between Jefferson and Hemings.[21]

It is in the context of this nineteenth-century manipulation of the "Jefferson image" that we must place the so-called memoirs of Madison Hemings, published on March 13, 1873, as the first of a series of interviews with former slaves titled "Life Among the Lowly," in the *Pike County* (Ohio) *Republican*, a partisan newspaper edited by Samuel F. Wetmore, a Republican Party abolitionist. As University of Virginia professor and historian Robert Turner concludes in his individual views in the Scholars Commission Report (2011), there are many good reasons to be highly skeptical of this 1873 newspaper article. One reason is that we are not sure the statements attributed to Madison Hemings really were his and not the words of the biased editor, Wetmore. Even if the statements were indeed Hemings's, Madison Hemings had no first-hand knowledge of a relationship between Jefferson and his mother, Sally Hemings, and certainly not of John Wayles or Betty Hemings. Indeed, there is no evidence that Sally Hemings herself claimed Wayles as her father. And, in fact, Madison Hemings's statements so closely resembled the original political smear against Jefferson from 1802 (for example, in their identical misspellings of John Wayles's name) that it is probable that Madison based his entire story on scandal-mongering journalist James Callender's allegations.[22]

There are other substantial inaccuracies contained in the Madison Hemings interview about John Wayles that weaken its credibility, according to historian Cynthia Burton. "Many portions of Madison's story are inconsistent," argues Burton, "with known facts such as his absurd claim that [John] Wayles owned and negotiated for Betty Hemings when she was born." Betty Hemings was only 11 years old and belonged to the Eppes family when her mistress, Martha Eppes, married Wayles, and thus he could not have owned and negotiated for her freedom.[23] More factually, Wayles was born in 1715 and first appears in Virginia records in 1741, and thus he could not have been fighting over the newborn Betty Hemings in the 1725–1735 time frame. Betty Hemings belonged to Martha Eppes Eppes (Wayles's first wife), as stated in the tripartite agreement of 1746.

Years later, one other direct observer of happenings at Monticello offered his testimony denying the Hemings's paternity allegation against

Thomas Jefferson. Edmund Bacon, who was Jefferson's slave overseer for many years, in a reminiscence first recorded in 1862, denied that Sally Hemings's daughter (presumably Harriet) was Jefferson's daughter. "She was not his daughter, she was ——'s daughter. I know that. I have seen him come out of her mother's room many a morning when I went up to Monticello very early."[24]

The late famed historians Douglass Adair and Dumas Malone researched these various paternity theories involving Wayles-Hemings and categorically debunked the errors and myths. Adair never published his essay on the "Sally story," although it was published posthumously.[25] One of the cornerstones of Adair's assessment of this situation had been the statements of both Isaac Jefferson and Madison Hemings (Sally's son, and both slaves at Monticello) that John Wayles was the father of Sally Hemings. Isaac Jefferson painted lively pictures of persons he knew, but Isaac specifically noted "folks said" that some of the Hemings children were "old Mr. Wayles," thus merely reporting the newspaper slander of Isaac's time rather than the detailed personal observations that character-ized most of his account of life at Monticello. Madison Hemings never explicitly stated any sources—although implying many, he never was quoted as saying, "my mother told me" or "my grandmother said."

In short, through exhaustive research in writing Martha's biography, I have simply found no evidence of John Wayles's being involved in such a sexual relationship with Betty Hemings, and found strong, although not incontrovertible, evidence against it. Wayles never spelled his name without the "y," and others before him in Lancaster, England, also used the "y" in Wayles. Interestingly, the 1805 newspaper article that first sug-gested that Wayles was the father of Sally made the same mistake as the Wetmore/Hemings article, spelling the name "Wales." Born in Lancaster, England, Wayles was not a "Welchman," no matter how the name was spelled. He was from the north country, most probably the Lake District, of England. There was, however, a man of Welsh ancestry in the family history: Daniel Lewellyn, who was grandfather to Lewellyn Eppes Jr., the first husband of Martha Eppes.

This passage from Madison Hemings implicating John Wayles with Betty Hemings, as famed Jefferson biographer Dumas Malone con-cluded, has the aura of abolitionist melodrama of the early nineteenth century. Malone, completing the final volume of his Jefferson biography in 1981, sought to formally debunk the 1873 memoir of Madison Hemings. In a journal article titled "A Note on Evidence," Malone and his research assistant, Steve Hochman, dismissed the Hemings memoir as a piece of propaganda. Malone wrote that the Hemings memoir "reminds us of the pedigree printed on the numerous stud-horse bills that can be seen posted around during the Spring season. No matter how scrubby the stock or whether the horse has any known pedigree," owners invent an exalted lineage for their property.

Madison Hemings's interview in the *Pike County Republican* was reprinted in historian Fawn Brodie's 1974 controversial book under the title "Reminiscences of Madison Hemings." She, as well as slave historian Annette Gordon-Reed, had described this as "the most important single document" relating to the story of Sally, and, except for a few minor inaccuracies, she accepted it as factually correct. Apparently, neither she nor any of the other historians who have cited this document in recent years inquired into the circumstances of its original publication, Malone and Hochman concluded. Any document must be viewed by the historian in its actual setting of time and place. This particular memoir refers to supposed happenings a score of years before Madison Hemings himself was born, Malone wrote. "Our concern here, however, is with the circumstances of its appearance rather than its contents. In its published form it was a report of an interview by the editor of the *Pike County Republican*, S. F. Wetmore. Judging from its title, 'Life Among the Lowly, Number One,' Wetmore hoped it would create sympathy for the freedmen just as *Uncle Tom's Cabin* did for the slaves."[26]

Malone expressed these views both personally and professionally. He told historian and journalist Virginius Dabney, "I don't want to claim too much about what we've got . . . but we have learned that it was solicited and published for a propagandist purpose. It seems perfectly safe to say however that it is a tradition of political, abolitionist propaganda."[27]

Thus, there is no verifiable, historical evidence that Wayles fathered any slave children with Betty Hemings, and, in all probability, the accusation was formulated as either a rumor among the slaves themselves or as abolitionist rhetoric to smear Thomas Jefferson and his father-in-law.

More importantly, in 2011, a new study and analysis of the Wayles-Hemings-Jefferson relationship was published by the Scholars

Commission (Carolina Academic Press), which consisted of a thirteen-member, blue-ribbon panel of prominent historians and scientists (white, black, male, and female) charged with analyzing the Jefferson-Hemings controversy as well as the 1998 DNA results. They evaluated all of the evidence in the controversy, including DNA, and concluded that what was presented as historical fact was based on a singular misleading headline in 1998, "Jefferson Fathered Slave's Last Child." After a year of investigating history's most famous paternity case, the independent historians tamped down the simmering allegation not only about Wayles, but about Thomas Jefferson and Sally Hemings:

> In the end, after roughly one year of examining the issues, we find the question of whether Thomas Jefferson fathered one or more children by his slave Sally Hemings to be one about which honorable people can and do disagree . . . With the exception of one member . . . our individual conclusions range from serious skepticism about the charge to a conviction that it is almost certainly untrue.[28]

APPENDIX A

CHRONOLOGY OF ALL CORRESPONDENCE ABOUT MARTHA JEFFERSON

1779 September 12. Maj. Gen. William Phillips to TJ: [Blenheim] "Major General Phillips wishes Mrs. Jefferson and the Governor a pleasant journey to Williamsburgh." [TJP]

Family thereafter moves to Williamsburg. They arrive by September 27. [TJA 486]

"Pd. Sam. Beall for wine from Cart. Braxton £151," 27 September 79; TJ "Pd. Miss Cook for a bonnet £36," 28 September 79; TJ "Pd. Miss Cook for 2 caps £40," 1 October 79; TJ "Pd. Chas. Taliaferro for 200 bush. coal £180," 2 October 79 [TJ continues to buy coal from Taliaferro throughout their time in Williamsburg]; TJ "Pd. James Wray repairs of palace £21-18," 21 October 79; TJ "Pd. Hanah Roberts fish & oysters to this day £14-3," 24 October 79; TJ "Gave T. Shackleford to pay for a bell £4-10," 3 November 79; TJ "Pd. Rob. Sandford for 8260 lb fodder £297-6," 12 November 79; TJ "Pd. Green the shoemaker 1 pr. shoes, makg. &c. £10-6," 13 November 79; TJ "Pd. Craig for mending pencil 24/," 24 November 79; TJ "Pd. Green for 1 pr. shoes, makg. &c. £10-6," 7 December 79; TJ "Pd. Mr. Prentis for hire of gardener £27-12," 20 December 79; TJ "Pd. Greenhow £7-10," 20 December 79; TJ "Pd. Nicholson for a book £6," 10 January 80; TJ "Pd. Giovanni making boy's clothes £21," 24 January 80; TJ "Pd. Giovanni for 2 pr. cotton stockings £60," 25

January 80; TJ "Recd. of Mrs. [Mary Cary?] Ambler in rent [for Governor's or Paspahegh lands in James City County between Jamestown and the Chickahominy] 12. barrels corn," 25 January 80; TJ "Pd. [Wiley] for shaving £5," 25 January 80; TJ "Recd. of Mrs. Ambler balance of rent 5. Barr. corn," 26 January 80; TJ "Pd. London [slave of James Wray] mending windows 30/" 26 January 80; TJ "Pd. Rob. Anderson (tavern keeper) in full £66-15," 27 January 80; TJ "Pd. Litchford for beer £6," 27 January 80; TJ "Pd. Giovanni for a book £45," 4 February 80; TJ "Pd. Giovannini in part of wages £90," 9 February 80; TJ "Pd. Dav. Middleton 10/6," 12 February 80; TJ "Pd. Litchford for 30. galls. ale £108," 15 February 80; TJ "Pd. Horton for beer £134," 19 February 80; TJ "Pd. Giovanni for thread £4-16," 20 February 80.

1779 October 9. TJ "Gave Mrs. Jefferson for houshold expences £11-2." [TJA 487]

NOTE: TJ also relies on Martin Hemings a great deal for handling household expenses. See memorandum book.

1779 October 15. TJ gave "Mrs. Jefferson to buy sundries £8-8. Pd. Mrs. Hallam entrance for Patsy £24." [TJA 487]

1779 October 16. TJ gave "Mrs. Jefferson £19-10." [TJA 488]

1779 October 24. TJ to Mary Willing Byrd: [Williamsburg] "Mrs. Jefferson presents her respects to yourself and the young ladies." [TJP]

1779 November 3. TJ "Gave Mrs. Jefferson for sundries £9-18." [TJA 488]

1779 November 8. TJ "Gave Mrs. Jefferson £15." [TJA 488]

1779 November 10. TJ "Gave Mrs. Jeff. 30/." [TJA 489]

1779 December 4. Baron Riedesel to TJ: [New York] "I presume to request you will present my respects and Madame de Riedesels best Compliments to Mrs. Jefferson, whose very amiable Character and the many proofs which we have experienced of Her Friendship can never be effaced from out of our Memory, and she will ever possess a high rank among Madame de R's particular Friends." [TJP]

1779 December 8. TJ gave "Mrs. Jefferson £70." [TJA 489]

1779 December 10. TJ gave "Mrs. Jefferson 30/" [TJA 489]

1779 December 20. TJ "Pd. Dr. Sequeyra 5. days attendance £45." [TJA 489]

1779 December 20. TJ "Gave Mrs. Jefferson £300." [TJA 489]

1779 December 25. TJ "Gave Christmas gifts 48/" [TJA 490]

1779 December 30. TJ "Recd. back of Mrs. Jefferson 30/ . . . Note of the £300 given Mrs. Jefferson ante December. 20. £8-8 was pd. in hhd. expen[ces]." [TJA 490]

1779 December 31. TJ "Pd. Dr. Mcclurgh for 5. visits £125." [TJA 490]

1780. Hessian officer, Jacob Rubsamen, who visits Monticello 1780, notes, "You will find in his house an elegant harpsichord piano forte and some violins. The latter he performs well upon himself, the former his lady touches very skillfully and who, is in all respects a very agreeable sensible and accomplished lady." [TJP]

1780 January 11. TJ "Gave Mrs. Jefferson for sundries £49-10." [TJA 490]

1780 January 15. TJ "Pd. Mrs. Hallam 1st. quarter for Patsy's dancing £20-2." [TJA 490]

1780 January 17. TJ "Gave Mrs. Jefferson £3." [TJA 490]

1780 January 28. TJ "Gave Mrs. Jefferson for sundries £22-14." [TJA 491]

1780 January 31. TJ gave "Mrs. Jefferson for sundries £21-6." [TJA 491]

1780 February 2. TJ "Pd. into Treasury in discharge of Mr. Wayles's debt to Farrell & Jones £1666-13-8." [TJA 491]

1780 February 4. TJ "Gave Mrs. Jefferson to pay for an apron £119-10s." [TJA 491]

1780 February 10. Baron Riedesel to TJ: [New York] "For your very polite recollection and kind Compliments as well, as those from Your Lady, to whom please to present my best respects, myself and Madame de Riedesel return you our most perfect thanks, requesting you will be persuaded that nothing can ever efface from our Memory the Esteem we have for so respectable a Family from whom we received so many instances of Friendship. Madme: de Riedesel, whose sentiments are united with mine, charges me with Her Compliments to Yourself and Mrs. Jefferson; and believe me to hear of the Continuation of the Health and Happiness of you and Yours will ever be most pleasing to us both." [TJP]

1780 February 11. TJ "Gave Mrs. Jefferson £2-14." [TJA 492]

1780 February 14. TJ "Gave Mrs. Jefferson £6-6." [TJA 492]

1780 February 15. TJ "Gave Mrs. Jefferson 6/" [TJA 492]

1780 February 16. TJ "Pd. [Beall] for Mrs. Jefferson £25-1." [TJA 492]

1780 February 19. TJ "Gave Mrs. Jefferson for sundries £30-12 ... Gave Mrs. Jefferson £24." [TJA 492]

1780 February 20. TJ "Gave our negroes to buy meat £14-15." [TJA 492]

1780 February 20. TJ leaves Williamsburg. Martha and family remain in town.

1780 March c15. TJ returns.

1780 March 20. TJ "Recd. from Greenhow what had been twice pd. £7-10."

1780 March 20. TJ gave "Mrs. Jefferson for sundries £3." [TJA 493]

1780 March 25. TJ "Gave Mrs. Jefferson to purchase sundr. £165-8." [TJA 494]

1780 March 26. TJ notes "Plumbs, peaches, cherries begin to blossom." [TJA 494]

1780 March c28. TJ leaves Williamsburg. Martha and family remain in town.

1780 March 30. Baron Riedesel to TJ: [New York] Cannot "refrain from once more addressing Your Excellency, and repeating my invariable Esteem for you, your Lady, and amiable Family, also testifying the lively rememberance i, and all mine have of your many Civilities and particular politeness to us." [TJP]

1780 April 3. TJ returns. "pd. household expences by Mrs. Jefferson in my absence £30–12 . . . Gave Mrs. Jefferson £3." [TJA 494]

TJ "Exchanged with Mr. Wythe my 3. year old roan horse colt at Elkhill for a sorrel horse (Thor) of his . . . ," 3 April 80; TJ "Pd. Jones the barber £12," 7 April 80; TJ "Pd. Mrs. Hallam 2d. quarter for Patsy £30," 7 April 80; TJ "Pd. Giovanni for cheese £32-8," 7 April 80; TJ "Pd. Craig for mendg. instrument case £20," 7 April 80; TJ "Pd. Wood & Maupin Sadler's acct. £166-8," 7 April 80; TJ "Pd. James Southall in full £125-8," 8 April 80.

1780 April 6. TJ "Gave Mrs. Jefferson £72." [TJA 494]

1780 April 8. TJ "Gave Mrs. Jefferson £26-4." [TJA 495]

1780 April 9. Family leaves Williamsburg for Richmond. [TJA 495]

The recollections of Isaac Jefferson (one of TJ's household slaves) contain the following account of the Governor's removal: "It was cold weather when they moved up. Mr. Jefferson lived in a wooden house near where the Palace (Governor's house) stands now. Richmond was a small place then: not more than two brick houses in the town. . . . It was a wooden house shedded round like a barn on the hill, where the Assemblymen used to meet, near where the Capitol stands now. Old Mr. Wiley had a saddler-shop in the same house." [TJP]

APPENDIX B

CHRONOLOGY OF THE JEFFERSONS, WAYLES, AND HEMINGS FAMILY

1741: John Wayles, Martha Jefferson's father, formerly of England, receives license to practice law in Virginia.

1743: Thomas Jefferson born April 13 in Albemarle County, Virginia.

1746: John Wayles marries Martha Eppes Eppes of Henrico County and signs a prenuptial agreement spelling out names of slaves coming to Martha from father and brother; list includes "Jenny" and "Betty, & Ben, a boy"; Wayles and wife to receive money from lease of the slaves.

1748: Martha Wayles (later to marry Jefferson) born in Charles City County; mother dies soon after the birth.

1749: John Wayles marries Tabitha Cocke after first wife dies; three more daughters from this marriage survive infancy.

1753: William Hemings, tavern keeper and merchant in Essex County, dies; his inventory lists "Bess and Ben, a boy."

1760: John Wayles marries Elizabeth Lomax Skelton—formerly of Essex County—after his second wife dies.

1760: John Wayles writes will and specifically asks that daughter Martha Wayles allow "Jenny the cook and Betty Hemings" to remain and care for his wife, Elizabeth, for the rest of wife's life, then to pass to Martha, as defined by the prior agreement.

1761: Elizabeth Lomax Skelton Wayles dies.

1766: John Wayles becomes involved in "Colonel Chiswell murder scandal" and meets Colonel Richard Randolph and Thomas Mann Randolph at Chiswell's home.

1766: Wayles settles some of Colonel Richard Randolph's debt owed to Bristol, England, merchants Farrell & Jones.

1766: Martha Wayles marries Bathurst Skelton, formerly of Essex County and younger brother-in-law of the deceased Elizabeth Skelton Wayles.

1767: John Wayles slandered unmercifully in *Virginia Gazette*, January.

1767: Francis Eppes (nephew of John and deceased Martha Wayles) begins to appear on legal papers as regular witness with John Wayles.

1768: Bathurst Skelton dies in Goochland County, leaving widow and son, along with estate of land and slaves (son, John, dies in 1771).

1772: Thomas Jefferson marries Martha Wayles Skelton on January 1.

1772: John Wayles "partnered" briefly with Colonel Richard Randolph by Farrell & Jones to arrange for sale of African slaves from the ship *Prince of Wales*; Farrell & Jones were insurers of the voyage.

1773: Wayles ill again in February and dies in May in Charles City County.

1773: Sally Hemings born to Betty Hemings.

1780: David Meade Randolph (son of Colonel Richard Randolph) marries Mary Randolph (daughter of Thomas Mann Randolph).

1782: Martha Wayles Jefferson dies at Monticello; three daughters survive.

1785: Thomas Jefferson goes to Paris, taking oldest daughter, Martha (daughters Mary and Lucy Jefferson stay in Virginia with "Aunt Eppes," Mrs. Elizabeth Wayles Eppes.

1786: Lucy Jefferson dies of whooping cough in Virginia at home of "Aunt Eppes" and (uncle) Francis Eppes in Chesterfield County.

1788: Polly "Maria" Jefferson goes to Paris, accompanied by Sally Hemings, as an older woman specified by Thomas Jefferson is pregnant and cannot travel.

1790: Jefferson returns to Virginia with daughters and entourage and becomes the first secretary of state.

1791: Martha "Patsy" Jefferson marries Thomas Mann Randolph Jr.

1791: Farrell & Jones file suit in federal court against Jefferson, et al., and David Meade Randolph, et al.

1791: Jefferson arranges appointment of David Meade Randolph as federal marshal of eastern district of Virginia.

1793: David Meade Randolph and brothers refuse to pay debts of Colonel Richard Randolph; debt holders take aim at Jefferson and brothers-in-law.

1793: Jefferson and Francis Eppes bring suit against Randolph brothers in Richmond over debts of Colonel Richard Randolph.

1793: High Court of Chancery decision goes to Jefferson and brothers-in-law; Randolph brothers appeal.

1797: Maria Jefferson marries John Wayles Eppes, son of Francis Eppes and Elizabeth Wayles Eppes; they live in Bermuda Hundred; Eppes practices law in Richmond and Chesterfield County.

1799: Virginia Court of Appeals sides with Randolph brothers and reverses Chancery Court decision, leaving Jefferson and brothers-in-law with a debt from Colonel Richard Randolph for which John Wayles was surety.

1799: David Meade Randolph and Molly leave Bermuda Hundred area for elaborate new home in Richmond.

1800: James T. Callender guilty of sedition in Richmond; nine months in jail.

1801: Thomas Jefferson elected third president of the United States of America in a multiple-ballot election in the U.S. House of Representatives.

1801: Jefferson fires David Meade Randolph as marshal in Virginia; accuses him of "packing juries."

1801: Jefferson pardons James T. Callender and another man on sedition charges; because both are already out of prison, fines are to be repaid to them.

1801: Callender demands job as Richmond postmaster (refused).

1801: Callender finally receives his $200 fine months later, returned by former marshal David Meade Randolph.

1802: John Wayles Eppes announces for Congress on June 25, 1802, to replace resigning Republican William Branch Giles, and is unopposed in district.

1802: James T. Callender prints the infamous "SALLY" story in *Recorder*.

1802: James T. Callender prints a diatribe about Ferdinando Fairfax, similar to ones against Jefferson, while admitting in the same issue that he knows nothing about Fairfax.

1802: Meriwether Jones at *Richmond Examiner* reports that David Meade Randolph had sent the subscription of Callender's *Recorder* to Ferdinando Fairfax; Fairfax sent the newspapers back to Callender as "bawdry."

1802: Story begins to circulate among Federalists that not only was Jefferson involved with "Sally," but that her father was Jefferson's father-in-law, John Wayles.

1804: Jefferson reelected president of the United States by "landslide," and Maria Jefferson Eppes dies at Monticello after childbirth.

1804: David Meade Randolph's grand house in Richmond auctioned for benefit of creditors in December.

1805: Smear against Jefferson in January Boston newspaper brings a defender in Massachusetts House to attempt to remove the printers of the paper from a state contract. Motion provokes debates in Massachusetts legislature about Jefferson's character. Motion on removing contract fails.

1805: Boston newspaper reprints the charges of Callender in May, although it adds to Callender's stories that "Wales" was father of infamous "Sally" and highlights Jefferson's attempted affair with Betsy Walker in 1767.

1805: Jefferson writes letter to two cabinet members twelve days after the *Washington Federalist* reprints the Boston article, and he denies all but one charge in the article (Jefferson says part of the Betsy Walker story was true, all else false). Newspapers with slanderous stories reach Monticello.

1809: Jefferson retires from presidency, but his party continues another sixteen years in the presidency, and the Federalist party disappears.

1826: Jefferson dies on July 4 at Monticello on fiftieth anniversary of the Declaration of Independence.

1861: War erupts between North and South.

1872: Thomas Jefferson Randolph opens the 1872 Democratic Party convention in Baltimore.

1873: Second inauguration of Ulysses S. Grant as president who ran again as a "Republican."

1873: Samuel F. Wetmore, printer and editor, features Madison Hemings's story in his *Pike County* (Ohio) *Republican* newspaper.

1951: Wetmore/Hemings article rediscovered in Ohio archives.

1974: Fawn Brodie book proposes thirty-eight-year-long affair between Jefferson and Sally Hemings based on Callender, Wetmore/Hemings article, and her psychological interpretations of Jefferson letters in Paris about other subjects.

1998: *Nature* article reports DNA evidence to "prove" Jefferson-Hemings liaison on eve of 1998 Congressional elections, just as original Callender story printed on the eve of 1802 Congressional election.

ACKNOWLEDGMENTS

This book could not have been written without the valuable assistance of Dr. Ken Wallenborn, whose meticulous research and valuable comments saved me from various errors and contributed immensely to improving my rough manuscript.

I am also grateful to several colleagues who lent their valuable time in critically reading all or part of the manuscript. I have benefited from their comments: Art Downey, Eric Petersen, Tom Fleming, and Cyndi Burton.

I would also like to thank Richard Dixon and the Thomas Jefferson Heritage Society for their support and guidance to scholarly materials. Similar gratitude is owed to the staff at the Alderman Library at the University of Virginia (Special Collections Department) who provided me with valuable research material.

No book is complete without the assistance of a passionate editor, Jon Sisk, who took a controversial manuscript and shaped it into a readable book. I also wish to thank my literary agent, Jim Fitzgerald, who began it all and kept me on track.

NOTES

PROLOGUE

1. David McCullough, *John Adams*, iBook edition, p. 22.

2. Gordon Wood, *Revolutionary Characters*, iBook edition, p. 198.

3. Jon Meacham, *Jefferson, The Art of Power*, iBook edition, p. 384; Merrill D. Peterson, *Visitors to Monticello*, pp. 8–9.

4. Virginia Scharff, *The Women Jefferson Loved*, iBook edition, p. 226; Ellen Randolph Coolidge, *Domestic Life*, pp. 43–44.

5. Scharff, *The Women Jefferson Loved*, iBook edition, pp. 226–27; Coolidge, *Domestic Life*, p. 66.

6. Henry Wiencek, *Master of the Mountain*, p. 31; Henry S. Randall, *Life of Thomas Jefferson*, vol. 1, p. 63.

7. Randall, *Life of Thomas Jefferson*, vol. 1, pp. 62–64; see, in general, Monticello's website, http://www.monticello.org/site/jefferson/martha-wayles-skelton-jefferson.

8. Thomas Fleming, *The Intimate Lives of the Founding Fathers*, iBook edition, p. 23.

9. Malone, *Jefferson The Virginian*, p. 397.

CHAPTER 1

1. Douglas Anderson, "Subterraneous Virginia: The Ethical Poetics of Thomas Jefferson," *Eighteenth-Century Studies* 33(2/Colonial Encounters: Winter 2000), 233–49. Published by Johns Hopkins University Press for the American Society for Eighteenth-Century Studies. http://www.jstor.org/stable/30053684. Accessed March 8, 2012.

2. See, in general, Annette Gordon-Reed (AGR), *The Hemingses of Monticello*, iBook edition, p. 147.

3. AGR, *The Hemingses*, iBook edition, p. 147.

4. AGR, *Hemingses*, iBook edition, p. 150.

5. Susan Kern, *The Jeffersons at Shadwell*, Kindle edition, pp. 608–12.

6. Kern, *The Jeffersons at Shadwell*, Kindle edition, p. 620.

7. Dan Guzy, "The 1736 Survey of the Potomac River," *Virginia Magazine*, 122(1): 11, 28.

8. Kern, *The Jeffersons at Shadwell*, Kindle edition, pp. 630–39.

CHAPTER 2

1. Rebecca L. McMurry and James F. McMurry Jr., *Anatomy of a Scandal: Thomas Jefferson & the Sally Story*.

2. Maurer Maurer, "A Musical Family in Colonial Virginia," *The Musical Quarterly*, 34(3/July 1948): 358–64, published by Oxford University Press. Available at http://www.jstor.org/stable/739548; accessed December 28, 2012; see also, G. Sonneck, *Early Opera in America* (New York, 1915), pp. 23–24, 44, passim; John Rogers Williams (ed.), *Philip Vickers Fithian Journal and Letters, 1767–1774* (Princeton, 1900), pp. 51, 56, 57, et seq.; Mary Newton Stanard, *Colonial Virginia: Its People and Customs* (Philadelphia, 1917), p. 313.

3. Maurer, "A Musical Family in Colonial Virginia," 358–64; see also, Sonneck, *Early Opera in America*; Williams, *Philip Vickers Fithian Journal and Letters, 1767–1774*; Mary Newton Stanard, *Colonial Virginia: Its People and Customs*.

4. AGR, *Hemingses*, iBook edition, pp. 154–56.

5. AGR, *Hemingses*, iBook edition, pp. 156–57.

6. P. Burwell Rogers, "Tidewater Virginians Name Their Homes," *American Speech*, 34(4/December 1959), 251–57, published by Duke University Press. Available at http://www.jstor.org/stable/453703; accessed December 28, 2012.

7. AGR, *Hemingses*, iBook edition, p. 136.

8. AGR, *Hemingses*, iBook edition, p. 136.

9. AGR, *Hemingses*, iBook edition, p. 154.

10. AGR, *Hemingses*, iBook edition, p. 154

11. AGR, *Hemingses*, iBook edition, p. 154.

12. AGR, *Hemingses*, iBook edition, p. 154.

13. AGR, *Hemingses*, iBook edition, p. 143.

14. Marie Kimball, *Jefferson: The Road to Glory, 1743 to 1776* (New York: Coward-McCann, 1943), pp. 169, 166–86.

15. Sarah N. Randolph, *The Domestic Life of Thomas Jefferson*, p. 343 (hereafter TDLTJ); Jon Meacham, *Jefferson and the Art of Power*, iBook edition, p. 324.

16. Meacham, *Jefferson*, iBook edition, p. 343; TDLTJ, p. 344.

17. Meacham, *Jefferson*, iBook edition, p. 343; see also Monticello website, http://www.monticello.org/site/jefferson/martha-wayles-skelton-jefferson.

18. Scharff, *The Women Jefferson Loved*, iBook edition, pp. 378–80.

19. Lucia Stanton, *Free Some Day*, pp. 103–4.

20. Gordon Wood, *Revolutionary Characters*, iBook edition, p. 34.

21. Wood, *Revolutionary Characters*, iBook edition, p. 35.

22. Randall, *Jefferson*, pp. 63–66; Jack McLaughlin, *Jefferson and Monticello: The Biography of a Builder*, p. 187.

23. McLaughlin, *Jefferson and Monticello*, p. 187.

24. See, in general, Jon Meacham, *Jefferson, The Art of Power*, iBook edition, pp. 390–416; Thomas Fleming, *The Intimate Lives of the Founding Fathers*, iBook edition, pp. 1134–54; Scharff, *The Women Jefferson Loved*, iBook edition, pp. 264–94; see, in general, Roberta Grimes, *My Thomas: A Novel of Martha Jefferson's Life*.

25. James A. Bear and Lucia Stanton, *Jefferson's Memorandum Book*, 2 volumes (hereafter MB) vol. 1, p. 334; Stanton, *Free Some Day*, pp. 33–34; see also, in general, Monticello website, http://www.monticello.org/site/jefferson/martha-wayles-skelton-jefferson; Scharff, *The Women Jefferson Loved*, iBook edition, p. 301.

26. MB, vol. 1, p. 334; Wiencek, *Master of the Mountain*, p. 35; Stanton, *Free Some Day*, pp. 33–34; see, in general, Monticello website, http://www.monticello.org/site/jefferson/martha-wayles-skelton-jefferson; Scharff, *The Women Jefferson Loved*, iBook edition, 301.

27. Barton, *The Jefferson Lies*, p. 91; Paul Leicester Ford, ed., *The Writings of Thomas Jefferson*, vol. 11, p. 264.

28. Barton, *The Jefferson Lies*, pp. 99–100; Ford, *The Writings of Thomas Jefferson*, vol. 11, p. 417; Andre Lipscomb, ed., *The Writings of Thomas Jefferson*, vol. 1, p. 4.

29. Barton, *The Jefferson Lies*, iBook edition, p. 99; Paul Leicester Ford, *The Writings of Thomas Jefferson*, vol. 1, p. 474.

30. Barton, *The Jefferson Lies*, iBook edition, p. 100; Julian Boyd, *The Papers of Thomas Jefferson*, vol. 1., p. 130.

31. Thomas Jefferson, *Rough Draft of the Declaration of Independence*; available at ushistory.org.

32. Thomas Jefferson, *Memoir, Correspondence and Miscellanie*, ed. Thomas Jefferson Randolph (New York: G& CH Carville, 1830), vol. 1, p. 16.

33. Monticello website, http://www.monticello.org/site/plantation-and-slavery/thomas-jefferson-and-slavery.

34. Virginia Act XXI. An Act to Authorize the Manumission of Slaves, University of Virginia, 1782, digital collection.

35. Ford, *The Writings of Thomas Jefferson*, vol. 11, p. 238.

36. Merrill D. Peterson, *Thomas Jefferson and the New Nation* (New York: Oxford University Press, 1970), p. 153.

37. Jack P. Greene, "The Intellectual Reconstruction of Virginia in the Age of Jefferson," in *Jeffersonian Legacies*, ed. Peter S. Onuf (Charlottesville: University of Virginia Press, 1993), pp. 229, 244.

38. Joseph J. Ellis, *American Sphinx: The Character of Thomas Jefferson* (New York: Knopf, 1997), p. 246.

39. Catherine G. Obrion, "Morris versus Cravens," *Library of Virginia Broadside*, Winter 2014, 2.

CHAPTER 3

1. Scharff, *The Women Jefferson Loved*, iBook edition, p. 203.

2. McMurry and McMurry, *Anatomy of a Scandal*, pp. 16–18.

3. Lancashire Record Office, Records of St. Mary's Parish, St. Mary Ref. PR3262/1/2, Jan. 1714–March 25/1724; AGR, *Hemingses*, iBook edition, p. 161.

4. Daniel Dafoe, *A Tour through the Whole Island of Great Britain*, ed. Pat Rogers (Exeter, 1989), 195, 193; AGR, *Hemingses*, iBook edition, p. 162.

5. AGR, *Hemingses*, iBook edition, p. 162.

6. AGR, *Hemingses*, iBook edition, p. 162.

7. AGR, *Hemingses*, iBook edition, p. 162.

8. Gordon-Reed, *The Hemingses of Monticello*, iBook edition, pp. 207–8.

9. Genealogical Notes of the Lee Family, Papers of Richard Bland Lee, MSS1L5153 b 13–16, VHS; AGR, *Hemingses*, iBook edition, p. 168.

10. "Virginia Gleanings in England," *VMHB* 19 (1911), p. 289. Charles Campbell, Life of Isaac Jefferson of Petersburg, Virginia, Blacksmith, *WMQ* 3rd ser. 8 (1951); AGR, *Hemingses*, iBook edition, p. 170.

11. Virginia B. Price, "Constructing to Command: Rivalries between Green Spring and the Governor's Palace, 1677–1722," *VMHB* 113 (2005), 2–45; AGR, *Hemingses*, iBook edition, p. 172.

12. "Williamsburg—The Old Colonial Capital," 9, 10. *WMQ* 16 (1907), 33; AGR, *Hemingses*, iBook edition, p. 180.

13. "Williamsburg—The Old Colonial Capital"; AGR, *Hemingses*, iBook edition, p. 180.

14. A. G. Roeber, "Authority, Law, and Custom: The Rituals of Court Day in Tidewater Virginia, 1720 to 1750," *WMQ* 3rd ser., 37 (1980), 29–52; AGR, *Hemingses*, iBook edition, p. 182.

15. AGR, *Hemingses*, iBook edition, p. 192.

16. McLaughlin, *Jefferson and Monticello*, iBook edition, p. 495.

17. Gordon-Reed, *The Hemingses of Monticello*, iBook edition, pp. 158–59.

18. AGR, *Hemingses*, iBook edition, p. 192.

19. Papers of William Jones, Somerset Record Office, Somerset, England; AGR, *Hemingses*, iBook edition, p. 198.

20. AGR, *Hemingses*, iBook edition, p. 199.

21. John M. Hemphill II, ed., "John Wayles Rates His Neighbors," *VMHB* 66 (1958), 302–6; AGR, *Hemingses*, iBook edition, p. 201.

22. Hemphill, "John Wayles Rates His Neighbors"; AGR, *Hemingses*, iBook edition, p. 201.

23. Hemphill, "John Wayles Rates His Neighbors"; AGR, *Hemingses*, iBook edition, p. 201.

24. Hemphill, "John Wayles Rates His Neighbors"; AGR, *Hemingses*, iBook edition, p. 201.

25. See, in general, ACR, *Hemingses of Monticello*; Jon Kukla, *Jefferson's Women*.

26. Scharff, *The Women Jefferson Loved*, Kindle edition, pp. 1259–260.

CHAPTER 4

1. Jon Kukla, *Jefferson's Women*, iBook edition, p. 211.

2. Roberta Grimes, *My Thomas*, iBook edition, p. 10.

3. Marie Kimball, *The Road to Glory*, p. 169.

4. Mrs. Mildred Campbell Whitaker, of St. Louis, Missouri. In her recent book on "Genealogy," in her letter published in the "Forum" of the *News Leader* (Richmond, Va.) January 24, 1929.

5. Albert J. Nock, *Mr. Jefferson* (Tampa, FL: Hallberg Publishing Corporation, 1983).

6. Mrs. Mildred Campbell Whitaker, of St. Louis, Missouri. In her recent book on "Genealogy," in her letter published in the "Forum" of the *News Leader* (Richmond, Virginia), January 24, 1929.

7. Kimball, *The Road to Glory*, p. 324 n. 11.

8. Kimball, *The Road to Glory*, p. 324 n. 11.

9. Scharff, *The Women Jefferson Loved*, Kindle edition, 1367–368.

10. Scharff, *The Women Jefferson Loved*, iBook edition, p. 243.

11. Grimes, *My Thomas*, iBook edition, pp. 36–37.

12. Grimes, *My Thomas*, iBook edition, pp. 37–38.

CHAPTER 5

1. TDLTJ, p. 20; Meacham, *Jefferson*, iBook edition, p. 99.

2. Cynthia A. Kierner, "'The Dark and Dense Cloud Perpetually Lowering over Us': Gender and the Decline of the Gentry in Postrevolutionary Virginia,"

Journal of the Early Republic 20 (2/Summer 2000), 185–217. Published by University of Pennsylvania Press on behalf of the Society for Historians of the Early American Republic. http://www.jstor.org/stable/3124701. Accessed August 15, 2012; 1 Marquis de Chastellux, *Travels in North America in the Years 1780, 1781 and 1782*, ed. Howard C. Rice Jr., 2 vols. (Chapel Hill: University of North Carolina Press, 1963), vol. II, p. 427.

3. McLaughlin, *Jefferson and Monticello*, p. 17.

4. Susan Kern, *The Jeffersons at Shadwell*, pp. 239–40.

5. Kern, *The Jeffersons at Shadwell*, p. 240.

6. Fleming, *Intimate Lives*, iBook edition, p. 890.

7. Fleming, *Intimate Lives*, iBook edition, p. 890.

8. McLaughlin, *Jefferson and Monticello*, iBook edition, p. 498.

9. Fleming, *Intimate Lives*, iBook edition, p. 890.

10. TJ to John Page, October 7, 1763, PTJ, vol. 1, pp. 11–12; Fleming, *Intimate Lives*, iBook edition, p. 898.

11. TJ to John Page, October 7, 1763, PTJ, vol. 1, pp. 11–12; Fleming, *Intimate Lives*, iBook edition, p. 898.

12. Gordon Wood, *Revolutionary Characters*, iBook edition, pp. 66–67.

13. Meacham, *Jefferson*; Kern, *The Jeffersons at Shadwell*, pp. 29, 33–38, 43.

14. Kern, *The Jeffersons at Shadwell*, Kindle edition, pp. 605–6.

15. Malone's unpublished manuscript, p. l-j–vi-14m, Merrill Peterson papers; see also William G. Hyland, *Long Journey with Mr. Jefferson*.

16. *Papers of Thomas Jefferson Retirement Series* (hereafter PTJRS), vol. VIII, p. 544; Meacham, *The Art of Power*, iBook edition, p. 33; "the Blue Ridge Mountains were named by European settlers because from a distance the atmosphere makes them look that color." Mazzei, *My Life and Wanderings*, p. 202.

17. Lee Wilkins, "Madison and Jefferson: The Making of a Friendship," *Political Psychology* 12 (4/December 1991), 593–608. Published by International Society of Political Psychology. http://www.jstor.org/stable/3791548, p. 595.

18. McCullough, *John Adams*, iBook edition, p. 456.

19. Kern, *The Jeffersons at Shadwell*, Kindle edition, p. 620.

20. Kern, *The Jeffersons at Shadwell*, Kindle edition, p. 383.

21. Kern, *The Jeffersons at Shadwell*, Kindle edition, p. 383.

22. Kern, *The Jeffersons at Shadwell*, Kindle edition, p. 383.

23. Kern, *The Jeffersons at Shadwell*, Kindle edition, p. 678.

24. Kern, "The Material World of the Jeffersons at Shadwell," *WMQ*, 3rd ser., 62 (2/April 2005), 213–42. Published by Omohundro Institute of Early American History and Culture. http://www.jstor.org/stable/3491600. Accessed January 14, 2012.

25. Randall, *Jefferson*, vol. 1, p. 2; Kern, *The Jeffersons at Shadwell*, Kindle edition, p. 832; Kern, "Archaeological Investigations at Shadwell," pp. 54–65; see footnote 5 for comparative sizes.

26. Randall, *Jefferson*, vol. 1, p. 2; Kern, *The Jeffersons at Shadwell*, Kindle edition, p. 832; Kern, "Archaeological Investigations at Shadwell," pp. 54–65.

27. Randall, *Jefferson*, vol. 1, p. 2; Kern, *The Jeffersons at Shadwell*, Kindle edition, p. 832; Kern, "Archaeological Investigations at Shadwell," pp. 54–65.

28. Mss 4726-a Randolph-Meikleham Family Papers, 1792–1882, ViU; Kern, *The Jeffersons at Shadwell*, Kindle edition, p. 3035.

29. Kern, *The Jeffersons at Shadwell*, Kindle edition, pp. 3027–33; Mss 4726-a Randolph-Meikleham Family Papers, 1792–1882, ViU.

30. *TDLTJ*, p. 38; Meacham, *The Art of Power*, iBook edition, pp. 60–61.

31. Meacham, *Jefferson*, iBook edition, pp. 200–201; *Papers of Thomas Jefferson*, vol. X, p. 308.

32. Meacham, *Jefferson*, iBook edition, p. 201.

33. Kern, "The Material World of the Jeffersons at Shadwell," *WMQ*, 3rd ser., 62 (2/April 2005), 217; Published by Omohundro Institute of Early American History and Culture. http://www.jstor.org/stable/3491600. Accessed January 14, 2012.

34. Kern, "The Material World of the Jeffersons at Shadwell."

35. Kern, "The Material World of the Jeffersons at Shadwell."

36. Old Style (O.S.) and New Style (N.S.) are sometimes used with dates to indicate that the start of the Julian year has been adjusted to start on January 1.

37. Kern, "The Material World of the Jeffersons at Shadwell."

38. Jefferson Randolph Anderson. "Tuckahoe and the Tuckahoe Randolphs," *Virginia Magazine of History and Biography* 45 (1/January 1937), 55–86. Published by Virginia Historical Society. http://www.jstor.org/stable/4244772. Accessed August 15, 2012, 65–67.

39. Anderson, "Tuckahoe and the Tuckahoe Randolphs."

40. Kern, *The Jeffersons at Shadwell*, p. 70.

41. Randall, *Jefferson*, vol. 1, pp. 16–17; Fawn Brodie, *Thomas Jefferson*, p. 41; Meacham, *The Art of Power*, iBook edition, p. 145.

42. Meacham, *The Art of Power*, iBook edition, p. 146; Kern, *The Jeffersons at Shadwell*, p. 64.

43. Meacham, *The Art of Power*, iBook edition, p. 140.

44. Jefferson, *Writings*, p. 3; Meacham, *The Art of Power*, iBook edition, p. 146.

45. Malone, *Jefferson the Virginian*, vol. 1, pp. 37–38.

46. *PTJ*, vol. 1, p. 409.

47. Kern, *The Jeffersons at Shadwell*; see also http://www.monticello.org/site/jefferson/jane-randolph-jefferson.

48. Albemarle County Will Book (hereafter AICWB), 2:42–43; Kern, *The Jeffersons at Shadwell*, Kindle edition, p. 859.

49. AICWB, vol. 2, pp. 42–43; Kern, *The Jeffersons at Shadwell*, Kindle edition, p. 859.

50. Kern, *The Jeffersons at Shadwell*, Kindle edition, pp. 859, 870.

51. Kern, *The Jeffersons at Shadwell*, Kindle edition, p. 870; see also Barbara G. Carson, *Ambitious Appetites: Dining, Behavior, and Patterns of Consumption in Federal Washington* (Washington, DC: American Institute of Architects Press, 1990) esp. 25–57, 59–70.

51. Kern, *The Jeffersons at Shadwell*, Kindle edition, p. 870; Carson, *Ambitious Appetites*.

CHAPTER 6

1. Kukla, *Mr. Jefferson's Women*, iBook edition, p. 213.

2. Jefferson, *Autobiography, Memoirs, Correspondence and Private Papers of Thomas Jefferson*, Volume 1, i. 4. Ford, ed. (1821); Ford, ed. *The Writings of Thomas Jefferson* (New York: Putnam, 1894).

3. See, in general, McLaughlin, *Jefferson and Monticello*, iBook edition, pp. 2102–3; pp. 2104–5; Thomas Fleming, *The Intimate Lives of the Founding Fathers*, iBook edition, pp. 1764–65; Jon Meacham, *The Art of Power*, iBook edition, pp. 3387–88.

4. Henry Stephens Randall, *The Life of Thomas Jefferson*, p. 63.

5. Randall, *Jefferson*, vol. 1, pp. 63–64; Meacham, *The Art of Power*, iBook edition, p. 339.

6. Randolph, *The Domestic Life of Thomas Jefferson*.

7. Malone, vol. I, p. 397.

8. *PTJ* vol. 1, p. 84; Meacham, *Thomas Jefferson*, iBook edition, p. 340.

9. Fleming, *Intimate Lives*, iBook edition, p. 908.

10. McLaughlin, *Jefferson and Monticello*, iBook edition, p. 20.

11. Ron Chernow, *Washington*, iBook edition, p. 1639: "Whatever their later differences, Jefferson started out by venerating Washington; he had once identified Washington, along with Benjamin Franklin and David Rittenhouse, as one of three geniuses America had spawned. 'In war we have produced a Washington, whose memory will be adored while liberty shall have votaries, whose name shall triumph over time.'"

12. *Life*, vol. 1, pp. 33–34; Scharff, *The Women Jefferson Loved*, iBook edition, p. 249.

13. McCullough, *John Adams*, iBook edition, p. 453.

14. Meacham, *Jefferson*, iBook edition, p. 340; *PTJ*, p. 84.

15. *TDLTJ*, p. 343; Meacham, *Thomas Jefferson*, iBook edition, p. 341.

16. Meacham, *The Art of Power*, iBook edition p. 341; *PTJ*, vol. 1, p. 247.

17. Meacham, *The Art of Power*, iBook edition, p. 341.

18. *PTJ*, vol. 1, pp. 62, 71; Meacham, *The Art of Power*, iBook edition, pp. 388–89.

19. Jefferson's stuttering marriage proposal to Rebecca Burwell while he was a student at the College of William and Mary ended in her flat rejection.

20. Randall, *Life*, 1:63–64.

21. Kukla, *Mr. Jefferson's Women*, pp. 214–15; Mary Deverell, "On Marriage, Addressed to a Sister," in *The Ladies Literary Companion* (Burlington, NJ, 1792), pp. 82–83.

22. Gordon Wood, *Revolutionary Characters*, iBook edition, p. 193.

23. Fleming, *Intimate Lives*, iBook edition, p. 897.

24. Although historical fiction, Martha Grimes's historical novel is both meticulously accurate and sheds light on the life of Martha Jefferson; see Grimes, *My Thomas*, p. 4.

25. To James Ogilvie, February 20, 1771, *PTJ*, vol. 1, p. 63; Fleming, *Intimate Lives*, iBook edition, p. 913.

CHAPTER 7

1. Grimes, *My Thomas*, iBook edition, p. 27.

2. Fleming, *Intimate Lives*, iBook edition, p. 914.

3. Scharff, *The Women Jefferson Loved*, iBook edition, 322.

4. *Life*, vol. 1, p. 65; Scharff, *The Women Jefferson Loved*, iBook edition, p. 258.

5. Fleming, *Intimate Lives*, iBook edition, pp. 16–18; Scharff, *The Women Jefferson Loved*, iBook edition, p. 258.

6. Fleming, *Intimate Lives*, iBook edition, p. 897.

7. Fleming, *Intimate Lives*, iBook edition, p. 1150–151.

8. Meacham, *Jefferson, The Art of Power*, iBook edition, 419–20.

9. Virginia Scharff, *The Women Jefferson Loved*, iBook edition, 315–16.

10. Sowerby, pp. 4, 445–47.

11. Sarah Randolph, *Domestic Life*, p. 39.

12. Meacham, *The Art of Power*, iBook edition, p. 386; *TDLTJ*, p. 47.

13. Andrew Burstein and Catherine Mowbray, "Jefferson and Sterne," *Early American Literature*, 29 (1/1994), 19–34. Published by University of North Carolina Press. http://www.jstor.org/stable/250569. Accessed August 24, 2012.

14. TJ to James Ogilvie, February 20, 1771, *Papers of Thomas Jefferson,* Julian Boyd, ed., vol. 1, pp. 62–63; Scharff, *The Women Jefferson Loved,* iBook edition, p. 255.

15. Fleming, *Intimate Lives,* iBook edition, p. 914; Marie Kimball, *Jefferson, The Road to Glory,* pp. 174–75.

16. Fleming, *Intimate Lives,* iBook edition, pp. 27–28.

17. Fleming, *Intimate Lives,* iBook edition, pp. 16–18.

18. *PTJ,* vol. 1, pp. 86–87; Meacham, *The Art of Power,* iBook edition, p. 372.

19. Grimes, *My Thomas,* Kindle edition, p. 53.

20. Scharff, *The Women Jefferson Loved,* iBook edition, p. 208; Ford, ed., *Autobiography,* vol. 1, p. 6.

21. *Virginia Gazette,* January 2, 1772; Meacham, *The Art of Power,* iBook edition, pp. 370–71.

22. Scharff, *The Women Jefferson Loved,* iBook edition, p. 275.

23. Scharff, *The Women Jefferson Loved,* iBook edition, p. 277.

24. Scharff, *The Women Jefferson Loved,* iBook edition, p. 277.

25. Scharff, *The Women Jefferson Loved,* iBook edition, p. 277.

26. Scharff, *The Women Jefferson Loved,* iBook edition, p. 342.

27. *Jefferson's Memorandum Book (MB),* vol. 1, p. 285; Scharff, *The Women Jefferson Loved,* iBook edition, p. 274.

28. McLaughlin, *Jefferson and Monticello,* iBook edition, p. 511.

29. McLaughlin, *Jefferson and Monticello,* iBook edition, p. 512.

30. Scharff, *The Women Jefferson Loved,* iBook edition, pp. 281–84; see also Kukla, *Mr. Jefferson's Women,* Kindle edition, pp. 1248–49.

31. Kukla, *Mr. Jefferson's Women,* Kindle edition, pp. 1256–57; Martha Jefferson Randolph quoted in Randall, *Life of Thomas Jefferson,* vol. 1, p. 64.

32. Kukla, *Mr. Jefferson's Women,* Kindle edition, p. 1255; Martha Jefferson Randolph quoted in Randall, *Life of Thomas Jefferson,* vol. 1, p. 64.

33. Scharff, *The Women Jefferson Loved,* iBook edition, pp. 281–84.

34. Kukla, *Mr. Jefferson's Women,* Kindle edition, p. 1255; Martha Jefferson Randolph quoted in Randall, *Life of Thomas Jefferson,* vol. 1, p. 64.

35. Scharff, *The Women Jefferson Loved,* iBook edition, pp. 281–84.

36. Scharff, *The Women Jefferson Loved,* iBook edition, pp. 283; Sarah Randolph, *The Domestic Life of Thomas Jefferson,* pp. 64–65; Parton, *Life of Thomas Jefferson,* p. 103.

CHAPTER 8

1. *Papers of Thomas Jefferson* (hereafter *PTJ*), vol. XXX, p. 15; Meacham, *Jefferson,* iBook edition, p. 338.

2. Meacham, *Jefferson,* iBook edition, p. 384.

3. Sarah Randolph, *The Domestic Life of Thomas Jefferson*, pp. 64–65.

4. Sarah Randolph, *The Domestic Life of Thomas Jefferson*, pp. 64–65; Parton, *Life of Thomas Jefferson*, p. 103.

5. Fiske Kimball, "Jefferson and the Arts," *Proceedings of the American Philosophical Society*, 87 (3/Bicentennial of Thomas Jefferson, July 14, 1943), 238–45. Published by American Philosophical Society. http://www.jstor.org/stable/984871. Accessed August 24, 2012.

6. Scharff, *The Women Jefferson Loved*, iBook edition, p. 239. Elie Weeks, "Thomas Jefferson's Elk-hill," *Goochland County Historical Society Magazine*, 3 (1/1971), pp. 6–11; Malone, vol. 1, p. 162.

7. Richard T. Couture, "Elk Hill." Paper, University of Virginia, 1965. (Located in VHLC Archives); Mrs. J. F. Bunnett, "Randolph Harrison's Elk Hill," *Goochland County Historical Society Magazine* 8 (1/1976), 3–4; Thomas C. Kennedy, "Randolph Harrison's Elk Hill." *Goochland County Historical Society Magazine*, 5 (2/1973), 3–7; Weeks, "Thomas Jefferson's Elk Hill," 6–8; Goochland County Deed Books 10, 12, 13, 17, 29, 40, 38. Goochland County Land Tax Books 1782–1850.

8. Couture, "Elk Hill"; Bunnett, "Randolph Harrison's Elk Hill"; Goochland County Deed Books 10, 12, 13, 17, 29, 40, 38. Goochland County Land Tax Books 1782–1850.

9. Mark R. Wenger, "Thomas Jefferson, Tenant," *Winterthur Portfolio* 26 (4/Winter 1991), 249–65. Published by the University of Chicago Press on behalf of the Henry Francis du Pont Winterthur Museum, Inc. http://www.jstor.org/stable/1181348. Accessed August 15, 2012; Thomas Anbury, *The Travels through the Interior Parts of North America* (London, 1789), 122–23. The woodwork in the riverfront wing suggests that Tuckahoe was probably expanded to its present form around 1750.

10. After Martha's death and upon his return from his five years in Paris in 1789, Jefferson made substantial architectural changes to Monticello; Marquis de Chastellux, *Travels in North-America in the Years 1780, 1781, and 1782*, 2nd ed., 2 vols. (London, 1787), II, 42; Duke de la Rochefoucauld Liancourt, *Travels Through the United States of North America . . . in the Years 1795, 1796, and 1797 . . .* , 2 vols. (London, 1799), II, 70; John Summerson, *Architecture in Britain, 1530 to 1830* (Harmondsworth, England), 5th ed., 1969, 341; "First Monticello," *Gene Waddell Journal of the Society of Architectural Historians* 46 (1/March 1987), 5–29. Published by University of California Press on behalf of the Society of Architectural Historians. http://www.jstor.org/stable/990142. Accessed August 15, 2012.

11. Chernow, *Washington*, iBook edition, p. 1941.

12. Chernow, *Washington*, iBook edition, p. 1942.

13. Chernow, *Washington*, iBook edition, p. 1942.

14. Fleming, *Intimate Lives*, iBook edition, p. 926; Julia Cherry Spruill, *Women's Life and Work in the Southern Colonies* (New York, 1972), pp. 56–57.

15. McLaughlin, *Jefferson and Monticello*, iBook edition, pp. 248–51.

16. McLaughlin, *Jefferson and Monticello*, iBook edition, p. 802.

17. Scharff, *The Women Jefferson Loved*, Kindle edition, pp. 1663–64.

18. Wiencek, *Master of the Mountain*, iBook edition, pp. 122–23; Bear, *Jefferson at Monticello*, p. 3; Meacham, *The Art of Power*, iBook edition, p. 382.

19. Mazzei, *My Life and Wanderings*, p. 14.

20. Mazzei, *My Life and Wanderings*, p. 209.

21. Mazzei, *My Life and Wanderings*, fn. 57, p. 405.

22. Mazzei, *My Life and Wanderings*, fn. 57, p. 405.

23. Mazzei, *My Life and Wanderings*, fn. 57, p. 405.

24. Mazzei, *My Life and Wanderings*, fn. 57, p. 405.

25. Adrian Higgins, "5 Myths about Cherry Blossoms," *Washington Post*, March 30, 2014, B2.

26. Mazzei, *My Life and Wanderings*, p. 212.

27. Mazzei, *My Life and Wanderings*, p. 212.

28. Mazzei, *My Life and Wanderings*, p. 212.

29. Mazzei, *My Life and Wanderings*, pp. 213–14.

30. Mazzei, *My Life and Wanderings*, fn. 61, p. 406.

31. Mazzei, *My Life and Wanderings*, fn. 81, p. 411.

32. Mazzei, *My Life and Wanderings*, fn. 81, p. 411.

33. Mazzei, *My Life and Wanderings*, p. 228.

CHAPTER 9

1. Meacham, *The Art of Power*, iBook edition, p. 287.

2. Richard Dixon, *Howell v. Netherland*, 1 Va (Jefferson) 49, Virginia Reports (Charlottesville: The Michie Company, Law Publishers, 1903).

3. William Waller Hening, *The Statutes at Large of Virginia*, vol. III, p. 447.

4. Richard Dixon, "Thomas Jefferson: A Lawyers Path to a Legal Philosophy," in *Thomas Jefferson and Philosophy: Essays on the Philosophical Cast of Jefferson's Writings* (Lanham, MD: Lexington Books, 2013).

5. Stanton, *Free Some Day*, p. 19.

6. Stanton, *Free Some Day*, p. 20.

7. Stanton, *Free Some Day*, p. 23. Martha also had a close relationship with servant Betty Brown, Betty Hemings's second daughter, who was given to Martha by her father, John Wayles, upon her marriage to Jefferson. Betty Brown was Martha's personal servant for many years and was apparently an accomplished seamstress. By the 1830s, Betty Brown ("Old Bett") was in her seventies and one

of the last remaining slaves at Monticello, having come to Monticello at the age of twelve.

8. Malone, *Jefferson the Virginian*, pp. 121–22; Thomas Fleming, *Intimate Lives*, iBook edition, p. 930–32.

9. Mazzei, *My Life and Wanderings*, p. 223.

10. Mazzei, *My Life and Wanderings*, p. 223.

11. Mazzei, *My Life and Wanderings*, p. 223.

12. Mazzei, *My Life and Wanderings*, pp. 223–24.

13. Mazzei, *My Life and Wanderings*, pp. 223–24.

14. Henry Wiencek, "The Dark Side of Thomas Jefferson," *Smithsonian Magazine*, October 2012.

15. Chernow, *Washington*, iBook edition, p. 311.

16. William Cohen, "Thomas Jefferson and the Problem of Slavery," *Journal of American History* 56(1969), 503–26; Wood, *Revolutionary Characters*, fn. 8, p. 286.

17. "Old Coke" was the English lawyer that all law students had to read.

18. Parton, *Life of Thomas Jefferson*, p. 101; Scharff, *The Women Jefferson Loved*, iBook edition, pp. 315–16.

19. Thomas Jefferson, Henry Augustine Washington, *The Writings of Thomas Jefferson*, inaugural addresses and messages, 394.

20. Kimball, "Jefferson and the Arts."

21. Wood, *Revolutionary Characters*, iBook edition, p. 199.

CHAPTER 10

1. Scharff, *The Women Jefferson Loved*, iBook edition, p. 368.

2. *Ask the Times*, *Tampa Bay Times*, March 30, 2014, 5P.

3. *PTJ*, vol. 1, p. 489; Meacham, *The Art of Power*, iBook edition, p. 633.

4. Jan Lewis and Kenneth A. Lockridge, "Sally Has Been Sick: Pregnancy and Family Limitation among Virginia Gentry Women, 1780–1830," *Journal of Social History* 22 (1/Autumn 1988), 5–19, at p. 6. Published by Oxford University Press. http://www.jstor.org/stable/3787949. Accessed August 24, 2012; Darrett B. and Anita H. Rutman have hypothesized that Chesapeake women of childbearing age were weakened by malaria. ("Of Agues and Fevers: Malaria in the Early Chesapeake," *William and Mary Quarterly*, 3rd ser., XXXIII [19761 51–2]); Allan Kulikoff, *Tobacco and Slaves: The Development of Southern Cultures in the Chesapeake, 1680–1800* (Chapel Hill, NC, 1986), p. 63. Approximately 30 percent of the women in our sample born 1710–1799 died before age 45; only about 10 percent of women in that cohort were preceded in death by their husbands (men who were, typically, several years older than their wives). The higher female mortality rate may well be related to childbirth and in particular, the debilitating effects of malaria.

For women's fear of childbirth, see also Judith Walzer Leavitt and Whitney Walton, "'Down to Death's Door': Women's Perceptions of Childbirth in America," from *Childbirth: The Beginning of Motherhood, Proceedings of the Second Motherhood Symposium,* April 1981 (Madison, 1982), in Judith Walzer Leavitt, ed., *Women and Health in America* (Madison, 1984), pp. 155–65; and Judith Walzer Leavitt, *Brought to Bed: Childbearing in America,* 1750–1950 (New York, 1986), pp. 20–35.

5. Lewis and Lockridge, *Sally Has Been Sick*; Rutman, "Of Agues and Fevers."

6. Lewis and Lockridge, *Sally Has Been Sick*; Rutman, "Of Agues and Fevers."

7. Lewis and Lockridge, *Sally Has Been Sick*; Rutman "Of Agues and Fevers."

8. Lewis and Lockridge, *Sally Has Been Sick*; Rutman "Of Agues and Fevers."

9. Lewis and Lockridge, *Sally Has Been Sick*; Rutman "Of Agues and Fevers."

10. Lewis and Lockridge, *Sally Has Been Sick*; Rutman "Of Agues and Fevers."

11. Gordon-Reed, *The Hemingses of Monticello,* iBook edition, pp. 462–64.

12. Gordon-Reed, *The Hemingses of Monticello,* iBook edition, pp. 462-465.

13. McLaughlin, *Jefferson and Monticello,* p. 188.

14. Monticello website, http://www.monticello.org/site/research-and -collections/Christmas.

15. Monticello website, http://www.monticello.org/site/research-and -collections/Christmas.

16. Monticello website, http://www.monticello.org/site/research-and -collections/Christmas.

17. Monticello website, http://www.monticello.org/site/research-and -collections/Christmas.

18. Monticello website, http://www.monticello.org/site/research-and -collections/Christmas.

19. Cynthia Kierner, *Martha Jefferson Randolph,* iBook edition, p. 214.

20. Jefferson was accused of a sexual affair with his slave in an 1802 *Richmond Recorder* newspaper article by muckraking journalist James Callender.

21. Martha Jefferson Randolph to Thomas Jefferson, October 29, 1802; Betts, *Thomas Jefferson's Farm Book,* p. 238; Cokie Roberts, *Ladies of Liberty,* iBook edition, p. 298.

22. Roberts, *Ladies of Liberty,* iBook edition, p. 299.

23. William H. Gaines Jr., *Thomas Mann Randolph: Jefferson's Son-in-Law.* Southern Biography Series (Baton Rouge: Louisiana State University Press, 1966); William H. Gaines, "Thomas Mann Randolph: Jefferson's Son-in-Law," *William and Mary Quarterly,* 3rd ser., 24 (1/January 1967), 150–51. Published by Omohundro Institute of Early American History and Culture. http://www .jstor.org/stable/1920577. Accessed August 15, 2012.

24. Kierner, *Martha Jefferson Randolph,* p. 5.

25. Kierner, *Martha Jefferson Randolph*, p. 5; Smith, "Carysbrook Memoir," pp. 74–75; 23–24, University of Virginia Special Collections Library.

26. http://www.monticello.org/site/jefferson/maria-jefferson-eppes.

27. http://www.monticello.org/site/jefferson/maria-jefferson-eppes; Jefferson Memorandum Book, vol. 2, p. 1125.

28. Marie Kimball, "A Playmate of Thomas Jefferson," *The North American Review*, 213 (783/February 1921), 145–56. Published by University of Northern Iowa. http://www.jstor.org/stable/25120674. Accessed August 15, 2012.

29. Kimball, "A Playmate of Thomas Jefferson," 145–56.

30. Kimball, "A Playmate of Thomas Jefferson."

31. Kimball, "A Playmate of Thomas Jefferson."

32. Kimball, "A Playmate of Thomas Jefferson," 145–56.

33. Jefferson's Scrapbooks.

34. Kimball, "A Playmate of Thomas Jefferson."

CHAPTER 11

1. *PTJ*, vol. X, p. 451; Meacham, *Jefferson*, iBook edition, p. 986.

2. Scharff, *The Women Jefferson Loved*, iBook edition, p. 308; "Jefferson Family," *Tylers's Quarterly*, 269–70.

3. McLaughlin, *Jefferson and Monticello*, pp. 182–83.

4. *PTJRS*, vol. VII, p. 191; Meacham, *The Art of Power*, iBook edition, p. 2295.

5. Fleming, *The Intimate Lives of the Founding Fathers*, iBook edition, pp. 1820–24.

6. TJ to Richard Henry Lee, July 29, 1776, *Papers*, vol. 1, p. 477; TJ to John Page, July 30, 1776, *Papers*, vol. 1, p. 483; Scharff, *The Women Jefferson Loved*, iBook edition, p. 372.

7. Scharff, *The Women Jefferson Loved*, iBook edition, p. 157.

8. *PTJ*, vol. I, p. 409; Meacham, *The Art of Power*, iBook edition, fn. 85, p. 2851; Marie Kimball, *The Road to Glory*, p. 278.

9. Scharff, *The Women Jefferson Loved*, iBook edition, p. 172; *MB* vol. 1, p. 415; TJ to Thomas Nelson, May 16, 1776, *Papers*, vol. 1, p. 292; TJ to William Randolph, ca. June 1776, *Papers*, vol. 1, pp. 408–10.

10. Scharff, *The Women Jefferson Loved*, iBook edition, pp. 332–33, 698–99; see also Meacham, *The Art of Power*, iBook edition, pp. 1094–97.

11. Scharff, *The Women Jefferson Loved*, iBook edition, pp. 177–78.

12. Scharff, *The Women Jefferson Loved*, iBook edition, pp. 177–78.

13. Scharff, *The Women Jefferson Loved*, iBook edition, p. 179; Kern, "The Jeffersons at Shadwell; The Social and Material World of a Virginia Family" (PhD dissertation, College of William & Mary, 2005), pp. 120–21.

14. Boyd, ed. *PTJ*, vol. I, p. 483; David McCullough, *John Adams*, iBook edition, pp. 600–1.

15. Fleming, *Intimate Lives*, iBook edition, p. 962.

16. Fleming, *Intimate Lives*, iBook edition, p. 962; *PTJ*, vol. I, pp. 524, 589.

17. Fleming, *Intimate Lives*, iBook edition, p. 962; *PTJ*, vol. I, pp. 524, 589.

CHAPTER 12

1. Mazzei, *My Life and Wanderings*, p. 200.

2. Meacham, *The Art of Power*, iBook edition, p. 2295; *PTJRS*, vol. VII, p. 191.

3. Brodie, *Thomas Jefferson*, p. 120; Scharff, *The Women Jefferson Loved*, pp. 342–43.

4. Scharff, *The Women Jefferson Loved*, p. 342.

5. Fiske Kimball; reproduced, with commentary, in his 1916 study, *Thomas Jefferson, Architect: Original Designs*.

6. George Morrow, *The Day They Buried Great Britain*, p. 19.

7. Fiske Kimball, "Jefferson and the Arts."

8. Kimball, "Jefferson and the Arts," pp. 238–45.

9. Kimball, "Jefferson and the Arts," pp. 238–45.

10. Wenger, "Thomas Jefferson, Tenant," 263–65; Mark R. Wenger, "Thomas Jefferson and the Vernacular Tradition" (Paper delivered at the University of Virginia Architectural Conference, Charlottesville, 1993), 25; Wenger, "Thomas Jefferson and the Virginia State Capitol," 82–89.

11. Stanley R. Hauer, "Thomas Jefferson and the Anglo-Saxon Language," *Publications of the Modern Language Association*, 98 (5/October 1983), 879–98. On the Summary Review of Rights, see Boyd, *Papers of Thomas Jefferson*, vol. 1, pp. 121–22, 37; Thomas Jefferson to Edmund Pendleton, as cited in John E. Selby, *The Revolution in Virginia, 1775–1783* (Williamsburg, VA: Colonial Williamsburg Foundation, 1988), pp. 139–40; Boyd, *Papers of Thomas Jefferson*, vol. 1, pp. 492, 38; On the revision of Virginia laws, see Selby, *Revolution in Virginia*, pp. 159–60; for the text of the bills, see Boyd, *Papers of Thomas Jefferson*, vol. 2, pp. 230–31, 492–507; on the University of Virginia, see Hauer, "Thomas Jefferson and the Anglo-Saxon Language," pp. 879–81, 242; *Winterthur Portfolio* 32, 4.

12. Kimball, "Jefferson and the Arts."

13. Kimball, "Jefferson and the Arts."

14. Maurer, "A Musical Family in Colonial Virginia."

15. Maurer, "A Musical Family in Colonial Virginia," 360–63.

16. Maurer, "A Musical Family in Colonial Virginia," 358–64.

17. Maurer, "A Musical Family in Colonial Virginia," 358–64.

18. Maurer, "A Musical Family in Colonial Virginia," 358–64.

19. Maurer, "A Musical Family in Colonial Virginia," 358–64.

20. Maurer, "A Musical Family in Colonial Virginia," 358–64.

21. James C. Darling and Maureen McF. Wiggins, "A Constant Tuting: The Music of Williamsburg," *Music Educators Journal* 61(3/November 1974), 56–61. Published by Sage Publications, Inc., on behalf of MENC: The National Association for Music Education. http://www.jstor.org/stable/3394620. Accessed December 28, 2012.

22. Darling and Wiggins, "A Constant Tuting."

23. Darling and Wiggins, "A Constant Tuting."

CHAPTER 13

1. Malone, *JHT*, vol. I, pp. 358–59; Meacham, *The Art of Power*, pp. 816–17.

2. Roberts, *Founding Mothers*, p. 564.

3. Roberts, *Founding Mothers*, iBook edition, p. 159.

4. Roberts, *Founding Mothers*, iBook edition, p.167.

5. Roberts, *Founding Mothers*, iBook edition, p. 71.

6. Roberts, *Founding Mothers*, iBook edition, p.73.

7. Grimes, *My Thomas*, p. 8.

8. Kranish, *Flight from Monticello*, p. 274; Mary Beacock Fryer and Christopher Dracott, *John Graves Simcoes, 1752–1806: A Biography* (Toronto: Dundurn Press, 1998), p. 75.

9. Fleming, *Intimate Lives*, iBook edition, p. 968.

10. TJ to Timothy Matlack, April 18 1781, *PTJ*, vol. I, p. 589; Fleming, *Intimate Lives*, iBook edition, p. 969.

11. Wiencek, *Master of the Mountain*, iBook edition, pp. 136–37.

12. Wiencek, *Master of the Mountain*, iBook edition, pp. 136–37.

13. Wiencek, *Master of the Mountain*, iBook edition, pp. 136–37.

14. Wiencek, *Master of the Mountain*, iBook edition, pp. 137–39.

15. Wiencek, *Master of the Mountain*, iBook edition, pp. 137–40.

16. Wiencek, *Master of the Mountain*, iBook edition, pp. 144–45.

17. Fleming, *Intimate Lives*, iBook edition, p. 977; Meacham, *The Art of Power*, iBook edition, pp. 734–35; Virginius Dabney, "Jouett Outrides Tarleton, and Saves Jefferson from Capture," *Scribners Magazine*, June 1928, 690–92.

18. Chernow, *Washington*, iBook edition, p. 726.

19. Kranish, *Flight From Monticello*, p. 283.

20. Kranish, *Flight From Monticello*, p. 283.

21. Kranish, *Flight From Monticello*, p. 283.

22. *PTJ*, vol. VI, p. 84; Meacham, *The Art of Power*, iBook edition, pp. 736, 738.

23. Fleming, *Intimate Lives*, iBook edition, p. 975.

24. Kranish, *Flight From Monticello*, p. 284.

25. Randall, *Life of Thomas Jefferson*. vol. 1, pp. 337–39; Wiencek, *Master of the Mountain*, iBook edition, pp. 142–43; Kranish, *Flight From Monticello*, pp. 280–84; Meacham, *The Art of Power*, iBook edition, p. 738.

26. TJ to William Gordon, July 16, 1788, *Papers*, vol. 13, pp. 363–64; Scharff, *The Women Jefferson Loved*, iBook edition, p. 426.

27. Kranish, *Flight From Monticello*, pp. 283–87.

28. Chernow, *Washington*, iBook edition, p. 1171.

29. Kranish, *Flight From Monticello*, pp. 283–87.

30. Thomas Jefferson and Norma B. Cuthbert, "Poplar Forest: Jefferson's Legacy to His Grandson," *Huntington Library Quarterly* 6 (3/May, 1943), 333–56, at 333. Published by University of California Press. http://www.jstor.org/stable/3815767. Accessed August 15, 2012.

31. Kranish, *Flight From Monticello*, pp. 283–87.

32. Douglas Anderson, "Subterraneous Virginia: The Ethical Poetics of Thomas Jefferson," *Eighteenth-Century Studies* 33(2: Colonial Encounters, Winter 2000), 233–49, at 235. Published by Johns Hopkins University Press for the American Society for Eighteenth-Century Studies (ASECS). http://www.jstor.org/stable/30053684. Accessed: August 3, 2012.

33. Kranish, *Flight From Monticello*, pp. 283–87.

34. Kranish, *Flight From Monticello*, p. 318.

35. Jefferson and Cuthbert, "Poplar Forest," 340.

36. Kranish, *Flight From Monticello*, p. 316; Closen, *Revolutionary Journal of Baron Ludwig von Closen*, pp. 186–87.

37. Mazzei, *My Life and Wanderings*, p. 283.

38. Kranish, *Flight From Monticello*, p. 318.

CHAPTER 14

1. Meacham, *Jefferson*, iBook edition, p. 758; Scharff, *The Women Jefferson Loved*, p. 151.

2. Scharff, *The Women Jefferson Loved*, iBook edition, p. 452; Randolph and Cary, "Reminiscences of THJ by MR," *Papers*, vol. 6, pp. 199–200.

3. Kukla, *Mr. Jefferson's Women*, iBook edition, p. 260; TJ to Marquis de Chastelluex, 26 November 1782, *Jefferson Papers*, vol. 6, p. 203.

4. Edmund Randolph to James Madison, September 20, 1782, in *Papers*, vol. 6, p. 199; Scharff, *The Women Jefferson Loved*, iBook edition, p. 451.

5. TJ to Elizabeth Eppes, October 3 (?) 1782, *Papers*, vol. 6, pp. 198–99; Scharff, *The Women Jefferson Loved*, iBook edition, p. 456.

6. Scharff, *The Women Jefferson Loved*, iBook edition, pp. 180–83.

7. McLaughlin, *Jefferson and Monticello*, iBook edition, p. 17.

8. Scharff, *The Women Jefferson Loved*, iBook edition, p. 460.

9. *PTJ*, vol. VI, p. 203; Meacham, *The Art of Power*, iBook edition, p. 796.

10. *PTJ*, vol. VI, pp. 198–199; Meacham, *The Art of Power*, iBook edition, p. 779.

11. Robert P. Watson, "The First Lady Reconsidered: Presidential Partner and Political Institution," *Presidential Studies Quarterly*, 27 (4), 805; "Rules of the Game: How to Play the Presidency" (Fall 1997), 805–18. Published by Wiley-Blackwell on behalf of the Center for the Study of the Presidency and Congress. http://www.jstor.org/stable/27551802. Accessed August 24, 2012.

12. Robert P. Watson, "The First Lady Reconsidered: Presidential Partner and Political Institution," *Presidential Studies Quarterly* 27 (4/Fall): 805.

13. Watson, "The First Lady Reconsidered"; "Rules of the Game," p. 806.

14. Mayo, "Influence and Power of First Ladies," p. A52.

15. Watson, "The First Lady Reconsidered"; "Rules of the Game," p. 806.

16. Watson, "The First Lady Reconsidered"; "Rules of the Game," p. 806.

17. Kukla, *Mr. Jefferson's Women*, iBook edition, 227–28.

18. Kukla, *Mr. Jefferson's Women*, iBook edition, 227–28; Scharff, *The Women Jefferson Loved*, iBook edition, 379.

19. Kimball, "Thomas Jefferson's Cook Book," 238–39.

20. Kimball, "Thomas Jefferson's Cook Book," 238–39.

21. Kimball, "Thomas Jefferson's Cook Book," 238–39.

22. Kimball, "Thomas Jefferson's Cook Book," 238–39.

23. Kimball, "Thomas Jefferson's Cook Book," 238–39.

24. Kimball, "Thomas Jefferson's Cook Book," 238–39.

25. Scharff, *The Women Jefferson Loved*, iBook edition, 482–98.

26. Scharff, *The Women Jefferson Loved*, iBook edition, 482–98; Kimball, "Thomas Jefferson's Cook Book," 238–39.

27. McLaughlin, Jack, Jefferson and Monticello, iBook edition, pp. 782–86.

28. McLaughlin, Jack, Jefferson and Monticello, iBook edition, pp. 784–86.

29. McLughlin, Jack, Jefferson and Monticello, iBook edition, pp. 788–92.

30. McLughlin, Jack, Jefferson and Monticello, iBook edition, pp. 788–92.

31. McLughlin, Jack, Jefferson and Monticello, iBook edition, pp. 788–93.

32. Kimball, "Thomas Jefferson's Cook Book," 238–39.

33. Fiske Kimball, "The Life Portraits of Jefferson and Their Replicas," *Proceedings of the American Philosophical Society* 88 (6/December 28, 1944), 497–534. Published by the American Philosophical Society. http://www.jstor.org/stable/985240. Accessed August 15, 2012, 498.

34. Scharff, *The Women Jefferson Loved*, iBook edition, 225; *Domestic Life*, 43–44; *Life*, 1:63–64; Bear, 5.

35. Kukla, *Mr. Jefferson's Women*, iBook edition, 244; see also Ana Maria Thornton, *Diary of Mrs. William Thornton, 1806–1863*, Records of Columbia Historical Society, 10 (1907), 88–226.

CHAPTER 15

1. "Home at Last for a Nation's Hero," *Historic Preservation* 39, 50–55. Robert L. Polley, ed. *America's Historic Houses: The Living Past* (New York: G. P. Putnam's and Sons, 1967), pp. 117–18. "The earliest reference to preparation for building at Monticello is a contract dated 15 May 1768. John Moore agreed to level a 250-foot square at the northeast (east) end of the mountain by Christmas of 1768; Uriah P. Levy, a commodore in the U.S. Navy, purchased the property in 1836. Monticello fell out of the hands of the Levy family for about seventeen years during and after the Civil War when the property was seized by the Confederacy and then disputed over in court. After the Civil War and years of litigation, Uriah's nephew, Jefferson Monroe Levy, assumed ownership of the property in the late 1870s. An ardent admirer of Thomas Jefferson, Commodore Levy believed that the houses of great men should be preserved as 'monuments to their glory,' and he bequeathed Monticello in his will to the 'people of the United States.' The government relinquished its claim to the estate, however, as litigation over the will deprived Monticello for 17 years of an owner to care for it. In 1879 Jefferson Monroe Levy (1852–1924), who shared his uncle Uriah's admiration for Jefferson, gained clear title to Monticello and began to make badly needed repairs. After adding considerable land from the original Monticello tract, he sold the house and 652 acres to the Thomas Jefferson Memorial Foundation in 1923. At two crucial periods in the history of Monticello the preservation efforts and stewardship of Uriah P. and Jefferson M. Levy successfully maintained the property for future generations."

2. *Architecture of A. Palladio; in Four Books*, trans. Giacomo Leoni, 3rd ed. (London, 1742), p. 56; *1 Quattro Libri dell'Architettura* (Venetia, 1570), book 2, p. 46. Earlier, Leon Battista Alberti had recommended an elevated site as ideal for health. *Della Architectura di Leon Battista Alberti* [The Architecture of Leon Batistta Alberti], trans. Giacomo Leoni (London, 1726), book 2, p. 79; see Fiske Kimball, *Architect*, fn. 5, p. 20; and David Irwin, ed., *Winkelmann: Writings on Art* (London, 1972), pp. 42–43, 61, 107–8, 113–14; Gene Waddell, "First Monticello," 5, 29.

3. Boyd, ed. *PTJ*, vol. VI, p. 203; McCullough, *John Adams*, iBook edition, p. 1352.

4. Seymour Howard, "Thomas Jefferson's Art Gallery for Monticello," *The Art Bulletin* 59 (4/December 1977), 583–600. Published by College Art Association. http://www.jstor.org/stable/3049712. Accessed February 26, 2013, 587.9.

5. Jefferson, *Writings*, p. 1321; Ron Chernow, *Washington*, iBook edition, p. 1640.

6. Howard, "Thomas Jefferson's Art Gallery for Monticello," 587; for Jefferson's remodelings of Monticello and his work on the University of Virginia, see *Eye of Jefferson*, 272ff., 284ff., 385ff. (biblio.). For the late eighteenth-century market in antiquities and reproductions of ancient sculptures in Rome and Florence, including pieces that Jefferson wanted, see, for example, A. Bertolotti, "Esportazione di oggetti di belle arti di Roma nei secoli XVI, XVII, e XVIII," *Archivio storico artistico . . . di Roma*, 1875, 173f., to iv, 1880, 74ff., passim; C. Justi, *Winckelmann und seine Zeitgenossen*, 5th ed. (Cologne: W. Rehm, 1956), ii, 290ff., 377ff.; Michaelis, 55ff.–128, passim; H. Ladendorf, *Antikenstudium und Antikenkopie*, 2nd ed. (Berlin, 1958), 62ff., 71f.; and S. Howard, "An Antiquarian Handlist and Beginnings of the Pio-Clementino," *Eighteenth Century Studies* VII, 1973, 40ff. (biblio.).

7. Roberts, *Founding Mothers*, iBook edition, p. 69.

8. Roberts, *Founding Mothers*, iBook edition, p. 77.

9. Marie Kimball, "Thomas Jefferson's Cook Book," *William and Mary Quarterly*, 2nd ser., 19 (2/April 1939), 238–39. Published by Omohundro Institute of Early American History and Culture. http://www.jstor.org/stable/1922859. Accessed January 14, 2012.

10. Kimball, "Thomas Jefferson's Cook Book," pp. 238–39.

11. Kimball, "Thomas Jefferson's Cook Book," pp. 238–39.

12. Kimball, "Thomas Jefferson's Cook Book," pp. 238–39.

13. Kimball, "Thomas Jefferson's Cook Book," pp. 238–39.

14. Kimball, "Thomas Jefferson's Cook Book," pp. 238–39.

15. Kimball, "Thomas Jefferson's Cook Book," pp. 238–39.

16. Kimball, "Thomas Jefferson's Cook Book," pp. 238–39.

17. Kukla, *Mr. Jefferson's Women*, iBook edition, pp. 227–28.

18. Kukla, *Mr. Jefferson's Women*, iBook edition, pp. 227–28; Scharff, *The Women Jefferson Loved*, iBook edition, p. 379.

19. Kimball, "Thomas Jefferson's Cook Book," pp. 238–39.

20. Kimball, "Thomas Jefferson's Cook Book," pp. 238–39.

CHAPTER 16

1. Julian Boyd, *The Papers of Thomas Jefferson* (Princeton: Princeton University Press, 1950–1974), vol. 1, p. 78; Kukla, *Mr. Jefferson's Women*, p. 64.

2. James A. Bear and Lucia Stanton, eds. *Jefferson's Memorandum Books*, vol. 1, p. 521.

3. Meacham, *The Art of Power*, iBook edition, p. 757; *PTJ*, vol. VI, p.186.

4. See, in general, McLaughlin, *Jefferson and Monticello*, iBook edition, pp. 752–892; Fleming, *The Intimate Lives of the Founding Fathers*, iBook edition, pp. 1226–246; Kukla, *Mr. Jefferson's Women*, iBook edition, pp. 319–32; Meacham, *The Art of Power*, iBook edition, pp. 858–82.

5. Meacham, *The Art of Power*, iBook edition, p. 619; *PTJ*, vol. I, p. 477.

6. Meacham, *The Art of Power*, iBook edition, p. 757.

7. Scharff, *The Women Jefferson Loved*, p. 444; *PTJ*, vol. 6, p. 196.

8. Scharff, *The Women Jefferson Loved*, iBook edition, p. 452.

9. Meacham, *The Art of Power*, iBook edition, p. 761; Randall, *Jefferson*, vol. I, p. 380.

10. Burstein and Mowbray, "Jefferson and Sterne," 19–34.

11. Randolph, *TDLTJ*, pp. 40–41.

12. Bear, *Jefferson at Monticello*, pp. 99–100; Meacham, *The Art of Power*, iBook edition, p. 767.

13. Scharff, *The Women Jefferson Loved*, iBook edition.

14. Interview with Ken Wallenborn, January 2014, former guide at Monticello and author of the minority report for the Monticello Foundation, 2000.

15. *MB*, vol. I, p. 521; see also Gordon Jones and James A. Bear, "Thomas Jefferson: A Medical History," unpublished manuscript, Thomas Jefferson Foundation, Charlottesville, VA.

16. Scharff, *The Women Jefferson Loved*, iBook edition, p. 454; *PTJ*, pp. 198–99.

17. Malone, vol. I, p. 397.

18. McLaughlin, *Jefferson and Monticello*, iBook edition, p. 689.

19. McLaughlin, *Jefferson and Monticello*, iBook edition, p. 676; *PTJ*, vol. 6, p. 196.

20. Malone, vol. I, p. 396.

CHAPTER 17

1. Malone, Unpublished memoirs, ch. ix—5, Merrill Petersen papers, UVA Special Collections.

2. Fleming, *The Intimate Lives of the Founding Fathers*, iBook edition, p. 1006.

3. Fleming, *The Intimate Lives of the Founding Fathers*, iBook edition, p. 1002.

4. Kukla, p. 357; Scharff, p. 558; *PTJ*, vol. 11, p. 612; McLaughlin, p. 753; see also, Kimball, *Jefferson, The Scene of Europe*, vol. 3 (New York, 1950), p. 9; Fleming, *The Intimate Lives of the Founding Fathers*, iBook edition, p. 1004.

5. Kimball, *Jefferson, The Scene of Europe*; Fleming, *The Intimate Lives.*

6. Elizabeth Wayles Eppes to TJ, October 13, 1784; *Papers*, vol. 7, p. 441; Scharff, *The Women Jefferson Loved*, iBook edition, p. 499.

7. Roberts, *Founding Mothers*, iBook edition, 86–87.

8. Meacham, Jefferson, *The Art of Power*, iBook edition, p. 996.

9. TJ to Maria Cosway, October 12, 1786; Kukla, *Mr. Jefferson's Women*, iBook edition, p. 262; http://www.monticello.org/site/research-and-collections/ maria-cosway-engraving.

10. Kukla, *Mr. Jefferson's Women*, pp. 266–67; this article is based on Stein, *Worlds*, pp. 176–77; Jefferson to Maria Cosway, Paris, October 12, 1786, in *PTJ*, vol. 10, p. 446, letterpress copy available online from the Library of Congress; John Trumbull, *The Autobiography, Reminiscences and Letters of John Trumbull* (New York: Wiley and Putnam, 1841), p. 118. Jefferson to Maria Cosway, Paris, October 12, 1786, in *PTJ*, vol. 10, p. 446, letterpress copy available online from the Library of Congress; Daphne Foskett, *Dictionary of British Miniature Painters* (New York: Praeger Publishers, 1972), vol. 1, p. 220; Stephen Lloyd, "Richard Cosway, R. A.: The Artist as Collector, Connoisseur and Virtuoso," *Apollo* 133 (June 1991), 398–405.

11. Kukla, *Mr. Jefferson's Women*, p. 272; Stein, *Worlds*, pp. 176–77; Jefferson to Maria Cosway, Paris, October 12, 1786, in *PTJ*, vol. 10, p. 446; Trumbull, *The Autobiography, Reminiscences and Letters of John Trumbull*; Foskett, *Dictionary of British Miniature Painters*; Lloyd, "Richard Cosway, R.A."

12. Kukla, *Mr. Jefferson's Women*, iBook edition, p. 286.

13. Kukla, *Mr. Jefferson's Women*, iBook edition, p. 286.

14. Kukla, *Mr. Jefferson's Women*, iBook edition, p. 286.

15. Dumas Malone, *Rights of Man*, p. 70; Kukla, *Mr. Jefferson's Women*, iBook edition, p. 286.

16. Kukla, Mr. *Jefferson's Women*, iBook edition, p. 286.

17. http://www.monticello.org/site/research-and-collections/maria-cosway -engraving.

18. Stein, *Worlds*, pp. 176–77; Jefferson to Maria Cosway, Paris, October 12, 1786, in *PTJ*, vol. 10, p. 446; Trumbull, *The Autobiography, Reminiscences and Letters of John Trumbull*, p. 118; Foskett, *Dictionary of British Miniature Painters*; Lloyd, "Richard Cosway, R.A."

19. Kukla, *Mr. Jefferson's Women*, pp. 95–114.

20. Jefferson to Maria Cosway, October 5, 1786, *PTJ*, vol. 10, pp. 431–32; Jefferson to Lewis Littlepage, October 10, 1786, *PTJ*, vol. 10, p. 442 ed. N., 453–54; Kukla, *Mr. Jefferson's Women*, iBook edition, pp. 296–97.

21. Kukla, iBook edition, p. 306; Malone, *Rights of Man*, pp. 75–76.

22. Kukla, *Mr. Jefferson's Women*, iBook edition, p. 313.

23. Stein, *Worlds*, pp. 176–77; Jefferson to Maria Cosway, Paris, October 12, 1786, in *PTJ*, vol. 10, p. 446; Trumbull, *The Autobiography, Reminiscences and Letters of John Trumbull*, p. 118; Foskett, *Dictionary of British Miniature Painters*; Lloyd, "Richard Cosway, R.A."

24. See Dumas Malone's *Miscegenation Legend* and William G. Hyland's *Long Journey with Mr. Jefferson*.

25. Anderson, "Subterraneous Virginia," 235.

EPILOGUE

1. Randall, *Jefferson*, vol. III, p. 551; Meacham, *The Art of Power*, iBook edition, p. 2376.

2. Meacham, *The Art of Power*, iBook edition, pp. 2396–97.

3. Meacham, *The Art of Power*, iBook edition, p. 2398; Randall, *Jefferson*, vol. III, p. 542.

4. Meacham, *The Art of Power*, iBook edition, p. 2408.

5. Meacham, *The Art of Power*, iBook edition, p. 2402.

6. Fleming, *Intimate Lives*, iBook edition, pp. 1118–19.

7. David N. Barton, *The Jefferson Lies*, p. 25; Charles Warren, *Odd Byways in American History* (Cambridge: Harvard University Press, 1942), p. 127; Malone, *Jefferson the President, First Term, 1801–1805*, vol. 4, p. 206.

8. AGR, *Hemingses*, iBook edition, p. 166.

9. Cynthia Burton, *Jefferson Vindicated*, p. 135.

10. McMurry and McMurry, *Anatomy of a Scandal*, pp. 118–19.

11. McMurry and McMurry, *Anatomy of a Scandal*, pp. 12–14.

12. McMurry and McMurry, *Anatomy of a Scandal*, pp. 13–15.

13. McMurry and McMurry, *Anatomy of a Scandal*, pp.13–15.

14. McMurry and McMurry, *Anatomy of a Scandal*, p. 128.

15. McMurry and McMurry, *Anatomy of a Scandal*, p. 128.

16. McMurry and McMurry, *Anatomy of a Scandal*, 161–64.

17. McMurry and McMurry, *Anatomy of a Scandal*, pp. 161–64.

18. McMurry and McMurry, *Anatomy of a Scandal*, pp. 161–64.

19. McMurry and McMurry, *Anatomy of a Scandal*, p. 128.

20. Wiencek, *Master of the Mountain*, iBook edition, pp. 514–15.

21. McMurry and McMurry, *Jefferson, Callender, and the Sally Story*, p. 105.

22. David N. Mayer, *The Thomas Jefferson - Sally Hemings Myth and the Politicization of American History, Individual Views of David N. Mayer, Concurring with*

the Majority Report of the Scholars Commission on the Jefferson-Hemings Matter. http://web.archive.org/web/20110725015820/http://www.ashbrook.org/articles/mayer-hemings.html#III.

23. Burton, *Jefferson Vindicated*, p. 163.

24. Rev. Hamilton Wilcox Pierson, "Jefferson at Monticello: The Private Life of Thomas Jefferson," manuscript of the recollections of Edmund Bacon, printed in James A. Bear, *Jefferson at Monticello*, p. 102.

25. See Adair, *Fame and the Founding Fathers*.

26. Malone and Hochman, *A Note on Evidence*; Malone, *Jefferson the President, First Term*, p. 526.

27. Hyland, *In Defense of Thomas Jefferson*, iBook edition, p. 347.

28. Turner, *The Scholars Commission Report*.

SELECTED BIBLIOGRAPHY

MANUSCRIPT COLLECTIONS

Adams Family Papers, Massachusetts Historical Society, Boston

Albert Gallatin Papers, New York Historical Society

American Memory (Library of Congress), George Washington Papers, Thomas Jefferson Papers

Coolidge Collection of Thomas Jefferson Manuscripts, Massachusetts Historical Society, Boston

Correspondence of Ellen Wayles Randolph Coolidge, Special Collections, University of Virginia Library, University of Virginia, Charlottesville, Virginia

Dumas Malone Papers, University of Virginia, Alderman Library, Albert and Shirley Small Special Collections Library—Special Collections MSS 12712-b, SC-STKS

Edgehill-Randolph Papers, Special Collections, University of Virginia Library, University of Virginia, Charlottesville, Virginia

Ellen Randolph Coolidge Papers, University of Virginia, Alderman Library, Albert and Shirley Small Special Collections Library

Family Letters Project (Papers of Thomas Jefferson: Retirement Series, Monticello)

John D. Rockefeller Jr. Library (Colonial Williamsburg Foundation), *Virginia Gazette* and index for 1736–1780

Merrill Peterson Papers, University of Virginia, Alderman Library, Albert and Shirley Small Special Collections Library

Nicholas Philip Trist Papers

Papers of Thomas Jefferson, Editorial Files, Princeton University, Princeton, New Jersey

Robley Dunglison Papers, College of Physicians of Philadelphia, Philadelphia, Pennsylvania

The Parke Rouse Papers, Mss 71 R75, William and Mary Library, Williamsburg, Virginia

The Tyler Papers, Mss 65 T97, Group b, William and Mary Library, Williamsburg, Virginia

Thomas A. Graves Papers, UA 2.16, Series 13: Accession 1985.037, box 1, folder 133, William and Mary Library, Williamsburg, Virginia

Thomas Jefferson Digital Archive (University of Virginia Library Electronic Text Center)

Thomas Jefferson Papers, Library of Congress, Washington, D.C.
TJP-ViU Thomas Jefferson Papers, University of Virginia
University of North Carolina, Southern Historical Collection, Chapel Hill
William A. Burwell Papers, Library of Congress, Washington, D.C.

BOOKS

Adair, Douglass, *Fame and the Founding Fathers.* New York: Liberty Fund, 1974.

Adams, Henry. *History of the United States of America during the Administration of Thomas Jefferson.* New York: Library of America, 1986.

Adams, John. *Correspondence of the Late President Adams.* Originally published in the *Boston Patriot* in a "Series of Letters." Boston: Everett & Munroe, 1809.

Adams, William Howard. *The Eye of Thomas Jefferson.* Washington, DC: National Gallery of Art, 1976.

———. *Jefferson and the Arts: An Extended View.* Washington, DC: National Gallery of Art, 1976.

———. *Jefferson's Monticello.* New York: Abbeville Press, 1983.

———. *The Paris Years of Thomas Jefferson.* New Haven, CT: Yale University Press, 1997.

Barton, David. *The Jefferson Lies.* Nashville, TN: Thomas Nelson Books, 2012.

Bear, James A., Jr. *Jefferson at Monticello.* Charlottesville: University of Virginia Press, 1985.

——— and Lucia C. Stanton, eds. *Jefferson's Memorandum Books: Accounts, with Legal Records and Miscellany, 1767–1826.* Princeton, NJ: Princeton University Press, 1997.

Bedini, Silvio A. *Declaration of Independence Desk.* Washington, DC: Smithsonian Institution Press, 1981.

———. *Thomas Jefferson: Statesman of Science.* New York: Macmillan, 1990.

Bernstein, R. B. *Thomas Jefferson.* New York: Oxford University Press, 2003.

Betts, Edwin M., ed. *Thomas Jefferson's Farm Book.* Princeton, NJ: American Philosophical Society/Princeton University Press, 1953.

———. *Thomas Jefferson's Garden Book, 1766–1824.* Philadelphia: American Philosophical Society, 1944.

——— and James Adam Bear, Jr., eds. *The Family Letters of Thomas Jefferson.* Charlottesville: University of Virginia Press, 1986.

Boorstin, Daniel. *The Americans: The Colonial Experience.* New York: Random House, 1993.

———. *The Lost World of Thomas Jefferson.* Chicago: University of Chicago Press, 1948.

Boyd, Julian, ed. *The Papers of Thomas Jefferson.* Vols. I–XX. Princeton, NJ: Princeton University Press, 1950.

Brodie, Fawn M. *Thomas Jefferson: An Intimate History.* New York: Norton, 1974.

Burns, James Macgregor, and Susan George Dunn. *Washington.* New York: Time Books, 2004.

Burstein, Andrew. *The Inner Jefferson: Portrait of a Grieving Optimist.* Charlottesville: University of Virginia Press, 1995.

———. *Jefferson's Secrets.* New York: Basic Books, 2005.

——— and Peter S. Onuf, eds. *Letters from the Head and Heart: Writings of Thomas Jefferson.* Charlottesville: University of Virginia Press, 2002.

Burton, Cynthia H. *Jefferson Vindicated: Fallacies, Omissions and Contradictions in the Hemings Genealogical Search*, foreword by James A. Bear Jr., emeritus director of the Thomas Jefferson Memorial Foundation, Keswick, VA, 2005.

Cappon, Lester J., ed. *The Adams-Jefferson Letters: The Complete Correspondence Between Thomas Jefferson and Abigail and John Adams.* Reprint, Chapel Hill and London, Published for the Omohundro Institute of Early American History and Culture at Williamsburg, Virginia, 1959.

Chase-Riboud, Barbara. *Sally Hemings: A Novel.* New York: Viking, 1979.

Chernow, Ron. *Alexander Hamilton.* New York: Penguin Press, 2004.

——. *George Washington.* New York: Penguin Press, 2011.

Coates, Eyler Robert, Sr., ed. *The Jefferson Hemings Myth: An American Travesty.* Charlottesville, VA: The Thomas Jefferson Heritage Society, 2001.

Crawford, Alan Pell. *Twilight at Monticello, The Final Years of Thomas Jefferson.* New York: Random House, 2008.

Cripe, Helen. *Thomas Jefferson and Music.* Charlottesville: University of Virginia Press, 1974.

Cullen, Charles, ed. *The Papers of John Marshall.* Chapel Hill: University of North Carolina Press, 1984.

——. *The Papers of Thomas Jefferson.* Vols. XXI–XXIII. Princeton, NJ: Princeton University Press, 1983.

Cunningham, Noble Jr., *In Pursuit of Reason, The Life of Thomas Jefferson.* Baton Rouge: Louisiana State University Press, 1987.

——. *The Jeffersonian Republicans in Power: Party Operations, 1801–1809.* Chapel Hill: University of North Carolina Press, 1963.

Dabney, Virginius. *Across the Years: Memories of a Virginian.* New York: Doubleday, 1978.

——. *The Jefferson Scandals: A Rebuttal.* New York: Dodd, Mead, 1981.

——. *Mr. Jefferson's University: A History.* Charlottesville: University of Virginia Press, 1981.

Dewey, Frank. *Thomas Jefferson, Lawyer.* Charlottesville: University of Virginia Press, 2005.

Durey, Michael. *With the Hammer of Truth: James Thomson Callender and America's Early National Heroes.* Charlottesville: University of Virginia Press, 1990.

Ellis, Joseph J. *After the Revolution.* New York: Norton, 1979.

——. *American Sphinx: The Character of Thomas Jefferson.* New York: Knopf, 1997.

——. *His Excellency: George Washington.* New York: Alfred A. Knopf, 2004.

Fleming, Thomas. *The Intimate Lives of the Founding Father.* New York: Smithsonian Books, 2009.

——. *The Man from Monticello: An Intimate Life of Thomas Jefferson.* New York: Morrow, 1969.

Ford, Paul Leicester, ed. *The Writings of Thomas Jefferson.* 10 vols. New York: G. P. Putnam's Sons, 1892–1899.

Ford, Worthington Chauncey, ed. *Thomas Jefferson and James Thomson Callender, 1798–1802.* Brooklyn: History Print Club, 1897.

Franklin, John Hope, and Alfred A. Moss Jr. *From Slavery to Freedom: A History of Negro Americans,* 6th ed. New York: McGraw-Hill, 1988.

Gordon-Reed, Annette. *The Hemingses of Monticello, The Story of an American Family.* New York: Norton 2008.

———. *Thomas Jefferson and Sally Hemings: An American Controversy.* Charlottesville: University of Virginia Press, 1997.

Grirnes, Roberta, *My Thomas.* iBook edition.

Halliday, E. M. *Understanding Thomas Jefferson.* New York: HarperCollins, 2001.

Hitchens, Christopher. *Thomas Jefferson: Author of America.* New York: HarperCollins, 2005.

Hyland, William G. *In Defense of Thomas Jefferson.* New York: St. Martin's, 2009.

———. *Long Journey with Mr. Jefferson.* Washington, DC: Potomac, 2013.

Jefferson, Isaac, and James A. Bear Jr., ed. *Memoirs of a Monticello Slave, in Jefferson at Monticello.* Charlottesville: University of Virginia Press, 1967.

Jefferson, Thomas. *Writings.* Edited by Merrill D. Peterson. New York: Library of America, 1984.

Justus, Judith. *Down from the Mountain.* Perrysburg, OH: Jeskurtara, 1990.

Kern, Susan. *The Jeffersons at Shadwell.* The Lamar Series in Western History. New Haven, CT: Yale University Press, 2010.

Kierner, Cynthia, *Martha Jefferson Randolph: Her Life and Times.* Chapel Hill: University of North Carolina Press, 2012.

Kimball, Marie. *Jefferson: The Road to Glory, 1743 to 1776.* New York: Coward-McCann, 1943.

———. *Jefferson: The Scene of Europe, 1784 to 1789.* New York: Coward-McCann, 1950.

———. *Jefferson: War and Peace, 1776 to 1784.* New York: Coward-McCann, 1947.

Koch, Adrienne, and William Peden, eds. *The Life and Selected Writings of Thomas Jefferson.* New York: Modern Library, 1944.

Kranish, Michael. *Flight from Monticello: Thomas Jefferson at War.* New York: Oxford University Press, 2010.

Kukla, Jon. *Mr. Jefferson's Women.* New York: Knopf, 2007.

Langhorne, Elizabeth. *Monticello: A Family Story.* Chapel Hill, NC: Algonquin Books of Chapel Hill, 1989.

Lanier, Shannon, and Jane Feldman. *Jefferson's Children.* New York: Random House Books for Young Readers, 2002.

Lewis, Jan Ellen, and Peter S. Onuf, eds. *Sally Hemings and Thomas Jefferson: History, Memory and Civic Culture.* Charlottesville: University of Virginia Press, 1999.

Lipscomb, Andrew A., ed. *The Writings of Thomas Jefferson.* Washington, DC: Jefferson Memorial Association, 1903.

———. *Anatomy of a Scandal: Thomas Jefferson & the Sally Story,* foreword by David N. Mayer. Shippensburg, PA: White Mane Publishing Co., 2002.

———. *1776.* New York: Simon & Schuster, 2005.

Malone, Dumas. *Jefferson and His Time.* 6 vols. Boston: Little Brown, 1948–1981. Individual titles and dates are *Jefferson the Virginian* (1948); *Jefferson and the Rights of Man* (1951); *Jefferson and the Ordeal of Liberty* (1962); *Jefferson the President: First Term,* 1801–1805 (1970); *Jefferson the President: Second Term, 1805–1809* (1974); and *The Sage of Monticello* (1981).

———. *Jefferson the Virginian.* Charlottesville: University of Virginia Press, 2006.

Mapp, Alf J., Jr. *Thomas Jefferson: A Strange Case of Mistaken Identity*. New York: Madison, 1987.

———. *Thomas Jefferson: Passionate Pilgrim*. New York: Madison, 1992.

Mayo, Bernard, ed., with preface by James A. Bear Jr. *Thomas Jefferson and His Unknown Brother*. Charlottesville: University of Virginia Press, 1981.

Meacham, Jon. *Thomas Jefferson and the Art of Power*. New York: Random House, 2013.

McCullough, David. *John Adams*. New York: Simon & Schuster, 2001.

McDonald, Forrest. *The Presidency of Thomas Jefferson*. Lawrence: University Press of Kansas, 1976.

McLaughlin, Jack. *Jefferson and Monticello: The Biography of a Builder*. New York: Holt, 1988.

McMurry, Rebecca L., and James F. McMurry Jr. *Anatomy of a Scandal: Thomas Jefferson & the Sally Story*, foreword by David N. Mayer. Shippensburg, PA: White Mane Publishing Co., 2002.

———. *Jefferson, Callender and the Sally Story: The Scandalmonger and the Newspaper War of 1802*. Toms Brook, VA: Old Virginia Books, 2000.

Miller, John C. *Alexander Hamilton: Portrait in Paradox*. New York: Harper & Brothers, 1959.

———. *Crisis in Freedom: The Alien and Sedition Acts*. Boston: Little, Brown, 1951.

———. *The Wolf by the Ears: Thomas Jefferson and Slavery*. Charlottesville: University of Virginia Press, 1991.

Mazzei, Philip. *My Life and Wanderings*, Amer. Inst. of Italian Studies, 1980.

Morrow, George. *The Day They Buried Great Britain*. London: Telford Publications, 2011.

Neff, Kelly Joyce. *Dear Companion, The Inner Life of Martha Jefferson*. Charlottesville: Hampton Roads Publishing Co., 1997.

Nichols, Frederick D., and James Bear Jr. *Monticello*. Charlottesville: University of Virginia Press, 1967.

Nock, Albert J., *Mr. Jefferson*. Tampa, FL: Hallberg Publishing Corporation, 1983.

O'Brien, Conor Cruise. *The Long Affair*. Chicago: University of Chicago Press, 1996.

Onuf, Peter, ed. *Jefferson Legacies*. Charlottesville: University of Virginia Press, 1993.

Parton, James. *Life of Thomas Jefferson*. Chicago: Houghton, Mifflin and Company, 1883.

Peden, William, ed. *Thomas Jefferson: Notes on the State of Virginia*. New York: Norton, 1982.

Peterson, Merrill D. *Adams and Jefferson: A Revolutionary Dialogue*. Oxford: Oxford University Press, 1976.

———, ed. *James Madison: A Biography in His Own Words*. The Founding Fathers. New York: Newsweek/Harper & Row, 1974.

———. *The Jefferson Image in the American Mind*. New York: Oxford University Press, 1960.

———. *Jefferson's Writings*. Washington, DC: Library of America, 1984.

———, ed. *The Political Writings of Thomas Jefferson*. Woodlawn, MD: Wolk Press, 1993.

———, ed. *The Portable Thomas Jefferson*. New York: Penguin, 1983.

———. *Thomas Jefferson and the New Nation*. London: Oxford University Press, 1970.

———. *Thomas Jefferson: A Reference Biography*. New York: Scribners, 1986.

———, ed. *Visitors to Monticello*. Charlottesville: University of Virginia Press, 1989.

Pierson, Rev. Hamilton W., ed. *Jefferson at Monticello: The Private Life of Thomas Jefferson.* New York: Michigan Historical Reprint Series, 1862.

Randall, Henry S. *The Life of Thomas Jefferson.* Vols. I–III. New York: Derby & Jackson, 1858.

Randall, Willard Sterne. *Thomas Jefferson: A Life.* New York: Holt, 1997.

Randolph, Sarah N. *The Domestic Life of Thomas Jefferson.* Charlottesville: University of Virginia Press, 1978.

Roberts, Cokie. *Founding Mothers.* New York: HarperCollins, 2003.

———. *Ladies of Liberty.* New York: HarperCollins, 2009.

Schachner, Nathan. *Thomas Jefferson.* 2 vols. New York: Appleton-Century, 1951.

Scharff, Virginia. *The Women Jefferson Loved.* New York: HarperCollins, 2010.

Shuffelton, Frank. *A Comprehensive, Annotated Bibliography of Writings Thomas Jefferson About Him (1826–1980).* New York: Garland Publishing Co., 1983.

———. *Thomas Jefferson, 1981–1991: An Annotated Bibliography.* New York: Garland Publishing Co., 1992.

Smith, Daniel Blake. *Inside the Great House: Planter Family Life in Eighteenth-Century Chesapeake Society.* Ithaca, NY, 1980.

Sowerby, Milicent, comp. *Catalogue of the Library of Thomas Jefferson,* 5 vols. Washington, DC: Library of Congress, 1952–1959.

Stanton, Lucia. *Slavery at Monticello.* Richmond, VA: Spencer, 1993.

Stein, Susan R. *The Worlds of Thomas Jefferson at Monticello.* New York: Abrams, 1993.

Tucker, George. *The Life of Thomas Jefferson, Third President of the United States.* 2 vols. Philadelphia: Carey, Lean, and Blanchard, 1837.

Turner, Robert F., ed. *The Jefferson-Hemings Controversy: Report of the Scholars Commission.* Durham, NC: Carolina Academic Press, 2011.

Wills, Garry. *Cincinnatus: George Washington and the Enlightenment.* Garden City, NY: Doubleday, 1984.

———. *Inventing America.* Garden City, NY: Doubleday, 1978.

———. *Negro President.* New York: Houghton Mifflin Company, 2003.

Wilson, L. Douglas, ed. *Jefferson's Books.* Lynchburg, VA: Progress Printing, 1986.

———. *Jefferson's Literary Commonplace Book.* Princeton, NJ: Princeton University Press, 1989.

Wood, Gordon S. *The Creation of the American Republic.* Chapel Hill: University of North Carolina Press, 1969.

———. *Empire of Liberty: A History of the Early Republic, 1789–1815.* New York: Oxford University Press, 2009.

———. *The Radicalism of the American Revolution.* New York: Knopf, 1992.

———. *Revolutionary Characters: What Made the Founders Different.* New York: Penguin Press. 2006.

ARTICLES

Anderson, Douglas. "Subterraneous Virginia: The Ethical Politics of Thomas Jefferson." *Eighteenth Century Studies* vol. 33, no. 2 (2000): 233–49.

Battle, J. D. "The 'periodical head-achs' of Thomas Jefferson." *Cleveland Clinic Quarterly* 51 (1983): 531–39.

Bear, James A., Jr. "The Hemings Family at Monticello." *Virginia Cavalcade* 29 (Autumn 1979): 78–87.

Beddow, Reid. "Dumas Malone, The Sage of Charlottesville." *Washington Post Book World*, July 5, 1981, vol. 11, no. 27.

Bradford, M. E. "The Long Shadow of Thomas Jefferson." *National Review* (October 2, 1981): 1146.

Bringhurst, Newell G. "Fawn M. Brodie: Her Biographies as Autobiography." *Pacific Historical Review* 59 (2/May 1990): 203–29. Published by University of California Press. http://www.jstor.org/stable/3640057. Accessed September 10, 2012.

Brodie, Fawn M. "The Great American Taboo." *American Heritage* XXIII (4/June 1972): 4–57.

———. "Jefferson's Biographers and the Psychology of Canonization." *Journal of Interdisciplinary History* 2 (Summer 1971): 155–71.

———. "The Political Hero in America." *Virginia Quarterly Review* XL (I/ Winter 1970): 6–60.

———. "Thomas Jefferson's Unknown Grandchildren: A Study in Historical Silence." *American Heritage* XXVII (October 1976): 23, 33, 94, 99.

Cohen, Gary L., and Loren A. Rolak. "Thomas Jefferson's Headaches: Were They Migraines?" *Headache: The Journal of Head and Face Pain* 46 (3): 492–97. doi:10.1111/j.1526-4610.2006.00292.x.

Dabney, Virginius, and Jon Kukla. "The Monticello Scandals: History and Fiction." *Virginia Cavalcade* XXIX (2/Autumn 1979): 53–61.

Ellis, Joseph J., and Eric S. Lander. "Founding Father." *Nature* (November 5, 1998): 13–14.

Foster, Eugene A., et al. "Jefferson Fathered Slave's Last Child." *Nature* 396 (6706): 198.

French, Scot A., and Edward L. Ayers. "The Strange Career of Thomas Jefferson: Race and Slavery in American Memory, 1943–1993," in *Jeffersonian Legacies*, ed. Peter S. Onuf (Charlottesville: University of Virginia Press, 1993), 418–56.

Graham, Pearl N. "Thomas Jefferson and Sally Hemings." *Journal of Negro History* 44 (1961): 89–103.

Hitchens, Christopher. "Jefferson-Clinton." *Nation* (November 30, 1998): 8.

Hyland, William G., Jr., and William G. Hyland. "A Civil Action: Hemings v. Jefferson," *American Journal of Trial Advocacy* 31 (Summer 2007): 1–68.

Jellison, Charles A. "James Thomson Callender: 'Human Nature in a Hideous Form.'" *Virginia Cavalcade* 29 (Autumn 1978): 62–69.

Jordan, Winthrop. "Review of Thomas Jefferson: An Intimate History, by Fawn Brodie." *William and Mary Quarterly*, 3rd ser., 32 (1975): 510.

Kern, Susan. "The Material World of the Jeffersons at Shadwell." *William and Mary Quarterly*, 3rd ser., 62 (2005): 213–42.

Kimball, Fiske. *Thomas Jefferson, Architect: Original Designs*. Boston: Da Capo Press, 1968.

Leary, Helen F. M. "Sally Hemings's Children: A Genealogical Analysis of the Evidence." *Jefferson-Hemings, A Special Issue of the National Genealogical Society Quarterly* 89 (3/September 2001).

Lewis, Jan, and Kenneth A. Lockridge. "'Sally Has Been Sick': Pregnancy and Family Limitation among Virginia Gentry Women, 1780–1830." *Journal of Social History* 22 (i/Autumn 1998): 5–19.

Malone, Dumas. "Mr. Jefferson's Private Life." *American Antiquarian Society Proceedings*, New Series 84 (April 1974): 65–74.

———. "Reflections." *The Virginia Magazine of History and Biography* 93 (1/January 1985): 3–13. Published by the Virginia Historical Society. http://www.jstor.org/stable/4248774. Accessed September 10, 2010.

———. "The Scholars Way Then and Now." *Virginia Quarterly Review* 51 (2/1975 Spring): 200.

——— and Steven Hochman. "A Note on Evidence: The Personal History of Madison Hemings." *Journal of Southern History* 41 (1975): 523.

Mayer, David. "The Thomas Jefferson-Sally Hemings Myth and the Politicization of American History." Individual Views of David N. Mayer, Concurring with the Majority Report of the Scholars Commission on the Jefferson-Hemings Matter, April 9, 2001 at http://www.ashbrook.org/articles/mayer-hemings.html.

Morgan, Marie, and Edmund S. Morgan. "Jefferson's Concubine." *New York Review of Books*, October 9, 2008; http://www.nybooks.com/articles/archives/2008/oct/09/jeffersons-concubine/?insrc=toc.

Neiman, Fraser D. "Coincidence or Casual Connection? The Relationship between Thomas Jefferson's Visits to Monticello and Sally Hemings's Conceptions." *William and Mary Quarterly* 57 (198/2000): 205.

Onuf, Peter S. "The Scholars' Jefferson." *William and Mary Quarterly*, 3d ser., 50 (1993): 671.

Peterson, Merrill D. "Dumas Malone: An Appreciation" *William and Mary Quarterly*, 3rd Series, 45 (2/(April 1988): 237–52. Published by Omohundro Institute of Early American History.

———. "Dumas Malone: The Completion of a Monument." *Virginia Quarterly Review: A National Journal of Literature and Discussion* (Winter 1982).

Randall, Henry S., *The Life of Thomas Jefferson*, Vols. I–III. New York: Derby & Jackson, 1858.

"Recollections of Israel Gillette Jefferson, Pike County Republican," December 25, 1873 (original in Ohio Historical Society).

"Report on Thomas Jefferson and Sally Hemings." Thomas Jefferson Memorial Foundation, January 2000.

Shuffelton, F. "Being Definitive: Jefferson Biography Under the Shadow of Dumas Malone." *Biography: An Interdisciplinary Quarterly* (Fall 1995) and *Library Journal* (September 1, 1996).

Wenger, Mark R. "Thomas Jefferson and the Virginia State Capitol." *Virginia Magazine of History and Biography* 101 (1993): 77–102.

Wills, Garry. "The Aesthete," Review of *The Worlds of Thomas Jefferson*, by Susan R. Stein." *New York Review of Books* 40 (August 12, 1993): 6–10.

———. "Uncle Thomas's Cabin," Review of Thomas Jefferson: An Intimate History, by Fawn Brodie. *New York Review of Books* 21 (April 18, 1974): 26.

Wilson, Douglas L. "Thomas Jefferson and the Character Issue." *Atlantic* 27 (5/November 1992): 7–74.

———. "Thomas Jefferson's Early Notebooks." *William and Mary Quarterly* XLII, 3rd ser., 4 (October 1985): 433–52.

Yoder, Edwin. "The Sage at Sunset." *Virginia Quarterly Review* (Winter 1982): 32–37.

ELECTRONIC SOURCES

American National Biography Online. http://www.anb.org/articles/03/03-00500.html.

Monticello. http://monticello.org/.

Monticello Explorer. http://explorer.monticello.org/text/index.php.

National Register of Historic Places. Edgehill Nomination. http://165.176.125.227/registers/Counties/Albemarle/002-0026_Edgehill_1982_Final_Nomination.pdf.

Oxford Dictionary of National Biography. http://www.oxforddnb.com.mutex.gmu.edu/index.jsp. Tay, Edrina, and Jeremy Dibbell. "George Wythe's 'legacie' to President Thomas Jefferson." Common-Place 10 (January 2010). http://www.common-place.org/vol-10/no-02/tales/.

The Thomas Jefferson Encyclopedia. http://wiki.monticello.org/mediawiki/index.php/Thomas_Jefferson_Encyclopedia.

Virginia Newspapers Project. http://www.lva.virginia.gov/public/vnp/.

NEWSPAPERS AND JOURNALS

Cavalier Daily
New York Times
The Pike County Republican
Richmond News Leader
Richmond Recorder
Richmond Times-Dispatch
Virginia Gazette (Williamsburg)
Washington (D.C.) *Federalist*
Washington (D.C.) *Gazette*
Washington (D.C.) *National Intelligencer*
The Washington Post
Washington Times

PERSONAL INTERVIEWS

Steve Hochman, Atlanta, GA
Ken Wallenborn, Charlottesville, VA
Edward M. Leake, Charlottesville, VA
Cynthia Burton, Charlottesville, VA
Herbert Barger, Charlottesville, VA
Robert F. Turner, Washington, DC
Taylor Stoermer, Williamsburg, VA

MISCELLANEOUS SOURCES

"Account Book of Peter Jefferson." The Huntington Library. HM912.

American Philosophical Society. Smith-Houston-Morris-Ogden Family Papers. Family Letters Project. Thomas Jefferson Foundation, at www.monticello.org/papers/index .html.

Anne Cary Randolph, 1805–1808. Household Accounts. Thomas Jefferson Papers. Series 7. Miscellaneous Bound Volumes. Library of Congress.

Coleman, Elizabeth Dabney. "The Carrs of Albemarle County." MA thesis, University of Virginia, 1944.

Coolidge, Ellen Randolph. Letterbook, Special Collections. University of Virginia Library. Accession 9090.

Correspondence of Ellen Wayles Randolph Coolidge. Albert and Shirley Small Special Collections Library. University of Virginia. Family Letters Project. Thomas Jefferson Foundation.

Edgehill-Randolph Papers. University of Virginia. "Thomas Jefferson Memorandum."

Elizabeth House Trist Papers. Virginia Historical Society. Family Letters Project. Thomas Jefferson Foundation.

Gilmer-Skipwith Papers. University of Virginia Library. "Dr. George Gilmer's Feebook, 1767, 1771–1775." MSS 6145.

Hochman, Steven. "Thomas Jefferson: A Personal Financial Biography." PhD diss., University of Virginia, 1987.

"Inventory of the Estate of Peter Jefferson." Huntington Library. HM912.

"Jefferson Family Bible, 1752–1861." University of Virginia Library. Accession 4726.

"Jefferson Papers." Huntington Library. HM5632.

Kern, Susan. "The Jeffersons at Shadwell: The Social and Material World of a Virginia Family." PhD diss., College of William and Mary, 2005.

Martha Wayles Jefferson. International Center for Jefferson Studies.

Martha Wayles Skelton Jefferson Account Book. Library of Congress.

Martha Wayles Skelton Jefferson, 1772–1782. Part B: Household Accounts.

Nicholas Philip Trist Papers. Southern Historical Collection. University of North Carolina. Family Letters Project. Thomas Jefferson Foundation.

Papers of Trist and Burke Family Members. Special Collections. University of Virginia Library. MSS 5385-f.

Robert Alonzo Brock Collection. Huntington Library.

Thomas Jefferson "Fee Book, 1764–74 [other accounts, 1764 to 1794]." Huntington Library. HM 836.

Thomas Jefferson Papers Series 7. Miscellaneous Bound Volumes. Library of Congress.

Thomas Jefferson Papers, 1606–1827, http://memory.loc.gov/ammem/collections/jefferson_papers

INDEX

ABOUT THE AUTHOR

William G. Hyland Jr., a native of Virginia, is the author of *In Defense of Thomas Jefferson* (2009), nominated for the Virginia Literary Award, and *Long Journey with Mr. Jefferson, The Life of Dumas Malone* (2013). Mr. Hyland is a practicing attorney and adjunct professor of law at Stetson University College of Law. He is a member of the Virginia and New York Historical Societies, serves on the board of directors of the Thomas Jefferson Heritage Society, and has lectured on CSPAN, the National Archives, and for the Colonial Williamsburg Foundation. He lives in Tampa, Florida.